The County Books Series

GENERAL EDITOR: BRIAN VESEY-FITZGERALD

SHROPSHIRE

THE COUNTY BOOKS SERIES

FOLLOWING ARE THE FIRST TWENTY
VOLUMES IN ORDER OF PUBLICATION

Sussex . . . . . Esther Meynell
Surrey . . . . . Eric Parker
Kent . . . . . Richard Church
Staffordshire . . . Phil Drabble
Shropshire . . . . Edmund Vale
Herefordshire . . H. L. V. Fletcher
Worcestershire . . . L. T. C. Rolt
Cheshire . . . Fred. H. Crossley
Gloucestershire . . . Kenneth Hare
Lowlands of Scotland . . George Blake
Cornwall . . . . Claude Berry
Devonshire . . . D. St. Leger Gordon
Dorset . . . . . Eric Benfield
Derbyshire . . . Crichton Porteous
Yorkshire, East Riding
               John Fairfax-Blakeborough
Hampshire and
   the Isle of Wight Brian Vesey-FitzGerald
Isle of Man . Canon E. M. Stenning
Cambridgeshire,
   Huntingdonshire and
   the Isle of Ely . . . E. A. R. Ennion
Essex . . . . C. Henry Warren
Western Isles . Alasdair Alpin MacGregor

PLEASE WRITE TO THE PUBLISHERS
FOR FULL DESCRIPTIVE PROSPECTUS

SHROPSHIRE

by

EDMUND VALE

Illustrated and with a Map

London
Robert Hale Limited
18 Bedford Square W.C.1

First published 1949

A CAUTIONARY WORD

T H E portrayal of a county offers the writer a wide choice which is only limited by the amount he happens to know. And that sum total is bound to be only a fraction of the truth, made up rather casually from gleanings out of printed matter, from hear-say, and from personal contacts with things and people. In topography, the personal element is generally kept out unless the form adopted is the itinerary or the gossiping guide. Perhaps this tradition which seems to be based mainly on the modesty of authors might be broken occasionally with advantage. I have my special plea for doing so, and here it is.

The request to write a book about Shropshire in the present series came to me during the war, when active sightseeing was difficult and when every place was suffering from that numbness of spirit which makes it seem dead to the world and dead to its own *genius loci*. With the young men and women all away and the elders living at home in discomfort on short commons, debarred from the exercise of hospitality, it was hard to recognize that Shropshire which used to be. The old Shropshire was a spirit so much bred in the blood and fortified by tradition that it would be bound to return after the war. But before that could happen this book would have to be written. Now it is not very satisfactory to try and present a thing as you see it today and as you remember it erstwhile, leaving out all reference to the reagent (which is one's self). It is simpler and more likely to make better reading to tell of one's contacts as a personal adventure. But it will not do to have everything in that vein, either. There will be numerous gleanings from books and transmitted information (knowledge at second hand), some fresh points observed and some new conclusions drawn, which will demand impersonal treatment. These cannot all be managed under classified headings as would be the case if the book were a well-regulated topography, county history, or guide-book. They will have to be worked in or put under separate cover of a chapter-heading as opportunity offers, and the reader with a quest must seek salvation in the index.

How well Shropshire has maintained its independence from the outside world with its narrowing conventions is shown by the fact that you may still go as you please with the spelling of many place-names. Caus Castle is thus spelt in *Burke:* it is Cause on the Ordnance map, while Sir Charles Oman (tempted perhaps by the famous crow emblem of the Corbet family) makes it Caws. And should it be Middle or Myddle? You can have it both ways; the sign-posts say so. The sign-posts also endorse the mixed formula Ruyton-11-Towns.

I should like to thank all those who gave me help, especially Miss Auden whose own name and that of her family have so long been associated with the archaeology of Shropshire, and Mr James the Librarian, who lent me the most inspiring room in Shrewsbury to work in, and Mr Sloane the Editor of the *Shrewsbury Chronicle* who came to the rescue with his camera-men when other appeals for photographs of the county failed and Miss Gaynor Jones.

E. V.
Nant Ffrancon

DEDICATED

*To the two Families who farm
the Upper Heath in Corvedale.
God bless their crops, their
flocks, and their bonny children!*

CONTENTS

ILLUSTRATIONS

ILLUSTRATIONS

ACKNOWLEDGMENTS

The illustrations above, numbered 13, 16, 20, 22, 24, 40, 41, 42, 43, 45 are reproduced from photographs by Mr Reece Winstone A.R.P.S.; 4, 7, 17, 18, 19, 28, 33, 34, 39 by The Shrewsbury Chronicle; 3, 7, 27, 30, 47 by Mr L. C. Lloyd F.L.S.; 5, 23, 37, 44 by Mr T. Edmondson; 25, 32 by Mr W. J. Mitchenall; 31, 46 by Mr H. J. Gornall; 1 by Mr G. Douglas Bolton; 36 by Eagle Photos; 9 by Mr D. C. Harries; 14 by Dr Watkins-Pitchford; 29 by Mr R. W. Lawton; 21 by Mr E. R. Westlake. The remaining 11 are reproduced from photographs supplied by Miss M. Wight.

CHAPTER I

WHO ARE THE PROUD SALOPIANS?

THE name Shropshire has a good sound. To me it has always brought mental images of trotting horses, running dogs, extra woolly sheep, a glimpse of red earths under foot and aquiline violet profiles on the horizon. Perhaps that is partly association and partly fancy, but I have a belief in the destiny of place-names if they are left alone by the pedant (who is so crazy about foundations and derivations that he will prefer a crude basic etymon to a well-matured euphony). I believe that a name, like a building, given time, will adapt itself to its surroundings and then begin to reflect the genius of its surroundings in itself. That is a branch of *evolution* which the poet rather than the scientist should develop, and it might well be a Shropshire poet, since it was a Shropshire lad, Charles Darwin, who first thought of the word.

There is no doubt but that Shropshire has a strong local flavour. The merest stranger will notice it. But the individuality of a county, like the personality of a human being, is difficult to hit off in a few words, and even more difficult to explain away. Yet there are two starting points on which one can, at least, build theories. The first relates to the basis on which the county was originally formed. Was it called after a people or a town? We have both sorts in England— Essex, the tribal land of the East Saxons, Cheshire, the county bounded by the sphere of influence radiating from Chester.

Shropshire belongs to the latter class. As the Roman was called after Rome although he might never have seen the

I

city, so the Shropshire man is one who is spiritually bound up with Shrewsbury (whether he calls himself a Shropshire man or a proud Salopian). In some counties the old centres of culture and shire-feeling have not kept their place as first-class county towns. In Shropshire, Shrewsbury is still pre-eminent. It is a distinctive town, not like any other in the county or indeed in England. It still radiates its peculiar Salopian flavour of culture, and the shire is still typical of it.

The other starting-point is with the people themselves; and who are they? When no clue of racial identity is given in the name of the county it would seem well to take up both threads at once and then cast an eye on the environment. In Shropshire all these factors are full of dramatic power, so much so, indeed, that if they were properly presented to a stranger he would expect to find the Salopians a romantic and distinctive people—and so they are. We begin, then, with the "shiring." This was a Saxon process which entailed breaking up the older kingdoms of the Heptarchy into "shares." Shropshire is a share of Mercia. And here (for the moment) let us make a fine distinction. Mercia was neither settled nor ruled by the Saxons but by the Angles. It is one of the many paradoxes of our paradoxical nation that, while the Saxons always get their name attached to the historical and architectural periods between Roman and Norman times, England and the English are called after the Angles. What the difference between these two kindred invaders really was has not yet been cleared up by the historians, but there does seem to have been a distinct cleavage in temperament and demeanour between the two which counts for something. I should like to emphasize this point about the Angles here because I shall not labour it as we go on. I think it better to use wrong labels with established meanings than to be constantly altering them. So, in future, I shall write *Saxon* in the usual way, I hope without prejudice. Be it said, though, that when musing on Anglian ingredients in the Shropshire make-up, and comparing Salopians with other Angles of Norfolk, Suffolk, Northumbria, and Eastern Mercia, it should be borne in mind that the old Viking blend is missing. You get it only in what I would call the New Norse Blend—from the Normans, a mere incidental "tone." Instead, you have the Celtic fusion from those aquiline violet profiles on the west horizon which I spoke of to begin with.

It is not known exactly when Mercia was cut up, but the carving had been done before Alfred's day, and Shrewsbury chosen as the focal point with at least one boundary fixed, as it was thought, for all time. This was the boundary in the west. It was fixed by Offa, the greatest of the Mercian rulers, towards the close of the eighth century, by the building of a huge earthwork known then, and known now, as Offa's Dyke. This was no inter-Teutonic affair but a formidable barrier made to seal off the dispossessed nation of the Ancient Britons (now called Welsh) from the English lands. Such a thing was not attempted in Devonshire against the Welsh of Cornwall or in Cumberland, Westmorland, and Lancashire against the Welsh of Strathclyde. But in Mercia the work was completed from one sea to another, that is, from the shore of the Bristol Channel to the Irish Sea at Prestatyn, in Flintshire, all that hundred and thirty odd miles, except where swamp or forest thicket rendered it unnecessary.

Offa's Dyke needs to be seen to be believed in, and the two best stretches lie in Shropshire, the most notable being the work between Lower Spoad Farm on the Clun-Montgomery road and Knighton. Here it still rises to about twenty-five feet above the ditch (always on the Welsh side); and the parapet is broad enough and level enough to walk on. It seems, however to have been a revised operation, for another, called Watt's Dyke, less advantageous to the Mercians, lies in a much more ruinous state a mile or two to the east.

3

Offa's Dyke must have been the western boundary of the new shire of Shrewsbury when it was first created, but it was the Saxons, and not the Welsh, who over-ran it, for by Harold's time the western border of Shropshire lay far beyond it into what is now Wales.

And how had Shrewsbury come to be, at so early a date, of sufficient importance to be named as the central source of influence? This answer would seem to go back to Roman enterprise. The Watling Street (A.5. in modern naming) is still one of the most conspicuous features in an up-to-date map of the English road system. It goes from London to Wroxeter, with a branch to Chester. By archaeological evidence it would seem to have reached Wroxeter by A.D. 50, only seven years after the Richborough landing in Kent.

Wroxeter is a small village on the site of the first Roman terminus of the road, called by our earlier antiquaries Uriconium, and corrected by our later archaeologists to Viroconium (to be pronounced Wiroconium). The place seems to have been a try-out as a garrison fortress. The Twentieth Legion was quartered there for a time and then moved on to the more impregnable key-position of Chester. But the settlement at Uriconium was not abandoned. It became one of the greatest Romano-British towns.

Light on the extraordinary speed with which the road was driven comes from Roman writers. It seems clear that it was connected with the affair of Caractacus, on whose romantic story school history books still dilate. He, the son of the pro-Roman King of Colchester, was the greatest patriot and non-collaborator of the British peoples. Being ousted from his kingdom in the east, he betook him to the most anti-Roman tribe in the west, namely, the Silures. Their country lay between Shropshire and the Bristol Channel, roughly just west of the line where, later on, Offa fixed his dyke. Their neighbours to the east were the Cornavii, who, one conceives, must have been partial to Roman aspirations.

4

Bases of forum colonnade, Uriconium

The Romans evidently made use of their good offices and based their attack on the Silures mainly from Uriconium. Caractacus was captured in 51 or 52 and the Romans then proceeded to settle down permanently in two legionary fortresses in the west, preferring Chester in the north to Uriconium, and chosing Carleon-upon-Usk in the south. The two were connected by a road which passed through Uriconium (which also had its water link via Severn and Usk). The road followed very nearly the subsequent line of Offa's Dyke, and the point to notice here is that even before the cleavage between Teuton and Welshman there was a semi-racial rift between the Celtic tribes. The Silures were Goidels (Gaelic-speaking "Q Celts"), the Cornavii were Brythons (Welsh-speaking "P Celts"). In fact, the Border was already established in the Iron Age.

The Roman towns of Britain were over-run by Angle and Saxon in the fifth century. Some were re-occupied by the newcomer, many more were derelict until rebuilt by the Normans. Uriconium was not revived by either. Only its name was preserved obliquely by the small village of Wroxeter. Viroconium (when pronounced Wiroconium) shows a distinct connection with its neighbour mountain, the Wrekin, and therefore Wroxeter, the *caester* (or fort) of Wiroc, is transparent. The Roman town was evidently called after the Wrekin (named probably by a still earlier race than the Celts), and so, after either the mountain or the town, was named one of the invading Teutonic tribes earliest heard of in English chronicle, the Wrocensetan.

When the Roman settlements were ravaged the native elements must have retired to places more fitted to natural defence such as they had been used to hold in the earlier days before the Roman Conquest, the same that are now known to archaeology as Iron Age forts; and that steep headland in the bend of the Severn only five miles away, where Shrewsbury now stands, was the most obvious retreat. Its many

5

Offa's Dyke Lane, occupying old frontier ditch

early churches seem to point to that. Whether this was indeed the Pengwern of the Princes of Powys in the ding-dong days, or not, is unconfirmed. But when the mists of the Dark Ages lift to show the extent of the new conquerors' domains the lion and the lamb are discovered lying down here together.

What a conjunction of highways there is at Shrewsbury! A first-class road going direct to London and the east, converging on a first-class waterway rolling down to Bristol and the west. Both routes brought in with equal facility the marauder, the missionary, and the merchant, and bore away the ever increasing bales of flannels, "cottons," friezes, and other cloth from the Welsh wool-growers and spinners and the Shrewsbury weavers.

Before the Norman incident the Saxons had done great things on their side of the Dyke in all four shires. Protected from meddlesome Welshmen, they had organized society, established Saxon manors and Saxon parishes and grouped them in "hundreds." Within this framework they were able to indulge their ruling passions for agriculture and building, both of which were, and still are, propensities alien to the Welsh way of life. They founded villages and named them. Some centuries later the Normans wrote these names down in their Domesday Book, and there they still are in our up-to-date maps and guide-books, very little altered.

So far as place-names go, Offa's Dyke continues to mark the Border, having Celtic topography on the west and English on the east. This speaks volumes for the conservatism (it would not smell as sweet if you called it prejudice) of both races, for the Border, proper, has swayed to and fro considerably since the eighth century and only at two places in Shropshire does it still coincide with the Dyke.

In 1935 Sir Cyril Fox carried out a systematic research of the ruins of the great barrier and gave it as his opinion that the line, although strategically drawn in general in favour of the Saxon, was not forced by him on his Cymric neighbour but negotiated by treaty. I should prefer to believe that this was not so, for, if it were, the English kept their bargain badly. By the time the Normans came they had over-run the line of the Dyke and penetrated far into Wales both from Shropshire and Herefordshire. It seems to me to be taking too optimistic a view of inevitables to believe that the Welsh of the eighth century would agree to have anything so injurious to their pride as a fixed boundary (with a ditch towards Wales) forced upon them, or that the English of that time would trouble to consult them in the matter. The mingling and mellowing that has gone on, on both sides of the Dyke, during the last twelve hundred years has modified characteristics on both sides but has not altered the tendency to react instantly and oppositely when the labels "English" and "Welsh" are displayed.

I am inclined to think that in all their dealings with the Welsh the Saxons were positive and blunt but generally true to their pledged word. They did not go in for compromise. It was the Normans who produced that melting-pot system which took the place of the Dyke between the two countries with results that have had a lasting effect, at least in Herefordshire and Shropshire and their opposite numbers in the west.

The Normans must have been a great surprise and puzzle to the Welsh. Ethnologically, they were Scandinavian sea wolves in Frenchmen's clothing. Since the days of the Roman occupation of Britain the Celtic speech had become saturated —by nearly three to one—with Latin words, so that the Norse-Frenchman and the Romanized Welshman had certain artificial foundations in common. Also the Normans, though barbarous at heart, had suave manners and a veneer of culture entirely agreeable to the Welshman. It was no small point in their favour, too, that the Norman had downed the hated Saxon.

7

From the Norman point of view, Wales was a very convenient reserve of territory into which supernumerary knights could be let loose after all the English manors had been distributed to William's most deserving friends. This did not happen immediately. First of all we hear of extraordinary excursions into Wales that were only lightly opposed and seem in places to have been even welcomed.

Roger de Montgomery, one of William's principal advisers and most resolute leaders in the Battle of Hastings, was made Earl of Shrewsbury. He very soon went down the Roman Watling Street and secured his headquarters at Shrewsbury by founding a castle with its huge earthwork motte, still surviving. Next, he took the other Roman road into Wales to the first important stop along that route where the Romans had secured their second passage of the Severn, and built another castle on the cliff that rises abruptly at that point. It was called after his home town in Normandy: Montgomery, a homely commonplace which recalls the doings of American pioneers of a later date. A little later he went on to mid-Wales and built another castle at Llandovery, ending his march on the Atlantic coast, where he built the castle at Cardigan. His nephew, Arnulph, carried on the good work in Pembrokeshire while the Welsh did little more than look on.

Hugh of Avranches, made Earl of Chester, set off west along his branch of the Roman road and reached that inner sanctuary of the mountain fastness, Carnarvon, without much difficulty. Here he built the wooden castle that was still standing in Edward I's time. Then he betook himself over the Menai Straits and built the very imposing motte near Penmon.

In the course of time the Welsh woke up to the fact that not only were the Normans no better than the Saxons, they were more dangerous and more unscrupulous. Then they set to, to throw them out. Meanwhile, a system of defence

8

for the Border had been established. It was based on the original idea that a knight who could make a conquest for himself in Wales could hold and rule his possession as an independent principality with the sanction of the King of England. There were, theoretically, three parties to the bargain, the King, the knight (now styled Lord Marcher), and his subjects (though these presumably were not consulted). The Lord Marcher must do homage for his Welsh land to the King of England; in return, the King would come to his aid if heavily attacked by the Welsh. He was to hold his own courts and dispense his own justice without reference to any of the King's officers. But if he became oppressive his subject had the right to go to the King and complain.

In the first great anti-Norman demonstration the Welsh either killed or chased out many of the foreigners who had established themselves in parts too remote to get help from the English crown. But most of them located on the actual Border, within easy reach of Chester, Shrewsbury, Hereford, or Gloucester were able to resist and remained with their powers unimpaired until the time of Henry VIII. Thus Shropshire was no longer sundered from Wales by a single line of earthwork, as in Offa's time, nor yet by a Debatable Land, as happened on the Scottish Border, but by buffer states ruled by the lords of Wigmore, Clun, Montgomery, Oswestry, and Whittington. The last two were always uncertain quantities, being not infrequently over-run by the Princes of Powys. But there would come inevitably the time when these princes became involved in a war with other Welsh princes and the Lords Marchers would come back into their own.

This method of defence was cheap so far as the English government was concerned, but it was not any more effective than the system of Wardens of the Marches on the Scottish Border. In war the Welsh came in force into Shropshire and could not be stopped, and in peace they slipped through by stealth or connivance and raided cattle in those fat pastures where dairy herds now graze. Return matches, such as made good ballad-singing in the Northern forays, were not fashionable, for the Welsh did not live in towns and villages and peel towers that you could set on fire. They dissolved into the mountains like mist and shadows, and then ambushed you in retreat. So they were given hard names—"Taffy was a thief." But to go to Taffy's house and beat about his head with a marrow-bone was easier for a Cheshire man to do than a proud Salopian.

When, in 1535, Henry VIII brought the whole of Wales under the English shire system the western boundary of Shropshire was enlarged to include the lordships of Clun, Chirbury, Oswestry, and Whittington as hundreds. It is difficult to picture what these communities can have been like which had lived for so long in their little worlds, where manners and traditions of the twelfth century were still preserved, while England had passed through the discipline and development of the whole of the Mediaeval period and now stood on the brink of the Reformation and the Renaissance movement. Even under such a tutelage and within such circumscribed bounds, the English and Welsh elements had not mixed. For in each lordship there was an Englishry and a Welshery. In the former a Norman interpretation of English law, as it was understood about the time of Henry II, mixed with what was called the "Custom of the March," was dispensed, while in the other the old tribal law of Wales, also modified by the Custom of the March, obtained.

One cannot know what the addition of these elements to the stable population of Shropshire, still mainly Saxon in thought, word, and deed, can have been; but one has a very strong feeling when wandering in the country of the old marchland with its magical environment, its sparkling air and clear distances, that the people match it because they have certain magical qualities of their own—not like those of any other people except the folk in the enlarged boundary of Herefordshire whose history was the same—men with an imagination founded on three creeds, a belief in God, in ghosts, and in the fairies: Saxons in craftsmanship, Normans in their craze for sport, and Welsh in wit and intuition.

Chapter II

THE MERES AND MOSSES

I REMEMBER the day I first went to Fenn's Moss. It was in the autumn of 1915. I was a young temporary lieutenant, then, quartered in the big camp lately erected at Prees Heath near Whitchurch. Owing, however, to a particular mystery in signalling which I professed, I was not so much mewed up as others of my kind; I was even allowed to be absent at will from the sacred function of the mess dinner, and I generally was.

In a lane turning off from the village of Prees there was one of those simple brick cottage-houses of the mid-nineteenth-century, so plentiful in North Shropshire, which are architecturally plain and yet have comfort and even charm, for there is always a setting of flower-garden, usually reinforced with jasmine trellises and bees, with a small orchard beyond, populated with pigs, hens, and ducks.

Here lived Mrs A., who was persuaded to let a sitting-room, and here I was generally to be found in off-duty times rather than in the mess ante-room. Another young officer with literary leanings shared the secret and the expenses of this retreat. Mrs A. would prepare tea and any number of poached eggs at any time, and when these had been brought in and she had made as though to go, she would generally halt in the doorway, holding the empty tray and looking at it with a slight pucker of the brow as if there were something invisible thereon which she had not yet served. It would immediately be forthcoming in the shape of a narrative which she had "just remembered."

These bits of news generally concerned the doings of local

12

heroes niched somewhere in the past, especially one John Thorne and the Reverend Mr Justice, and about the people who lived on the Moss. Her favourite characters were very real to her. She knew their general appearance and tricks of speech as if she had been personally acquainted with them. John Thorne was "a big, handsome, black-looking man." He came to Whitchurch and no one knew anything about him except that he was married and that his wife had a flourishing milliner's shop in Chester with a "large connection." He had the reputation of possessing an unusual gift of clairvoyance which he was able to transmit to anyone who came to consult him, so that they saw a vision within his sanctum as though seated in a camera-obscura. Here is a sample of the Thorne saga.

Farmer Booth lived at Twemlows. He was a very stern old man, and he had the finest wheat crops in the county. About 1830 there was a great scarcity of wheat in Shropshire, and at the same time there had been an outbreak of rick-fires in the neighbourhood. Booth swore that he was not going to be robbed in that manner. He would watch, himself, and any man he caught should hang for it. But he trusted in men's fear of him and went to bed. On that very night there was a ball at Whitchurch and someone brought word to the revellers that there was a fire at Twemlows. The people forsook their dancing and ran to Prees Heath with the idea of saving the property, "but most out of curiosity to see the fire and how Booth took it." However, Booth was not there; he was hurrying to Whitchurch, where he went straight to Thorne's house. Says he, "I want to know who's set my ricks afire."

To which Thorne replied casually, "I don't know who done it."

"Can't you do owt to help me?"

"Oh, perhaps, but you must take a solemn oath that you won't bring my name into a court of law."

A Bible was fetched and Booth swore. Then Thorne took him into a little room. "Do you know this place?" says he. "Why, yes," said Booth, "it's my stack-yard." In the dim light he could see his ricks in two long rows. Then Thorne took him out and disappeared for a few minutes, after which he brought him back again. There was his stack-yard once more. And now he could make out two men groping cautiously about. Presently a point of light glowed.

"Do you know them men?" said Thorne.

"I know enough" says Farmer Booth, and went straight back to Twemlows. "The next day," recounted Mrs A. solemnly, "he summonsed two young men from Tilstock, Lee and Grindley, and in open court accused them with having burned his stacks. He swore on oath that he had seen them setting the blaze. They were both condemned to be hanged on his accusation, and when on the scaffold they confessed to the deed."

I should not burden the reader with this story in the hopes that as a narrative it would be worth his perusal. The historic details may or may not be true; a little research (which I have not attempted) would soon decide. What counts for me is the magical element in it which Mrs A. firmly believed in and I know a great many of her neighbours did. Such stories were current and easily accessible in 1915 and perhaps still are, though, like the local dialect, they have gone further "underground" since then. They are an expression of that leaning towards the mystical which is typical of Shropshire. And if the stories are no longer current they must have been replaced by some other form of expression, for the feeling that there is but a thin partition between matters of fact and matters of fate is still prevalent. That is the note which Mary Webb strikes with such tremendous effect, making it issue not only from the people but from the scenery. Incidentally, there was another Thorne story so exactly parallel to that in which the more worldly enchanter

Beguildy conjures the vision of a maiden in *Precious Bane* that I am convinced Mary Webb drew it from that source.

Folklore is, after all, of most interest as an outward sign of the way in which people think and frame imaginative ideas. Everywhere there are the great traditional myths that seem to have had far-off beginnings in the forests of Germany or the lands east of Europe and to have been brought here by Saxon or Celt, but these are not of the same local significance as stories of recent date. Mrs A.'s other hero, Mr Justice, sometime Rector of Ightfield, fitted another category. They resembled the Johnny Cant stories of Monmouthshire brought up to date, but they were more sinister, for this clergyman was said to have secret dealings with the Devil and he was always referred to by the black name of the Old Rook. I will not detain you with more than one of these accounts.

The rector had a boy to work in his garden from the Sandhole. It was reported to him that this boy had whispered something about his master which was discreditable. The Old Rook sent for him and turned him away from his service and the boy returned home. One day Mr Justice was driving from Prees and passed the lad wheeling a barrow. He stopped and asked him what he was doing these days. The boy replied that he was trying to get a new place.

"You'll never get another place," said the Old Rook, and drove away.

Some time after, the boy was found sitting on the shafts of the barrow, pale and trembling. He said he felt ill. He was taken home and put to bed. The doctor was sent for. He came and examined him.

"You've had a fright, my lad," said the doctor. "What has scared you?"

The boy told of the meeting with the Rector and how after he had driven away a strange shadow had suddenly appeared in the road beside him. It was a strange shadow, nothing more, only it stayed by his shadow and would not go away. Three days afterwards he died. But while he lived he never stopped trembling.

Mrs A. had many tales about people living on the Moss. And she said that there used to be fairies there. If there were none there now it was quite certain that they used to frequent that part because things belonging to them had often been found. And what were these objects? Well, they were pipes. Pipes? Did not Pan have pipes, and did not Tennyson write of the "horns of Elfland faintly blowing"?

It was a still autumn afternoon when I first went to the Moss, a huge expanse of primaeval peat-bog extending for some four miles east and west and for some two miles or more in breadth. Only part of it is in Shropshire, the main bulk, called Fenn's Moss, lies in that detached part of Flintshire known as the Hundred of Maelor. Though no other part of the Border was strictly a no-man's-land, as in the Scottish Border, this was. One finds it referred to by both sides in ancient documents as the Wilderness.

It was indeed like another world. In the blue haze of that afternoon the horizon seemed to extend endlessly, dotted with dwarf birch spangled in gold. The silence was profound; one seemed to inhale it with the scent of the bog plants and the faint whiff of peat smoke. From the lane-end a path led away over firm ground towards a gaunt image in the blue that was the target of a rifle range. I detached myself with silent footfalls from the last signs of life represented by cottages at the lane's end, and they vanished immediately behind a screen of birch, not to reappear. The illusion of complete isolation was perfect. It was all the more striking because Fenn's Moss was not the first large peat-bog I had been on. I had seen some of the great ones in Ireland and also the peat-hags in Scotland where the Covenanters hid in the time of Claverhouse. But Fenn's Moss was not like them. Their desolation was wild and monotonous. This desolation was beautiful and solemn. So much drowned land, so much lurking treachery, such endless vistas of melting blue must inspire feelings of sadness. But they were tempered by the quality of the air which acted on the imagination as lyrically as lark-song.

Throughout the whole of human history man has only succeeded in making four marks on Fenn's Moss. Telford cut a corner of it with his canal, the Cambrian Railway engineer secured a passage along the northern fringe, there was the rifle range, and there were the peat-cutters. Otherwise it was as untouched as the sea, and its survival from primaevalism gave it something of the same elemental grandeur.

My next memory is of a Moss-man. He lived at one of those cottages at the lane-end, just within the Shropshire boundary, though whether I came across him on that first visit I can't remember. He was the jolliest fellow himself with a large jolly family of boys and he had a name I have never heard of before or since, Almark. It was the fairy pipes I wanted to know about. Had he ever seen or heard of such things? Oh, yes, he had plenty put by in a box. The large family, awed into silence by the presence of a strange soldier-man in their midst, turned and made a dash for the dresser. In an instant fairy pipes were being held aloft by every child, faces all aglow with excitement and expectancy in the generous flickering light of the peat fire. But they were in no sort those horns of elfland I had fancied; they were tobacco pipes; parts and pieces of tiny clay pipes with sloping bowls that were barely half an inch in diameter. I knew the kind, for they were common museum pieces, referable to the seventeenth century, and must have been cast away by workmen cutting peat all that long time ago.

I paid many visits to Fenn's Moss, saw many grand sunsets there and heard many strange tales about the doings of the old people and the fairies in the Moss, seated in the hospitable Almark circle. There was no radio to distract in those days.

In 1944 I came again to these old haunts. The heath at Prees had now been completely obliterated by a bomber airfield. But the Moss was just the same. It was a spring morning and the birches were just come into their new foliage, the ling and water-plants had that same heady smell, faintly spiced with peat smoke. The blue distances and the air of primaeval endlessness were all there as before. I met a man who gave me news of the Almark family, now dispersed. The Dutch firm were still steadily cutting the peat, mostly for litter (stable-bedding). It did not seem to have made any difference to the general appearence, nor had the bombers made any impression on it, for they had used part as a range. And peat-diggers still found fairy pipes.

To the west of the Moss, and a witness to the same geological phenomenon, is a cluster of meres, Ellesmere, Blake Mere (an archaic spelling for Black, one suspects), White Mere, Newton Mere, and Cole Mere. There are two outliers, Crose Mere to the south and Hanmer Mere to the north, in the Hundred of Maelor.

This little Lake District is situated among miniature hills that are no more than knolls. They are just big enough to show the lakes off to advantage. Their peculiar humpiness gives them a distinction and character and their gradients are steep enough for wooded dells to lie secretively and snugly.

These lakes, like some other Shropshire meres, have no feeder streams to speak of and no outlet drainage. They have lain here since the meltings of the last glaciers in the Welsh mountains flooded the land, having long ago struck a balance between rainfall and evaporation which has enabled them to stabilize their margins. Green sheep-pastures roll down to screens of alder and ash which venture to within the water's lap, reluctantly giving place to bulrush and sedge. On the bare bosoms of these reflecting and reflective waters

18

is always seen a host of visiting and resident waterfowl with its nobility of swans.

At certain times of the year, usually the late summer, there is a strange troubling of the waters, which become opaque, and a dark green scum rises to the surface. This is called the "breaking of the meres" and is caused by the sudden multiplication of an alga. The water becomes unusable for man or beast, and the fish lose their appetite for bait. The breaking lasts for varying lengths of time and clears as suddenly as it started, leaving the water more limpid than before. The provision is a remarkable one, for if it were absent the decaying vegetation which accumulates in these pools which have no outlet would certainly contaminate them. But the carbonic acid dissolved in the water is the very thing which promotes the propagation of the alga, and then the action of the chlorophyll in these minute plants disposes of the carbon and liberates the oxygen, rendering the water sweet. The occurrence is common to other Shropshire meres and probably to those of Staffordshire and Cheshire, though it was first studied in this county.

The manor of Ellesmere was part of the dowry of King John's bastard daughter, the Princess Joan, whom he gave in marriage to Llewelyn ap Iorwerth (the Great), Prince of Wales. A relic of the castle mound survives. The little town at the head of the mere derives much of its charm from that sheet of water with its swans and its boating. But it has something innate which makes it typical of the region of meres and mosses and not quite like anywhere else.

The only comparable neighbour is Whitchurch. That town has more half-timbered buildings than Ellesmere but is neither so pretty nor so homely. There is more stir and bustle in Whitchurch, though it is not an industrial place. It has, however, one trade which is an odd one. In old days it was famous for its grandfather clocks. When the railways came, one of these clockmakers was asked to provide timepieces for the stations and also to wind them up, for as the guard of a coach had not been thought sufficiently intelligent to wind up a clock provided for its journey by the post office, neither was a railway servant—not even a station-master. The railway became absorbed in the London and North-Western system and grew, and with it the business. The maker of grandfather clocks became a specialized railway horologist. He devised such masterpieces for whiling away the weary hours as the great clocks at Crewe, which, although they look so big and wide, are only empty drums round whose faces the giant hands are driven by a torque rod from machinery in the refreshment-room block.

Roads from Whitchurch and Ellesmere converge southward and meet at Wem. The inside of this triangle has always been cut off from the north by the barrier of Fenn's Moss and it remains, like parts of Essex, whose rivers have kept the London roads away, a district of untouched rural simplicity. It has never had but one important thoroughfare, the Shropshire Union Canal, and that has now sunk into picturesque desuetude. The little wharf at Edstaston with its old bridge and warehouses would be a favourite haunt of artists, if they knew of it. The offices and dwellings of the management have become the homes of cottagers who have the Shropshire taste for bright old-fashioned flower gardens, a hive or two of bees, and a bit of orchard, but the warehouses are still used. It shows how tenacious is tradition. A barge rarely if ever comes down this spur of the canal, but the place has remained a centre for farmers to get their stuff from. Now it comes there in motor-lorries, a factor arranges matters, and it is fetched away as of yore.

Edstaston itself is only just off the Whitchurch-Wem road and it has one of the most remarkable churches in Shropshire, whose foundation, however, is shrouded in complete mystery. It is described on page 92. But I fancy it is seldom

20

visited by strangers, for there is nothing to indicate its presence, not even a steeple.

The canal and its spur wind about in that triangle of by-roads which the traffic routes reck nothing of, among large brick farmhouses of Queen Anne and Georgian date with stately byres of half-timber. Swans nest in the basins by the old lime-kilns, and there is a general feeling abroad that Mrs A.'s stories may still be current at Welshend, Whixall, and Paddolgreen, if they are not indeed, as the Irish say, still "creating" there.

Much of the land here, too, was under water at one time and the soil is still rich in alluvium. It used to be one of the greatest barley lands in Shropshire and that is why there is a brewery at Wem. And because of the brewery and Wem Ales, whose legend appears so frequently, Wem is a famous place. Now, I fancy, the barley or its malt comes from elsewhere and the ancient water-mills have ceased to grind. The brewery remains, but the name of Wem is coupled today with a more teetotal beverage, namely, milk. It is the main centre of the Shropshire dairy-farming country, a pasture-land browsed by pedigreed herds whose respective merits are still a matter of keen speculation.

The three favourites are Frisians, shorthorns, and Ayrshires. The owners of these several herds hold strong views as to which is the "best" for the farmer to keep on these rich dairy pastures. The three breeds vary quite a lot in the three essential points, which are milk-yield in volume, milk-yield in fat (cream) content, and the posthumous yield of the animal itself in beef.

The contest of personal and expert opinions is all the keener because several new factors have come into the dairy-farming industry all at once. Chief among them are the petrol engine, the milk factories and cheese-making establishments, and mechanical milking. These have revolutionized the farm routine, made it less leisurely and less self-support-

21

ing, and though it has eased burdens in some directions it has created others, especially financial ones. The farmer's wife has probably come off best. It used to be her part to see to the cheese-making. This was a very exacting addition to her many other duties. She generally had a particular recipe which must be followed assiduously according to a family tradition. And then when the cheeses had been made they had to be pressed, and when they had been pressed the real hard work began, namely, the turning of them every so often. And the turning of three hundred heavy cheeses was no light job. But the consumer, both on and off the farm, had something that he can't get now-a-days, something that would ripen and mellow as lusciously as the cheeses of Cheshire, over the Border. The milk-collecting lorry has spoilt all that. No factory cheese can ever rival the farm-made article, nor can shopping rival in its social contacts such gatherings as the cheese-fairs of Ellesmere, Whitchurch, and Market Drayton. It is difficult to believe that the High Cheese party will ever be able to persuade the farmer's wife to return to her wring.

Mechanical milking has caused another sort of revolution. In addition to the pneumatic plant necessary for the operation it is desirable to have a large milking hall instead of the old-fashioned shippon, and this means a rather drastic conversion of the established farm buildings which form such a picturesque feature of the Shropshire farms. If you go in for a pedigreed herd it will seem a pity not to take the next step and install a pneumatic milker, and, having done that, it will not seem economical to carry on in the old cramped style which was very well for a cowman or a dairy-maid with a pail. All this means more capital outlay, and then more speeding-up and competition, out of which the small farmer comes off badly and so does the county feeling, for, when all's said and done, the milk, the condensed milk, and the butter and cheese which are products of the factory do not stay in the district or appear on the stalls of the picturesque local markets. And farming is apt to become, not a happy rustic living, but a branch of town-controlled industry. On the other hand, no one can complain of good and keen farming, with well-tended pastures, well-kept hedges, and prosperous-looking farmhouses and buildings. There is something typical of Shropshire in that.

Chapter III

RUYTON-ELEVEN-TOWNS

In 1929 I undertook a literary commission which enabled me to visit the greater part of Shropshire. During the recent war years military duties often took me to the county and I then constantly had in mind several oddments of interest whose detail was clear enough in my memory but not the place-names with which they were associated. Gradually I recovered all these identities whose labels were lost except one. It was an effigy in a church that the vicar assured me was made of iron. There are several grave-slabs made of iron, as in Sussex, though in this county I have not seen one earlier than the seventeenth century. The church was a small sandstone building whose ground-course throughout the whole of its perimeter was fluted with those mysterious grooves and cuts which are said to be the result of arrow-sharpening. I wanted to see this collection again to test a new theory, not related to lethal weapons but roasting-spits.

I never rediscovered that church, but if the effigy (early nineteenth century I think) were of cast iron like the grave-slabs, then it was one of the most wonderful castings I have ever seen. They were very painstaking in this debased art in Shropshire. At Cleobury North, for instance, a mediaeval parclose screen has been used to rail in a family pew. As there was not enough of the original tracery to go round they imitated a section in cast iron, and the restoration is quite indistinguishable except that the pattern repeats itself.

I found one of my oddments at Loppington. There it was, in the middle of the road, just as I remembered it sixteen years ago, an iron ring secured to an eye-bolt, lying flush

with the road-surface. It was a relic of that most barbarous
diversion that ever disgraced the name of sport—bull-baiting. I had looked so long in various villages for this object
without success that I feared it had been swept away by road
improvements. Indeed, the landlord of the Dicken Arms Inn,
opposite to which the ring is located, told me that this would
have happened when they last made up the road but for his
protests. The workmen had had orders to remove it and his
remonstrances would not have prevailed but for a point connected with a householder's technical ownership of the surface of a public way opposite his dwelling. He deserves high
commendation from those interested in the preservation of
ancient monuments. A bull-ring *in situ* is now very rare indeed, and though it may not be a highly esteemed "monument" with the antiquaries, it has its own peculiar value as a
reminder of our failings and is a salutary antidote to com-
placency in our record of humanitarianism.

Be it remembered that bull-baiting was so far from being
shameless as to be a municipal matter. If one turns up an
account of the expenses of the Corporation of Oswestry in
1682 one finds this:

For stone for the Bull-ring   0 : 2 : 6.

For eighteen pound of iron to make the ring   0 : 3 : 0.

Pd Kinge for working of it   0 : 1 : 6.

And yet almost stranger than the tolerance of this horrible
barbarity is the extenuating circumstance. When I was glancing through the old bylaws of Barnstaple I found under
1690, "Also it is ordained that no Butcher or Victualer shall
sell in the market within this Borough the flesh of any Bull,
or offer the same to sell, except the same Bull immediately
before the slaughter be beaten or chased with dogs for the
space of one hour, at the Bull Ring and usual place appointed
for the same purpose within this Borough upon paine of for-

feiting 6s 8d for every such default." A sanitary precaution!
The odd fact is borne out by like bylaws elsewhere.

But the iron ring is the only ugly thing in Loppington. The
turn to it is off that road from Ellesmere to Wem mentioned
in the last chapter. Probably this byroad is a very ancient
one, for it threads its way obliquely to the Welsh Border
where the county boundary still rests on Offa's Dyke and
where there must have been a way through when that barrier
was effective. It goes through an unspectacular countryside
but one which has that same wistful charm of detachment
about it which characterizes Fenn's Moss and the meres. It
has all been fenland in historic times, parts of it having been
drained and reclaimed within the last two centuries. But,
unlike the eastern fens, it has a sweeter and more invigor-
ating air for it is on an elevated plateau. Fenn's Moss itself
is three hundred feet above sea level and is on the actual line
of the water-parting which separates the basin of the Dee
from that of the Severn.

Going on down that byway to Wales which I have just
mentioned, you come to a group of four small meres. One of
them is called Marton Pool and should not be confounded
with the other mere of that name near Worthen, an easy
mistake to make as both have prehistoric associations.
These four meres are evidently the relics of a great lake and
fen which, having nearly dried up, has exposed one of the
most remarkable prehistoric relics we have. This is the
Berth. It is not approached by a road but stands in a clear
triangle formed by roads which must have been devised when
the ground was still too wet to cross. At first sight it appears
to be a large rounded shape rising from a saucer-like depression of meadow-land. At the foot of it, a ruffle of blue among
waving water-flags, is the Berth Pool. The Berth is so big
that the pool is called after it. In old days it must have been
quite the other way round.

In those days the Berth was evidently an island which had

been shaped and trimmed, scarped in one place and levelled in another, so that the upper part served as a platform for a habitable settlement. One guesses that the population must have been Celtic (late Iron Age) well established before the coming of the Romans and perhaps remaining in possession for long afterwards. It is a guess that does not require much detective work, for, standing on the Berth and gazing out over the surrounding expanse of green grass where the water-floods once rolled, one sees two great raised causeways approaching. One joins the island with the high ground on the east, the second goes to another raised platform which seems to bear some resemblance to an earthwork boat-harbour. The Glastonbury lake dwellings and the Irish lake cranogs spring to the mind.

The Berth is not quite like either of the above. Of its kind, it is unique, and of course one longs to know more. Many a less worthy relic has received meticulous attention from the excavator within the last thirty years, while the Berth has remained untouched. And yet the very fact that its mystery remains, that its secret lies hidden in the greensward we scan and tread, adds a charm to its natural beauty and solitude that could not be put back again with the earth when its treasure had been rifled. Among the ancient monuments we preserve some ought to be scheduled specifically as "Playgrounds for the Imagination" and kept free of diggers, fact-hunters, notice-boards, and custodians.

About a mile farther along the road is Baschurch. It was a place of considerable importance in Saxon times and the church was collegiate when its advowson was handed over to the new abbey at Shrewsbury at the time of the Norman Conquest. The origin of this "college" is as obscure as that of Pontesbury, where the rectory is still held by three priests. Both may have deeper roots than most of these ecclesiastical institutions and have sprung from a Celtic monastic foundation. If so, one would jump to the conclusion that the old

importance of Baschurch was not unconnected with the Iron
Age stronghold of the Berth. There are no Saxon remains in
the large, sombre-looking church, but there is a look of "has-
beens" about the curiously laid out little village. Its decline must have begun in the twelfth century when as a parish
it lost the whole of its western area through the rise of its
neighbour Ruyton to parochial and also military dignities of
its own.

Ruyton-of-the-Eleven-Towns (which looks even more impressive on the sign-posts marked Ruyton XI Towns) is
along the same road within two miles. Just before getting
there a stream is crossed called the River Perry, and by that
crossing the name Plattmill appears on the map. This is the
old boundary between mediaeval Shropshire and the
Marcher lands which lay like a buffer state between this part
of England and the Welsh kingdom of Powys. And the fore-
bear of this bridge by Plattmill must be identified with that
Platt Bridge which is constantly turning up in old documents
relating to security against Border raids. The survival of the
name Platt is interesting. Richard Gough, the seventeenth-
century local historian of Myddle, calls to mind that every
hamlet kept a light horseman fully armed in readiness to
ride at a moment's notice to a rendezvous, which was the
Platt Bridge. The alarm would mean that a raiding party
from Wales was on the move and any Welshman who was
found on the eastern side of the River Perry was to be slain
at sight. It is reminiscent of the old code relating to Offa's
Dyke, but more drastic, for then the Welshman was to lose
one hand only. But Gough must have been speaking of a
longer memory than anything in his own childhood, an echo,
in fact, from the early fifteenth century when Marcher rule
west of the Perry had been suspended for a while by that of
Owen Glendower.

At any rate, the name Platt is still on the map, though the
bridge was probably a little farther up-stream so that it

could be commanded by Ruyton Castle. It is really astonishing how these names stick in this part of the world. In the middle of the twelfth century the three manors of Ruyton, Wykey, and Felton were united to form one manor of Ruyton, the whole comprising eleven townships named Cotton, Eardiston, Shelvock, Shotatton, Wykey, Haughton, Rednal, Sutton, Tedsmore, West Felton, and of course Ruyton. And all the eleven still appear on the one-inch ordnance map, perpetuated in most cases by a single farmhouse, brave survival of a millennium of stormy history.

Ruyton is grouped round a sharp little hill on which stands the church and what is left of the castle. There is a generous space between the foot of the rock and the houses where the once famed market of the borough was held. The place can hardly be called a "town" in the modern sense (in spite of its multi-urban name), but it looks of more consequence than a village and, with its peculiar lay-out and setting, would be very picturesque if it had managed to keep some of its older houses.

All that is left of the castle is a fragment of the basement of its single square tower, a featureless thing from which even the casing of ashlar has been robbed. It is one of those bits of the lumber of the past which remains only because it has always been there. It does no "good" to anyone and is so ragged as to be quite impossible to tidy up, so why not tidy it away? I would vote for its retention—just as it is. Not for the same reason that I would wish to keep the bull-ring at Loppington, nor on academic grounds, but just for sentiment's sake. All the associations of Old Ruyton are centred round this stump which you can see and touch. And some may think that these associations are things worth knowing. I would like to say exactly what they are. But that entails a whole chapter on the March itself by way of introduction. Therefore I will proceed to it forthwith.

CHAPTER IV

BORDER CASTLES

THERE is a history of England and a history of Wales, but no history of the March. Its affairs come into prominence during a national crisis and then lapse into a long interval of silence. It is a sort of blind tract forming the margin of both main histories. Into its veiled seclusion went many political fugitives from both sides to seek oblivion or renew their strength. And out of it came many a dark horse. Nor could we know very much even if an eager historian were forthcoming, for gifted chroniclers were lacking, bards were forbidden, and the record-making, never a strong point in the March, has mostly perished by flame and neglect.

But what has been lost to the historian in technical matter is perhaps not so regrettable as what has been lost to the romancer in the stories of lives, loves, and deaths of the people who abode under that peculiar regime where one man could be oppressed and another find himself freer and more independent than anywhere else in feudal Europe. What we have to reckon with today is the impression which that lost world has left behind as a surviving influence.

Abstracts are so elusive that it is sometimes easier to assert them in the negative than in the positive. Let us begin by saying that the Shropshire man is less stolid than his Cheshire neighbour and less commercial than his neighbour of Staffordshire. Positively, though, he is more genial than either, more romantic, more fatalistic. He is very near akin to the Herefordshire man. There is no March now—has not been since 1535. In the west you step out of Shropshire into Wales. But it would never do to compare the Salopian with the Welshman. Such an assessment would seem to him monstrous and insulting. And one has to remember that loyalty to a traditional feud bears no relation to common sense. I know several places on the old Border elsewhere than in Shropshire where everyone has a Welsh name and also Welsh ways. But for generations they have been on the English side in all the broils and turmoils, and they will not hear a good word said for a Welshman.

But in Shropshire one may mention A. E. Housman and Mary Webb with impunity. And what witness do they bear to the inner nature of the proud Salopian? The Shropshire Lad sings of death with a gay ballad lilt. And in "Gone to Earth" and "The Golden Arrow," while the heart takes in those unutterable pangs, the mind seems to hear the brisk pluckings of a harp and the trills of an elfin chorus. This gaiety and sadness going hand in hand is in the people and in their scenery. You feel it by the Wrekin and on the Clee Hills. But it is an emanation that comes from the west and not from the east, from Radnor Forest, the Kerry Hills, and the Berwyn Mountains.

Let us take romance for granted when we find it; it is a rarity. And when it has mystery as beautiful and incalculable as woman let us accept it with all thankfulness and pass on to facts and figments.

One wonders what Duke William's thoughts were in regard to Wales before he launched his attack at Hastings. What was his intelligence about that western lobe of Britain which the Saxons had never succeeded in conquering, though they had mastered his own hardy forebears the Vikings? He seems to have had quite definite plans, in which he paid Wales the compliment of confronting her with three of his most powerful backers in the English venture, namely, William Fitz Osbern, who led the right wing at Hastings, Roger de Montgomery, who contributed sixty ships to the invasion fleet and took a leading part in the battle, and Hugh of

Avranches, who contributed a further sixty ships. These three were made respectively earls of Hereford, Shrewsbury, and Chester.

But it looks as if the plan were in being well in advance of the main operation, because a Norman knight is discovered already installed in his castle even before Harold began his brief reign. This was Richard le Scrob, whose Christian name survives at Richard's Castle in the very south-western tip of Shropshire. The place is just halfway between the estuaries of Dee and Severn and one cannot avoid the thought that it was a well-chosen listening-post for gossip about the strength of the Border and a ready-made base for future uses. It was not the only pre-Conquest Norman castle on the Border. Another was made at Ewyas Harold in south Herefordshire.

When looking at the castles of Shropshire on the map it is tempting to try to deduce from their positions and relationship some scheme of defence of the Border. And something of the sort no doubt there was, but only in a very general sense, the fortuitous element always taking first place. There can have been nothing like a strategic plan such as that shown in the chain of castles built by Edward I in North Wales. The establishment of the March was accidental, a temporary measure (in the eye of the English king, at least) to consolidate, for it must always have been hoped that, when circumstances permitted the next great campaign against Wales, the conquest would be completed and all petty sovereignties could then be abolished. As this hope showed a chronic tendency to fail, men made the best of a miscellaneous equipment that was partly designed as base for attack and partly made to suit the local tactical needs of a manor. Perhaps the last thing that the English king and his officials ever dreamed of was that the March would not be eliminated until a sovereign of Welsh descent sat upon the throne; but so it was.

The story of the March begins at Richard's Castle and it is by castles that I would like to try and expound it, so far as it relates to Shropshire, and I hope the reader will be as much impressed as I am by the way in which it is always dominated by fortuity rather than strategy, for that, of course, is part of its secret of romance.

Richard le Scrob was one of those tame Norman knights whom Edward the Confessor, noted for his pro-Norman sympathies, liked to have about him at his court of Westminster. It seems very odd that he should manage to find his way to this out-of-the-way part of the world and fix his abode there; it was not even on the Watling Street. I have hinted that Duke William might have wished for news from such a quarter and perhaps had other designs, and one wonders to what extent these were furthered by the saintly but Norman-struck Edward. Richard's Castle is eight miles from Ludlow, and there flourished there as early as the eleventh century the great Palmer's Guild, an institution in which the Confessor was probably interested. In the guild chapel at St Lawrence Church you will see a window of early fifteenth century date, which tells the story of a ring, in which the Confessor figures prominently. This would seem to provide at least an excuse for a tour of pilgrimage to South Shropshire. Naturally Richard would not find a Saxon town a good site for one of those earthwork and palisade castles that the Normans were already in the habit of building, though he might well choose that hill-top in the heart of the forest eight miles away.

At any rate he came and installed himself there and it is notable that when the exiled Earl Godwin came back into favour he saw to it that the other Norman castle which had been put up at Ewyas Harold (above mentioned) was destroyed, though he did not manage to eject Richard le Scrob.

The motte-and-baily type of castle was one of those simple devices which people do not copy because they seem too

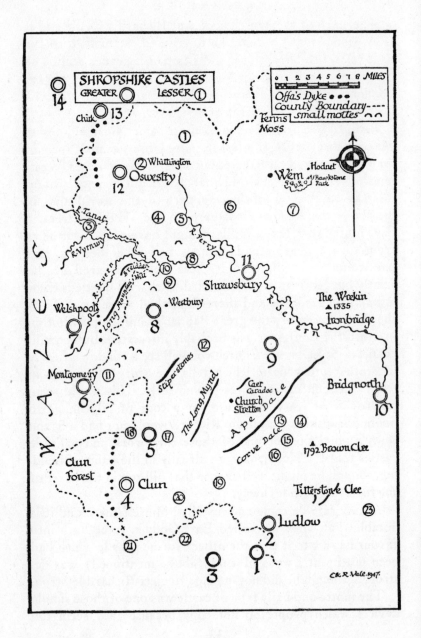

THE GREATER CASTLES (numbered from bottom to top)

1. Richard's Castle. Earthworks only.
2. Ludlow. A fine ruin.
3. Wigmore. Earthworks and fragments of masonry.
4. Clun. An impressive ruin.
5. Bishop's Castle. Platform of shell-keep only.
6. Montgomery. Fragmentary ruin.
7. Powys Castle. A Welsh castle. Residence of Lord Powys.
8. Caus Castle. Earthworks and stumps of masonry.
9. Acton Burnell. A "greater castle" by courtesy, actually a fortified bishop's residence. Much left of interest.
10. Bridgnorth. Wrecked keep only. A little down stream is the motte at Quatford, not indicated on the map.
11. Shrewsbury. Much restored.
12. Oswestry. Little but the motte left.
13. Chirk. Very complete. Still a private residence.
14. Dinas Bran, a Welsh castle. Very fragmentary ruin. Llangollen.

THE LESSER CASTLES (numbered from top to bottom)

1. Ellesmere. Motte only.
2. Whittington. A picturesque ruin but little left except gatehouse and moat.
3. Site of Carreghofa Castle. No remains.
4. Knockin. Earthworks only.
5. Ruyton-of-the-Eleven-Towns. Stump of tower only.
6. Middle. One tower (Tudor date) only.
7. Moreton Corbet. Ruin of Tudor mansion and part of earlier castle.
8. Shrawardine. Motte and stump of tower.
9. Wattlesborough. Norman tower and other ancient parts intact. The adjacent Rowton Castle is not shown. It is a modern residence. No remains of the fortilace are extant and its history is very obscure.
10. Alberbury. Ruined tower.
11. Chirbury. Motte only.
12. Castle Pulverbatch. Motte only.
13. Lower Millichope. Interesting remains. Usually mentioned as a "hunting lodge" but I think entitled to castle rank.
14. Holdgate. Motte of first castle. Part of second castle (thirteenth century) incorporated in adjacent house.
15. Broncroft Castle. A fourteenth century work with modern additions. Inhabited.
16. Corfam Castle. Faint remains of earthworks.

35

17. Lea Castle. Norman tower.
18. Bishop's Moat. Motte only.
19. Stokesay Castle. A fortified manor-house well preserved.
20. Hopton Castle. Motte and tower.
21. Knighton. Site only.
22. Brampton Brian. Interesting remains. Inhabited.
23. Cleobury Mortimer. Earthworks only.

The picturesque little thirteenth century ruin in Hawkestone Park called Red Castle has not been given a number. It lies just above the e in Wem. Its notoriety is based rather on its connection with Arthurian knights and Welsh giants than anything else, and these heroes are not so fashionable as they were.

Broncroft Castle

obvious to be believed in. The Normans thought of them first and the English disdained to copy them, partly no doubt because of the reason already given, and partly because they were foreign. They proved to be the chief instrument for the securing and maintaining of the Norman power after the Conquest. The principle is that you raise a mound, the same shape as a sand-castle, forming a ditch about it in the process. That is the "motte." Then you enclose a piece of ground with a rampart of earth, throwing up the earth from the outside so as to form a ditch round that. In this rampart you plant a wooden palisade, carrying it up on either side of the motte and round the flat platform on top, in the midst of which you set a wooden tower to command the whole work with archery. This enclosure is called the "baily" or ward and is usually supplemented by a second similar enclosure in which the entrance gate is set. The speed with which such a castle can be raised by a well-trained team is indicated by the time it is known to have taken King William to build his second castle at York, which was just eight days. And this had to accommodate a garrison of several hundred men.

The March is full of examples of these motte-and-baily castles of all shapes and sizes. Shropshire has two outstandingly huge ones, at Richard's Castle and Caus. In their way they are more impressive to contemplate than the great stone works at Ludlow, though it is not easy to say how much is original work and how much ought to be ascribed to the consolidators of the twelfth century. But at Shrewsbury, in spite of all the additions and alterations to the castle, the veritable motte of Roger de Montgomery is still extant.

The accompanying map shows the principal castles in Shropshire which may be thought of as being connected with the defences of the Border. Seven of these, and two beyond the present boundary, are indicated as prime key-points founded in the late eleventh century. I will give a brief account of them and the personalities connected with them,

37

Chimney Piece, Lower Spoad Farm

and the reader may then judge how far their arrangement is strategic and how far it is governed by local and personal considerations.

It would be natural to expect that as soon as the Conqueror appeared in person le Scrob of Richard's Castle would have an eye to the manor of Ludlow, a much more populous, and therefore profitable, holding than his eyrie on the forest hill-top. And we do, in fact, find in the Domesday Book that William had awarded it to Richard's son Osbern Fitz Richard, though he did not take possession himself but enfeoffed it to Roger de Lacy, whose name is perpetuated in the neighbouring parish of Stanton Lacy. This Roger got into trouble in the reign of Rufus by backing Robert of Normandy and had to leave the country in 1095, but his brother Hugh was allowed to keep Ludlow. One of these two, probably the former, began building the castle in stone, for the basement storey of the keep shows distinct eleventh-century work.

The situation of Ludlow on an eminence in the Teme Valley which opens a pass between England and Wales through the hills, and its station on the road leading from Shrewsbury to Hereford, at the break of the two counties, would seem to mark it down as an ideal site for a base of campaigning against Wales. But Ludlow was already an important place through its trade and church connections before the castle was built. It was a rich gift to a deserving family.

Clun was also a place of established importance, though its origin and that of its name are both obscure. It was awarded not by the Conqueror but by Roger de Montgomery to a follower, Picot de Say. Clun was never a base for any main operation against Wales and the de Says do not appear to have been very ambitious in trying to add to their lands at the expense of the Welsh, which might well have been expected of them, as their barony was not a rich one, con-

38

sisting for the most part of wild and unprofitable hill-country. So it is somewhat surprising to find one of them setting to work early in the twelfth century to build the huge and expensive fortress whose ruin is still formidable. It is doubtless the work of one who believed that money was better spent on house-pride than adventure. But Fate with its usual irony decreed that the male line of the de Says should fail in the middle of the same century. The heiress, Isabella, then allied herself to William Fitzalan, Lord of Oswestry, and there is nothing in the ruin of Clun Castle to suggest that anyone at a later date was sufficiently interested in it to do more than keep it in repair, an obligation which all Lords Marchers owed to the English crown.

The two Corbet brothers, Roger and Robert, came in for rich spoils at the hands of the Earl of Shrewsbury, Roger getting twenty manors in Shropshire and Robert fifteen. In the holding of the former was Westbury (which still keeps its Saxon name). About a mile and a half from here Roger built his castle of Caus, which really does seem to have been sited strategically, and built as a unit in a definite plan of campaign. The Corbets hailed from that eastern province of Normandy on the right bank of the Seine Estuary called Pays de Caux, a name which Roger transferred to his castle. It would seem to have been the custom to give your castle a name just as it is today to do the same for a house. Most of these familiar appellations have been lost for a long while, the buildings being known by the places where they stand. But charters preserve the names of two others in Shropshire and we know that Shrawardine Castle was properly Castle Isabella and Oswestry Castle, Castle Philip.

The site of Montgomery Castle (called after Roger's home town) was an inevitable one. The Romans had thought of it before (in terms of the Cornavian-Ordovician border and the ford of the Severn). Their fort, known in later times as Caer Fflos, was the next station west from

Uriconium. Its substantial ramparts are plainly visible in the fields close to the road leading from Montgomery to Chirbury, and most of the finds from the last excavation are in the Powysland Museum at Welshpool. But then the Celts were there before the Romans. They occupied the high ground behind the ruin of the mediaeval castle called Fridd Faldwyn and built there a strong "Iron Age fort." Excavations carried out in 1928 showed it to have been in occupation for a considerable time before the Romans arrived. In fact this site was of such importance geographically, both in war and commerce, that the crown appropriated it at the first opportunity and made Montgomery a royal castle.

Now, turning to the map once more, the eye catches Bishop's Castle. It looks uncommonly like a halfway house that has been fortified to serve as a convenient strong-point between Montgomery and Clun. But this conjecture is not borne out by its story, which is rather an odd one.

The relentless Offa, who flourished towards the close of the eighth century and built the Great Dyke, had gotten Ethelbert King of the East Angles into his power. The *Anglo-Saxon Chronicle* for the year 1794 mentions that Offa ordered the head of his royal prisoner to be struck off. The deed was done near Hereford and in that city the Anglian king was buried. Very soon miracles began to happen and a certain pilgrim went there out of West Shropshire called Egwin Shakehead whose ailment is indicated by his name. He was cured of his palsy. In return he gave the whole of his large manor of Lydbury (eighteen thousand acres) to the bishops of Hereford.

Shakehead's manor house and chief town must have been at Lydbury North and probably the Saxon bishops of Hereford had a palace here. What happened when the Norman regime came in is obscure. Three Norman castles exist within a short distance of each other. At Bishop's Moat, on the present border-line of the county, there is a large motte-and-baily earthwork which looks like a work of the eleventh century. Lea Castle, a mile and a half to the east of Bishop's Castle, shows a square Norman keep such as one associates with the early twelfth century. At Bishop's Castle itself there are the remains of a shell-keep which can hardly be earlier than the latter part of the twelfth century. All three appear to have been built with a main regard to the local tactical defence of the episcopal manor, though no doubt this was reinforced with a plea of "essential service" in defence of the Border, for the bishop was granted the usual seignorial rights of a Lord Marcher within this detached domain.

Probably in early Norman times Lea Castle was a residence and Bishop's Moat a frontier post. But when the new borough of Bishop's Castle was established the amenities of life and the necessities of defence were concentrated here. This is a site which must have been deliberately chosen after the first excitements of Border warfare had died down and after the first great English rebellions when the Lords Marchers took sides for and against the king and each other. It is a natural market centre and it must have been selected particularly with a view to trade. And though it has had its periods of depression, Bishop's Castle has always had trade. You may compare it with Caus (strategically chosen) which has now no near neighbour to its demolished castle but a single farmhouse.

To my thinking Causland (as the old marcher lordship was called) presents the most interesting problems of all these ancient defence zones and it is the region where the happy motte-hunter will find most virgin ground for research and speculation. It is on record that William, the son of Roger Fitz Corbet, who built Caus Castle, built Wattlesborough. This is a square tower which has become dovetailed into other buildings which comprise a farmhouse, so that in one storey at least it is still in use, and it has had only two changes of ownership since it was built, circumstances which make it one of the most picturesque buildings in Shropshire.

Presumably Wattlesborough was made for the dwelling-house of the lords of Causland, for though it was neither so grand nor so spacious as Caus Castle it was no doubt more peaceful and more convenient to Shrewsbury. As late as Elizabethan times, the high sheriff of the county, Sir Thomas Leighton, was content to live there. But it lay open to two valley routes from Wales towards Shrewsbury which were no doubt the trails of least resistance for raiding parties from the principality, and both by-passed Caus Castle. Along these two roads there are, at intervals, motte mounds —or so they appear to be. The last edition of the one-inch ordnance map, which is being issued while I am writing this, marks each of them as either "tumulus" or "beacon." But they certainly look as if they were of Norman make and the *Victoria County History* (1908) has taken them for granted as such and put them in its list of Norman mottes. They are very small, however, and if a palisade were erected on top you would think that there could hardly be room for half a dozen men to stand within it and draw bows.

Elsewhere in the March one finds mottes of this size that are said to have been used as the "caput" of a manor, or they are lightly written down as "adulterine" castles, meaning such as were raised without the proper royal licence to crenelate, and are conveniently attributed to King Stephen's reign. But the proximity and arrangement of the mounds in question would seem to suggest that neither explanation fitted them and that they were permanent defence-posts for the security of Wattlesborough. If so, then what were the practical details of the scheme? Who kept watch? How was the alarm raised? What was the drill for mustering? At what date was the plan conceived of, and for how many centuries did it last? I have not been able to find an answer to any of these questions. But the imagination is stimulated by the thought of the many brave tales that have been lost of those skirmishes to prevent the entry of raiders or to cut them off on the way home.

I last saw Wattlesborough on a spring evening in 1944, when the wild daffodils were out on the bank sides of the old moated garden, and the sun was setting, touching the Norman tower of red sandstone with a mellow glow, and glancing on the pale shining gold of the straw sticking out of the mixen in the cobbled farm-yard. The cattle were filing in from the fields for milking, and the rooks were moving from their feeding-grounds to some rookery which was probably as ancient and undisturbed as the tower, cawing lustily with satisfaction over our war-time policy of grain-production. I had just been walking through those fields and by those rook-woods which, as I have said, have changed hands only twice since the Conquest (and then through the marriage of heiresses—which is no change at all where kinship counts). I had noted that the lie of the hedgerows in one or two places bespoke great antiquity, survivals, probably, of pre-enclosure days, linking up with the three-field system, marks which could hardly have remained except on land so long in undisputed possession. Even banks and ditches can achieve a beauty in maturity which cannot be imitated for all the wealth in the world. So that when I saw the flame-colour on that twelfth century tower and heard cattle still lowing about it (and it was cattle that the Welshman usually came for) I thought that that sunset had been better spent by me at Wattlesborough than probably by anybody else in any other place.

So much for the principal early castles within the bounds of Shropshire—Oswestry we can leave for the moment. There was one in the neighbouring county of Hereford which we ought to take account of now because it nurtured a family destined to rule the fortunes not only of Shropshire but also of Wales and England. This was the castle of Wigmore, not quite so ruinous as Caus and Richard's Castle and perhaps even more impressive in its early motte and fosses.

The Conqueror's first operations against Wales were conducted from Hereford and not Shrewsbury. We have seen that in 1066 there was already a Norman strong-point at Richard's Castle, and another at Ewyas Harold, though it had been temporarily dismantled, and there is good reason to think that strong pro-Norman elements had been planted in Hereford City. At all events, while Shrewsbury had to wait until 1071 for the creation of Earl Roger and his arrival to take the initiative, William Fitz Osbern had been made Earl of Hereford as soon as the new king was crowned, and he set about at once making inroads into the Welsh lands and securing his gains by motte-and-baily castles. A knight in his train, who was his kinsman, bore the name of Ralph de Mortemer-en-Brai, a place in the Pays de Caux, from whence the Corbets came.

Fitz Osbern was the closest of William I's personal friends as well as his strongest man of war. He carried out his first campaign against Wales with great success and then managed to keep the whole realm of England in order while the King was away in Normandy. In 1071 he was killed fighting abroad. His son turned rebel; but in this affair Ralph de Mortemer sided with the King and not with the new Earl who was defeated and deprived of his honours and lands, some of which were handed to Ralph as rewards. Among these were the town and castle of Cleobury in Shropshire and the town and castle of Wigmore. In the time of his successor, Hugh, the family name was Anglicized into Mortimer.

It was perhaps Hugh Mortimer who built the formidable shell-keep on the great motte at Wigmore. He was much more active in annexing Welsh territory on the west than his neighbour de Say of Clun. He took advantage of the anarchy in King Stephen's reign and went so far as to seize the royal castle at Bridgnorth. For this he was called to account by the vigorous and order-loving Henry II. Hugh did not give way. He defied the King from his three castles of Wigmore, Cleobury, and Bridgnorth, but the royal power was too much for him and he had to submit. And now for the first time there appears the strength of a marcher baron. Henry II did not let rebels off lightly. But Hugh, although he had to give up Bridgnorth Castle (which wasn't his by rights, but the King's), was allowed to keep Wigmore and also Cleobury. Royal clemency of this sort was not extended to English nobles defeated after rebellion, no matter how high their rank—unless they had large holdings in the Marches of Wales. In such case, though, one observes time and again how the offence was either forgiven or condoned. For a large stake in the March gave a man an incalculable reserve of power both politically and in effective armament, and no English king relished a punitive expedition in those parts, for it was by no means certain that one of the Welsh princes would not join in the fray against the royal army.

The reader will find it easier to grasp the extraordinary story of the Mortimers by looking at the annotated pedigree (see page 228). It will be seen there how, by the peaceful means of marriage alliances, they secured the friendship of the ruling princely house of Wales and acquired those marcher lordships on the west, bordering their country, which took them right down to South Wales. And how, by the same means, they gained part of a province in Ireland and (more important to this story) the castle at Ludlow, whence they moved their headquarters from Wigmore. In the fourteenth century the most ambitious and the most unkind of them found himself in a position to assassinate the King of England which he did not scruple to take advantage of, thereafter having himself created Earl of March, a title equivalent to the old Saxon one of Earl of Mercia. Even so, although this Mortimer was brought to justice by Edward III and hanged on the common gallows at Tyburn, and though Wales (though not the March) had been conquered, the old superstition about doing away with a powerful marcher family still held good; and the son of Edward II's murderer was restored to all his honours and estates.

Finally, it will be seen how in Richard II's time the young Earl of March was acknowledged both by King and Parliament as heir to the throne of England, a hope deferred by the usurpation of the House of Lancaster. And how the male line failed just short of the realization of royalty, though the last of the Mortimers, Anne, provided the link which gave the victor of the Wars of the Roses his double title to the crown.

There is a small, armed figure standing in the northern gable of the old market-hall of Shrewsbury. It was taken from the mediaeval Welsh Bridge, dismantled at the end of the eighteenth century, and represents Richard Duke of York, the son of Anne Mortimer and the father of Edward IV. It is the nearest thing left to us of a portrait of any of the elder branch of that remarkable family, for all the splendid effigies which must have existed at Wigmore Abbey, where their bodies were brought for burial—even from the wilds of Ireland—have vanished. No doubt the Mortimers had a lot to do with the old prosperity of South Shropshire. Richard Duke of York was himself a good friend to Shrewsbury, and so was Edward IV, and the Tudors did not forget the claims of their Mortimer blood.

CHAPTER V

THE HUNDRED OF OSWESTRY

A F T E R this brief excursion among the castles of the Shropshire Border we may return to Ruyton-of-the-Eleven-Towns and ask why a castle should have been built there. True, the Hundred of Oswestry was march-land in the Middle Ages and not part of Shropshire until 1535. But the March was officially pro-English, so why fortify a bridgehead at that point? The answer would seem to be that in the first instance the little hill offered an irresistible perch for a motte emplacement when the Normans first came into that part, and that the stone castle was made when the place was created a borough to give it the seal of dignity. There were four boroughs in the March adjacent to Shropshire, Oswestry, Ruyton, Bishop's Castle, and Clun, and they were all prerogative creations of the Lords Marchers. It was the latest of the four. The other three had powerful castles, and that this should have at least a token castle must have been thought a *sine qua non*.

Ruyton received its first charter in 1308 from Edmund Fitzalan. A reaffirmation copy of it is extant showing it to be a very fair and liberal deed. We may note one point of it in passing, namely that the terms indicate that brewing was even in those days a main local industry. How conservative a thing is trade! In reading this charter one seems to hear ancestral voices prophesying Wem Ales.

I would not wish to weary the reader by giving him an overdose of mediaeval history about the March all in one place, but as the Mortimers have taken a turn on our small stage something ought to be said about the Fitzalans, and

47

I must admit that to me the chief interest of the stump of the tower at Ruyton is its memorial link with Edmund Fitzalan.

The first of the line to come into prominence in English politics was John Fitzalan, the son of that William who had married Isabella de Say (p. 39) and thereby augmented his power by the addition of the honour of Clun. Oswestry Castle can never have been such an imposing edifice as Clun Castle, but it was a strategic point and more than one main attack on Wales by the English Army had been prepared and launched from there. It was no doubt this reason, added to John Fitzalan's own force of character, which brought him to Runnymede as a witness to Magna Carta.

There was only one way of making a great fortune quickly in the Middle Ages and that was by marrying a great heiress. It was in this way that the second John Fitzalan became Earl of Arundel in 1243. Edmund was his great grandson. It was a great thing to be Count of Sussex, but much greater to be all that and, in addition, have two lordships in the Marches of Wales. If the times in which he had lived had been normal, this Earl of Arundel might have used the power which came to him and his natural ability to have served the country in a great capacity. But he lived in one of the worst periods of history, when neither power nor ability nor good will could do more than serve the ends of a party faction. Surely there are tragedies of the body corporate as well as the individual.

In public life of the early fourteenth century (as reflected in the textbooks of English history) the name of this Edmund Earl of Arundel is apt to crop up three times. In 1310 he is one of the Lords Ordainers (that body beloved of school exam'-setters, which tried to govern England when Edward II had failed to do so). At that time he was on good terms with Henry of Lancaster, whose government of the country eventually superseded that of the Lords

48

Ordainers. Then he appears as one of the judges who condemned Lancaster to death at Pontefract. Later on it is
the famous Despensers who govern in the King's name and
the whole country is divided. The barons of the Welsh
Marches take sides and Arundel is found in a different camp
from the Mortimers of Wigmore and Chirk. Civil war begins again. King Edward captures Bridgnorth and comes to
Shrewsbury. Arundel comes to his castle at Shrawardine and
joins forces with him. Many great men of the anti-Despenser
party are slain and both the Mortimers are captured and
doomed to perpetual imprisonment in the Tower of London.
Arundel is now given large rewards from the Mortimer
lands and made Justice of Wales and Warden of the Welsh
Marches. He is, in fact, next to the Despensers probably
the most powerful man in the realm.

But in 1324 Roger Mortimer of Wigmore escaped from
the Tower and managed to make his way into France. About
that time there was a small local broil in the little town of
Saint Sardos in Guienne between the people and their English seneschal. This came to the ears of the French King,
Charles IV. He bethought him of the trouble there had
been between his father and that of the present king of
England, only partly healed by the Treaty of Chartres in
1299. He reviewed the present state of affairs in the rival
country across the Channel and forthwith summoned Edward to come to Paris and do homage for Guienne. Edward
was quite prepared to do so, but the Despensers dissuaded
him. Instead his queen, Isabella, sister of the French king,
was sent as plenipotentiary.

When Queen Isabella came to the French court she found
there Roger Mortimer and fell violently in love with him.
Between them they thought out a way of converting the business of her embassy into the means to quite another end.
Letters were sent to London urging that Prince Edward
should be sent over to France to represent his father in do-

49

ing homage for Guienne. The scheme worked and the boy, who was only thirteen, joined his mother in Paris. In 1326 Mortimer, the Queen, and the captive prince landed in Suffolk and were joined by their friends. The rest is recorded in every history textbook, a few mention in aside that on November the seventeenth the same year Edmund Earl of Arundel was captured at Shrewsbury and beheaded in the market-place at Hereford by order of Roger Mortimer, who was the virtual ruler of England and already contemplating the murder of Edward II.

So it would seem that the creation of the borough of Ruyton-of-the-Eleven-Towns was the only lasting public benefit that this man of great opportunities and (I believe) good will was able to bestow, and the old stump of a castle is a rather touching memorial to one who might have figured in a great play or a great novel.

The Fitzalans and the Mortimers reached pinnacles of fame and vanished from the lands which knew them. They had much to do with the making of Shropshire, but not nearly so much to do with keeping things going there as the Corbets of Caus, the Sandfords of Sandford, the Plowdens of Plowden, and others who are still living on their lands of Norman gift. These have not cut such figures in the national history. They have not even, in the course of all these ages, become ennobled. But they have been constantly active in the affairs of the county, watching its interests since the days when the first model Parliament was summoned by Edward I at Acton Burnell, and ensuring in their quiet way the persistence of that distinctive individuality which still impresses the stranger.

Oswestry was the centre of the Fitzalan lordship and was then, as now, the centre of the hundred of that name. It is the only hundred-centre which is still represented by a town of any importance, and this is reckoned the second town in Shropshire. The place has had three names, all of them unusually pregnant with interest to the student of antiquities. At the time of the Domesday survey (1085) it is called Meresberie, the hundred being called Meresete. That is of interest because, like the Wrocensetan (p. 5) it betokens the presence at an early date of one of the Saxon tribes (similar to the reminiscence preserved in the names Somerset and Dorset). But at the end of the eleventh century it is mentioned in a charter granted to Shrewsbury Abbey by Earl Hugh de Montgomery (Roger's son) as Oswaldstre. By a similar name the Welsh appear to have known it for some time—Croes Oswallt (Oswald's Cross).

It is matter of history that Oswald, the Christian king of Bernicia, brought his army all the way from Northumberland to attack the pagan ruler of Mercia, the famous Penda, and was slain by him at the Battle of Maserfield. That this site is to be identified with Oswestry there is less doubt than in most instances of this kind. Oswald was regarded as a martyr and duly canonized, a fact of which the Mercians were probably not very proud, and it is perhaps not to be wondered at that although Oswald was killed in 642 his name was not mentioned in association with the site of his martyrdom until the coming of the pious Normans. All the same, it was not by either of these names that the place seems to have been generally known in the twelfth and early thirteenth centuries, when it was constantly referred to as Blanc Minster (the White Church), sometimes causing confusion with its namesake Whitchurch.

Oswald's well (reputed for miraculous cures even in the Venerable Bede's time) is still shown. It is not quite adjacent to the church, as one would expect, though at no great distance from it. But the church is nearer to the well than it is to the castle and stands in quite an unusual relation both to this and to the present town, which must indicate that the original place was of ecclesiastical rather than of military or urban importance.

And there is another sidelight on that remote affair of the seventh century which I hope the reader (who has not already skipped) will allow me to mention. At Woolstan, less than two miles to the south-west of the town, there is a charming little half-timbered building standing over a well. In post-Reformation times this pool was enlarged and altered and used rather like a modern "swimming pool." Parties came here not only to dip but to drink and roister. Local ale houses, which in the eighteenth century numbered five, kept open well into the small hours and the place got into such bad repute that revels had to be officially banned in 1755. This small house contains the timbers of a mediaeval building which served the bathers when the spring was a holy one. It has been associated with the cult of St Winifred but there does not seem to be any sure foundation to this tradition. At any rate, the name Woolstan appears in the Domesday Book as Osulvestone. This is evidently Oswald's Stone and must somehow have been connected in the story of the Battle of Maserfield with Oswald's Tree, the tree presumably being of the species gallows-tree on which the remains of the defeated hero would be exhibited by the ferocious Penda after the manner of the time.

But the town of today has a singularly blithesome air about it that I would ascribe partly to the happy Anglo-Celtic mixture of its people and partly to its delightful situation. It is a very English place in its good Salopian tradition of building and in the brisk business-like air of its shop-keepers (two traits which are absent in a very Welsh place) and yet it gives the impression of being nearer to the Wales of romance and legend than any other town on the Border. It is situated on the very edge of the Shropshire Plain at the foot of the first foot-hill. Up this the road to the west goes with hardly a break until it reaches the summit (just about a thousand feet). Here you find yourself on a long flat-topped ridge called "The Racecourse." An expanse of heather and

Llanymynech Hill
A Border nag

gorse stretches to north and south parted by a clear belt of mountain greensward as smooth as a well-kept putting-green —the old racecourse.

From here there is one of the most astonishing views in England. To the east the Shropshire Plain rolls its green farmlands into the aetherial blue in which the pyramid of the Wrekin stands some thirty miles away. The dim crest of Wenlock Edge lies to the south-east, and the humped Breiddens rise on the Montgomeryshire border. Westward, the scene is all mountain from the jags of Cader Idris (clearly seen when fine) to the Berwyn massif, while the hills in the near foreground are of a vigorous and determined down on the other side of the ridge, you can see Offa's Dyke shape such as impressionist artists dote on.

If you go to the brow of the hill where the road pitches a couple of hundred yards away, now acting as a hedge bank. It is rather less than a fair sample of the great Saxon earthwork. The present boundary between Shropshire and the principality is barely a mile beyond it.

On the other side of the town, crossing the Shrewsbury road at right angles, can be seen that still earlier boundary called Watt's Dyke, about which neither history nor legend has anything to say. Some mystery still attaches to these two earthworks but it is doubtful if they conceal any treasury of secrets for the spade to unearth. Very different is the case of Old Oswestry, that heavily fortified hill lying on the northern outskirt. Here are found vallum and ditch as impressive in size as those of Maiden Castle in Dorset, the work of those same Celts of the Iron Age. Very little excavation has been done here and it is difficult to believe that this tremendous hill-fort will not yield a rich hoard for the archaeologist when the time comes for its long silence to be broken.

Henry, the last Fitzalan, who lived as dangerously as Edmund and earned a much longer notice in the Dictionary

53

Shipton Hall, Corvedale
Entrance to tower, Upper Millichope Farm

of National Biography, died in 1580, leaving an heiress who married Thomas Howard, Duke of Norfolk, one of the friends of Mary Queen of Scots, who lost his head on that account. His son Philip, however, was allowed to keep the earldom of Arundel together with the baronies of Clun and Oswestry. But he ended his days mysteriously in the Tower of London, leaving behind one of those inscriptions in the Beauchamp Tower which are still quite legible. The forfeited honours were restored by James I to his son, Thomas Howard, who made a name for himself in a very different way from that of previous lords of Oswestry. He was a connoisseur and might perhaps be called the father of English museums. But he sold "all that Lordship, manor and Castle of Oswestrie, alias Oswester" to Dame Elizabeth Craven and it passed in the female line to the Herbert family and the present Earl of Powys.

There is scarcely anything left of the castle except the original motte. But the old outer baily keeps its shape and also its name—the Baily Head—and is the seat of the present borough government of the town and still the place of the ancient feudal market. Oswestry is a busy "market town" at the present day, meaning by that expression a selling centre for the agricultural produce of north-west Shropshire. Its older trade was more vital to the nation at large, being one of the chief marts for wool and woollen cloth from Wales, and here the Shrewsbury factors and merchants came to stock up the old Market House in the Square and carry the "cottons" for the noted company of Sheermen in Shrewsbury to dress. In pre-Tudor times this merchant trek was a hazardous one, even for armed parties, for the king's writ did not run in the Hundred of Oswestry and the sheriff of Shropshire could take no action beyond the Severn at Montford. Constant prayers were therefore said in the chapel of the Holy Trinity at St Mary's Church belonging to the Drapers' Guild for the safety of passengers along that road.

Wayfaring was no joke in the March. If you happened to be in a jurisdiction that was friendly to you, you might so easily stray out of it by taking a wrong turning.

Only two miles away to the east of Oswestry is Whittington, the head of a different lordship with a much more exciting history. It was constantly being "seized and held" either by the Prince of Wales or the King of England or that marcher baron who happened to be the rightful owner, and it is proper that it should have the most romantic-looking castle in Shropshire. There lies the flooded moat guarded by two swans and reflecting the twin towers of an embattled gatehouse and an ivied ruin peeping from an enchanted wood. And when the guide-book mentions such names as Marmion and Peveril of the Peak you must feel that a spell of Merlin's grammarie still prevails. So be content! Close the guide-book and ask no more of it. Gaze on the swans and on the gatehouse with its ancient wooden door still hanging. Think on the trophied halls of chivalry within the wood, but cross not the moat to seek them out.

The high ground on which the old Racecourse of Oswestry is situated breaks off at its south-west end to form a gap where two of the larger tributaries of the Severn, the Tannat and the Vyrnwy, meet just west of Llanymynech. The main street of this village has both pavements in Montgomeryshire but the houses on the eastern side are in Shropshire, which enables an inn-keeper on English ground to serve his customers on a Sunday, provided they can gain access through a side-street and not over the Welsh pavement. One inn-keeper has a porch with two Doric columns which rest on this holy ground. He pays rates for his inn to Shropshire but the Montgomeryshire County Council charge him one pound per annum for this two-legged embellishment to his house while banning its use for fifty-two days out of the three hundred and sixty-five. It is an acid test for the decorative value of a façade in terms of hard cash, and perhaps he could not have borne such an anti-aesthetic tyranny if he had not happened to have a corner stance with a door in England.

The end of the hill behind Pant and Llanymynech is car-boniferous limestone and is pitted with quarries old and new. But its upland is strange wild country with a luxuriant flora, woods of scrub birch, and yew trees growing from nooks in the cliffs of the old quarries. I have never seen cowslips grow so thickly and extensively as I saw here one spring during the war.

Offa's Dyke traverses this high ground, though not much of it is left. As a boundary it has been disregarded here for a long while and Shropshire makes a sharp salient into the old Welsh territory, though the place-names and even the names of farms remain Welsh. It reaches its farthest point west in the parish of Llanyblodwel through which that old road goes that we met at Baschurch and Ruyton, a way that takes you to Bala and on down to the seacoast. Llanyblod-wel, with its pretty little angler's inn by the old bridge on the banks of the clear, rushing Tannat, is much more like a Welsh than an English place. But the church shows you what the English could do in the mid-Victorian period with neo-Gothic restoration. What with marbles, paintwork, texts, and flamboyant tracery, *and* such a steeple, it is surely one of the most cheerful failures of the Gothic Revival which is to be seen anywhere. It is a fantasy, and somehow seems to fit in with the name Church-among-the-Flowers.

If we had come along the old road instead of follow-ing the Fitzalans to Oswestry, we should have gone by Knockin with its pleasant approach through a highroad avenue. There is the low flat-topped motte of the later Norman type there, now overgrown in a wood, where the L'Estranges had their old headquarters. They were sub-tenants of the Fitzalans and were lords of many manors both in Shropshire and that bit of Flintshire called the Hundred of Maelor which used to be in the March when the Welsh were not in possession. That late but interesting and nearly perfect churchyard cross at Hanmer bears their coat of arms, which is probably the reason for its survival. The religious Puritans who would smash a Christ or a saint let the L'Estrange greyhound be.

The Breidden and Moel y Golfa are the next landmark going south. I have noticed that while this group is called by the foreigner the Breidden Hills the Salopian calls it merely the Breidden (the double *d* pronounced as a thick *th*). There is some significance in that. They also say the Wrekin instead of Wrekin Hill, and the Clee. It is a far harkback to the Celtic manner of naming. The Welsh prefix the names not only of hills but places with the article *the*. Even the Normans said Le Rekin.

The sudden round-topped Breidden and its sharply peaked neighbour cut a very fine figure in the landscape from all points of view. The extensive quarrying operations which are eating them slowly away ought to be stopped and the wireless station recently established which tends to dwarf their mountain look ought to be moved on elsewhere. Its presence is entirely due to war shortages. An emergency arose when material was only available to build one mast. The difficulty was solved by finding a hill of the right height to act as second mast for a long aerial and in such a position that screening would not affect incoming waves.

The little range is a most delightful one to explore on an early summer's day when the bluebells are out. It is full of nooks and green dells sheltered by gnarled trees that the timber merchant has looked askance on. On the south side is a flat-topped detached hill crowned by an Iron Age fort with single rampart and ditch, with two great stones standing side by side in the middle of it. They were probably put there in the Tudor Period. They mark the boundary between Shropshire and Montgomeryshire.

Structurally these hills are volcanic lavas heaved up and cooled below the crust of the Ordovician world. The sharp-featured Moel y Golfa is an andesite, and Breidden Hill a dolerite, a hard, heavy, greenish rock so good for road metal and ballast that the attack on it is heavy. The Celtic fort just mentioned is not so much worth seeing as the fine stretch of wall (of the same period) near the top of the hill. On the very summit is a monument to Admiral Rodney. This tells you that it was put up in his honour by the gentry of Montgomeryshire and that it was done up later on by the gentry of Montgomery and Shropshire. I have not discovered yet why Admiral Rodney should have been commemorated here, as he does not seem to have had any association with either county, but I have been told more than once that the admiration he aroused by purchasing timber from the local woodlands for the Navy was what stirred subscribers to erect the Doric column even more than his victories at sea.

CHAPTER VI

THE RYELANDS

THE north-eastern corner of the county presents a very
different appearence from any other part. It is more solid
and Midlandish. If you should be journeying north from
Market Drayton up into Cheshire it is worth while to take
the byroad via Lonslow which brings you out on the main
road again by Adderley Church. West of this route three
estates adjoin one another and present a continuous view of
rich park lands and works of the landscape gardener that are
a little reminiscent of the Nottinghamshire Dukeries. Two
of the houses are visible, the moderate-sized one called the
Styche and the great one called Shavington Manor.

At the Styche, in 1725, was born Robert Clive, to whose
spirit and energies we undoubtedly owe—for better or worse
—our rule over the Empire of India. A momentous thing,
at all events, and something that could never have happened if our modern test for ability, the school-certificate,
had been in existence. The East India Company could have
made it a *sine qua non* for its clerkships and Robert would
surely have failed to satisfy the examiners. The Clives had
been long established here and were dyed-in-the-wool Salopians, Robert being twenty-first in descent from Henry de
Clive of Clive, a gentleman who lived in the twelfth century.

Robert Clive after his tremendous adventures in the East
returned home and represented Shropshire in Parliament
from 1760 until his death in 1774. He bought Walcott from
the ancient family of that name. But he died in London and
his body was brought to the little church of Morton Say,
in which parish he was born. Clive was ennobled in 1762,

being made Baron Clive of Plassy in the peerage of Ireland. His son Edward came to greater honours through less exertions. He was created Baron Clive of Walcott in the peerage of Great Britain in 1794. Later, on his marriage with the heiress of Powys, he was made Baron Powys of Powys Castle, Baron Herbert of Chirbury, Viscount Clive of Ludlow, and Earl of Powys in the County of Montgomery. Robert's statue stands in the Square at Shrewsbury, a good bronze of 1860. In that rather flowery period of commemorative art it is striking to note an inscription that conveys the spirit of the hero so perfectly. The plinth bears the single word, "Clive."

The manor of Shavington was acquired by the Needhams, a Cheshire family, in 1506. Sir Robert was sheriff of Shropshire and died in 1556. His brass at Adderley Church shows him dressed in Tudor armour. Shavington remained in the Needham family until 1885 and was then bought by Mr A. P. Heywood-Lonsdale. When the house changed hands a rich store of muniments was found relating to all the affairs of the previous owners during the three and a half centuries of their occupation as lords of the manor. These were documented and annotated by a very competent archivist, Mr H. D. Harrod, F.S.A., privately printed in two volumes at the expense of Mr Heywood-Lonsdale under the title of *The History of Shavington* and must rank only second in interest to the Ottley Papers (p. 150) among like county collections.

Among other matters of note which stand revealed in this hoard of old deeds and documents is the story of an ancient grudge. A branch of the family of Corbet lived (and still lives) at Adderley Hall (the third house mentioned above). They had been settled on their land since early feudal days and at some time in the remote past the lord of the manor of Shavington had held his land from a Corbet and owed the twentieth part of a knight's fee to his overlord. The feudal tenure of a knight's service consisted in accompanying the lord to the wars for a period of forty days. In some cases this had been commuted to a sum of money payable annually. By Tudor times, however, the due had generally lapsed and been forgotten. It does not seem to have been demanded from the new owners of Shavington until friction arose on other grounds.

The Corbets had always worshipped in the parish church, but before the Reformation there had been a private chapel at Shavington and a resident priest. In Queen Elizabeth's time, however, the use of such chapels was forbidden and it was made compulsory for everyone to attend public worship. There was no direct road from Shavington Hall to Adderley church, but there was a short cut through Adderley Park and this the Needham family made regular use of.

Under the new regime the squire of Adderley was also patron of the church and, as was the custom of the time, the Corbets chose to have their family pew erected in the place of highest honour, namely, the chancel. In this quarter the vicar was also allowed to have his pew, but no thought was taken for the needs of the Needhams. They had to put up with the humiliation of sitting in the nave until the vicar in Christian charity put his own pew at their disposal. Then an unfortunate thing happened. The vicar got married, and social considerations dictated that the Needhams had to retire once more into the nave. Sir Robert thought it was high time to make serious complaint and roundly tackled the squire of Adderley. A formal complaint was then laid before John Corbet, who retorted by demanding the old feudal due for that fraction of knight's service. This was refused. Corbet then blocked up the short cut to church. Insistence on its being a right of way met with contempt. In 1625 Sir Robert Needham was ennobled and became Viscount Kilmory in the peerage of Ireland. This made the Sunday situation almost insufferable, and matters were not improved in 1627 when John Corbet was created a baronet.

Lord Kilmory now made every effort to have the old privilege of a private chapel at Shavington restored and made interest with the Bishop of Coventry and Lichfield to this end. We have an account of a dinner in the Palace at Lichfield at which the legal aspect was discussed over good wine and by candlelight. The bishop was convinced that he might sanction the use of the chapel, and masons were set to work in haste. In 1629 he came to Shavington and consecrated the rebuilt chapel. Sir John, however, seems to have made interest elsewhere. In 1630 Sir Henry Martin, Dean of Arches, quashed the licence which had been granted and decided that only a limited consecration was valid for "celebrating the Lord's Supper and divine prayer and preaching the Word of God purely and sincerely." Early in 1632 Lord Kilmory died.

Although the Needham triumph had been somewhat diminished by the action of the Dean of Arches, it was nevertheless clear that the master of Adderley had been worsted. Sir John did not either forget or forgive. He had been heard to say with conviction that an English baronet was better than an Irish peer. In 1633 one of his footmen died. He sent for the vicar and gave explicit instructions that this man was to be buried in the chancel by the very place where Lady Kilmory lay. It came out later that the vicar expostulated in these words, "The chancel is the best part of the church and the best man could not have more honour than to be buried there. I pray you think of some fitter place for him."

To which Sir John replied, "I will have him buried there." This being the positive decree of the patron of the living, the vicar could do no other than obey. The interment took place at night and the matter was kept dark for a little.

When wind of what had been done got round to the new

viscount, he appealed through the proper channels and an enquiry was held in the parish church at Market Drayton on Sept 9, 1633. It was then ordered that the poor footman should be removed from the chancel. But this decision was reversed by higher authority.

Lord Kilmory was now in a dilemma as to the best legal procedure to take. There were several ways open, any one of which, if tried first, might spoil his chances of success with the others. Contrary to the advice of his lawyer, he applied direct to the Earl Marshal of England (Lord Arundel) who, as luck would have it, took a strong view and acted with great speed. In March 1634 the Earl Marshal promulgated a decree which could not be gainsaid, and the corpse of the lackey was removed. This success gave the second viscount courage to attempt a still bolder move, which would have the effect of carrying the feud into the enemy's country. He revived an idea of his father's, which was to have a splendid and roomy chapel added to the church itself. It was a thought full of subtle attraction from the worldly as well as the heavenly point of view but it had always been regarded as a chimera from the hard fact that where there is a patron of a church his leave must be sought before any building can be added to the fabric.

Lord Kilmory had learned that processes and "proper channels" were only snares. In 1635 he petitioned the King. The matter was unfolded to the Archbishop of Canterbury. Laud was at that time pursuing a vigorous policy in church matters in which the disciplining of patrons was a prominent feature. Accordingly he issued a licence in July of the same year, and plans were passed for the chapel to be erected at the head of the nave on the north side adjoining the chancel arch.

The chapel was completed in 1637 and no pains were spared to make it look like a house fit for a nobleman to worship in. In compliment, no doubt, to the archbishop's High

Church leaning, the old Gothic style was used and the exterior freely decorated with Needham heraldry and initials. Across the opening into the church an oak screen in the best Jacobean manner was erected.

This magnificent move was not quite checkmate. The debatable right of way could still be used to harass the enemy. Otherwise things quietened down on the surface until 1642. In that year national politics took a grave turn. The King and his Parliament were drifting asunder. Presently there would be a call to arms, and men would have to decide for whom they would stand. There would be no doubt about Lord Kilmory, for had he not obtained great benefits by petitioning the King?

On March the sixth, having got the key of the Kilmory chapel from the parish clerk, Lady Corbet arrived betimes with her family and servants and occupied the whole of it. On March the thirtieth the Needhams arrived in force and drove the Corbet retinue out of church, not without bloodshed. The next Sunday (the third before Easter) the congregation was told that the church had been profaned and no more services would be held there until it had been reconsecrated. At what date the bishop was fetched over to do this we know not, but on the ninth, at dead of night, the churchwarden entered with a gang of workmen and removed the massive oak screen of the chapel, re-erecting it before daybreak at the west end of the church. By May the eighth the building was presumably fit for the Divine Presence once more, for service was held and Lady Corbet with her family sat in the Kilmory chapel. She had, however, taken the precaution of placing a guard outside the church. Twenty armed men stood there all morning and forty all afternoon.

Lord Kilmory wrote off to Laud at once. But before his appeal reached Lambeth the archbishop had been carried off to the Tower. In the great Civil War most Shropshire gentlemen stood for the King, but Sir John Corbet was for the Parliament, which is not, perhaps, surprising in view of the facts narrated. He laughed last, and Lord Kilmory was fined by the triumphant government of Cromwell.

The tower of Adderley church was rebuilt in Queen Anne's reign and the nave in 1801, with a transept in the south wall opposite to that of the Needham chapel, to contain the Corbet pew. But the screen was not put back until 1822. And now there is little in the church to recall the doings of the ancient grudge. But the brass of old Sir Thomas must have seen it all happen. And when the Shavington estate was acquired by the present owners in 1885 a notice board stood on that short cut to church whose rights were never cleared up, bearing this inscription.

> This road is impassable
> Not even jackassable
> Who on it would travel
> Must bring his own gravel.

But that no longer applies. It forms part of the route that I suggested the reader should take with his car.

Market Drayton has a good deal of local character and preserves some picturesque half-timbered houses. I have only been able to pay it two fleeting visits and forgot each time to ask whether its mayoral procession on fair days and its ancient Court of Pie-powder were still held, and also to try and find out which of the gurgoyles on the church tower it was that Robert Clive as a boy climbed to and sat astride of while the townsmen held their breath.

The old battlefield of Blore Heath is only two miles away over the Staffordshire border. A mediaeval cross still stands on the spot where Lord Audlem was killed. It was here in 1459 that the Yorkists took a bad knock and the Lancastrians were able to march triumphantly down to the heart of the enemy's country at Ludlow and sack the town.

The farming between Drayton and Newport, and beyond, is chiefly arable and methods adopted are the most modernized in Shropshire. One of the big men in this industry kindly took me over his farms in 1945 and showed me what was doing. He had a highly mechanized equipment, mustered an electric welder among his farm hands, and owned among other machines a harvesting combine which I had not seen previously except on the Canadian prairie. It seemed odd to me that one could succeed in arable farming on the soil of this part of Shropshire, which is much lighter than elsewhere. But it is just here where mechanization tells over the older horse-drawn ploughing. The drainage is rapid, but if the soil can be made sufficiently retentive by a constant filling of humus it will yield magnificently. This can only be done by green crops being raised and ploughed in speedily, a problem to be resolved by tractors and capital. In pre-tractor days it was considered poor from the arable point of view, only fit to grow rye—hence the area names which you still hear occasionally—the Ryelands as opposed to the Wheatlands, south of Wenlock (where the Wheatland pack hunts, and there is a sign of the Wheatland Fox).

I could not help feeling, though, when I saw the potato-digger at work, that something of the slavery of industrialism was threatening the land-worker. The task is set by the speed of the machine and the reward is paid on results—piece-work. So that if the machine digs just a little bit faster than the labourer ought to work, the human being must compete with the machine. The agricultural industry is the last stronghold of the free man, the last place where he is not forced to work in artificial surroundings cut off from the contacts of nature, the last place where he can justifiably take his own time to do things. It used to be a "life" (the most complete and satisfying that a man could live). Is it

66

now to follow the inevitable lead of all machinery and become a "business"?

One feels this qualm especially in Shropshire. Here one is constantly reminded of the old struggle of sword versus plough and reaping-hook. Here one sees so well how triumphantly the struggle has ended. How whole families (squire, yeoman, and labourer) have remained on their land to ensue the peace, and how the best framework Nature could give for a county setting has been even more beautified by a rich tilth, a well-nourished pasture, and the contentment of all who get their living therefrom.

At Edgmond, near Newport, is the Harper Adams Agricultural College, founded by a private benefaction at the end of the nineteenth century.

Edgmond church is of interest to the collector of gurgoyles (if such a specialist exists) and there is a font here which is comparable with that at Stottesden. The carving of the interlace is more controlled and reminiscent of the Saxon tradition, though it must have been made in Norman times.

There are those who despise the "flat country" under any circumstances, and there are others who discriminate and are specially partial to old drowned lands reclaimed from the fen. For such, the country just west of Edgmond will seem romantic and picturesque. It is not like that other old fenland about Baschurch and the Berth (p. 26). It has its own regional flavour. Though here also is a great earthwork which has never been touched by excavation and its date is less easy to guess than that of the Berth. It is called simply Wall. The farm of this name stands on the crown of a small hill that was an island in the old fenland and often regains its insularity in wet weather. It is surrounded by a large earthwork bank with a wide flat top and of great breadth at the base and its circumference is just over one mile. The usual clues to Iron Age fortification are missing. One won-

ders whether it might not be Saxon. Archaeology is silent
on the subject.

The district is very Saxon in its names and suggestive of
its fenniness. To begin with, the whole area is called the
Weald Moors. Those who complain of the length of Welsh
names should remember that the English can produce one
or two. Ruyton-&c. we know, and here are Eyton-upon-the-
Weald-Moors and Preston-upon-the-Weald-Moors. And
these moors are moors in the old English sense, which does
not mean waste ground covered with heather but a swamp.
The word in its proper sense survives in the name of the
bird of that ilk, the moor-hen, a creature that is never seen
in places where the heather grows. And Sedgemoor preserves
the same usage. On Sedgemoor the ditches and trickles are
called rhines, and there is a Strine Brook on the Weald
Moors. Also, as in the other fens, it keeps its old island
names in *ey*, Kinnersley (Kinnard's Island), Adney (Ed-
win's Island), Butterey (the Isle of Butter, a lush pasture),
and Eyton (the Island Tun).

I must admit that the region fascinates me. If you can
enjoy the small things of exploration and go on foot or on
a bicycle, there is plenty to discover and probably tales to
hear like those which still hover round Fenn's Moss. And the
House that Jack built is at Cherrington.

There used to be a chain of lakes here of which only one
survives, Aqualate Mere, just over the Staffordshire border.
It is worth noting that some of this water of the Wild Moors
was put to economic use and was the first cause of the three
fishes which appear on the arms of Newport town. It was
by purveyance of fish to the king's court that the burgesses
held their ancient liberties. This supply came from a vivary
just outside the town whose last relic was destroyed by the
making of the Shropshire Canal in 1836. We, who have been
brought up to eat mainly sea fish caught by trawlers and
conserved by artificially made ice, may wonder how in the

Weather-board farm buildings in Corvedale
Ornate half-timber work in Shrewsbury

IN EXPECTATION

OF THE SECOND COMING
OF OVR SAVIOVR IESVS
CHRIST HERE LYETH
THE BODY OF MR CORNE
LVS ACTON LATE APO
THECARY IN THIS TO
WN WHO DEPARTED TH
IS LIFE APIL THE 9 1701
IN THE 40 YEARE OF HIS
AGE HERE ALSO LYETH
THE BODY OF THOMAS HIS
SVN HEE DEPARTED IAN
VARY THE 1 1695 IN
THE 2 YEAR OF HIS AGE

most remote places people could rely on making a Friday
meal of fish, to say nothing of eating it all Lent, which they
were compelled to do by law. And it may be mentioned that
there will be found in the church registers of Stanton Lacy
(early seventeenth century) a certificate granted by the
vicar declaring that "Dame Anne Foxe of Whichcote in the
parish of Stanton in respect of some indisposition of health
is to enter into a course of physicke this lente time and that
she may not eate fish during that course without prejudice
to her health and prejudice to her recoverie." But there
were from earliest times stews, fishponds, and weirs of all
sorts in all inland places which first fell into disuse when the
fish-eating acts were annulled and, finally, when rapid transport from the coast was established.

The vivary at Newport was a specially large one. The
chief official was an important man ranking with a forester
of the Wrekin and, with the men and contrivances at his
disposal, was able to supply a large regular weekly yield of
fish. It is a pity that this local amenity has gone even more
completely than the windmill, and there seems to be no
reason for it except the growth of commercial monopolies
and the inscrutable ways of fashion.

If we had taken the middle way out of Market Drayton
we should have come to Hodnet, one of the most picturesque
villages in North Shropshire. The guide-book will have
much to say about the church but will not tell you who made
the east window, which was put in in 1846 to the memory of
Reginald Heber, the author of some of our best hymns. Nor
can I find out from the present incumbent. But I think it must
be a late work of David Evans, the Shrewsbury glass-stainer.
It is not only a remarkable attempt to imitate the mediaeval
feeling (so much better than most Victorian experiments),
but also highly original and imaginative. It well deserves
scrutiny through binoculars.

Hawkstone Hill is just behind Hodnet. It is one of the

Iron grave slab, St Leonard's Church Bridgnorth
Font. Holdgate, 12th Century

three sandstone hills of North Shropshire and makes one of the most remarkable pieces of compact scenery in England. It is part of the park belonging to that famous Shropshire family, the Hills, whose most notable and popular member is commemorated on the large column at the eastern entrance to Shrewsbury. The house is now occupied by a Roman Catholic seminary.

But Hawkstone Hill has always been open—with certain limitations—to the public, and the variety of its sights is such as to require the services of a guide. This office has long remained in one family who live in the village of Weston on the southern slope of the hill. Some of these sights I may never have visited as I have not been guided. But in 1915 when I was quartered at Prees Heath camp I used to go to this strange place very often both by sunlight and moonlight and have never seen its like elsewhere. When Dr Johnson perambulated the grounds with his host and saw the woods, the rocks, the caves, and the subterranean passage, and gazed on the ruined tower of Red Castle (haunted by Knights of the Round Table), he wrote a most hair-raising account and was moved to use more epithets as to grandeur, beauty, and horror than in all his description of the Scottish Highlands.

The other two principal sandstone eminences are at Clive, where the Grinshill quarries are, spoken of elsewhere (p. 75) and at Nesscliff. Here is Kinnerston's Cave nearly opposite the Three Pigeons Inn on the Holyhead Road. It is the association with the outlaw Kinnerston of Tudor times which brings visitors to see it, for his initials and a date are plainly carved on the wall. The year, however, is subsequent to his death and perhaps a greater interest lies in the strong probability that this was the cell of an early religious recluse.

Between Nesscliff and Grinshill is Myddle. It is a charming little place and worth a visit for its own sake. But it has a very particular interest through having possessed a local historian who wrote an intimate account of it in 1701. This *Antiquities and Memoirs of the Parish of Myddle,* by Richard Gough, is a model work of its kind, and it is a pity we have not more like it. The author set about it in an original way that I don't think has been imitated. After a historical and topographical preamble in the accepted manner, though leavened by Gough's natural charm and wit, he comes to his real theme. This he introduces by giving a plan of the interior of the church, showing the pew seatings named and numbered to indicate which families occupied them. The rest of the book deals with the fortunes of those families, about which he gives all the facts and gossip that he knows. His comments are searching and although tempered with much sympathy are quite unsparing.

Gough had lived through one of the bitterest periods in our history and seen all accepted standards of life in decency, loyalty, and religion reversed and revalued. Yet, like Izaak Walton, he managed to keep his own natural equanimity and human kindness untainted by cynicism. The reader who has not seen Gough's book may like to hear how he remembers the impact of the great Civil War affected an out-of-the-way place like Myddle in 1644. So I quote:

"There happened noe considerable act of hostility in this parish dureing the time of the warres, save onely one small skirmage in Myddle, part of which I saw, while I was a schoole boy at Myddle under Mr Richard Rodericke, who commanded us boys to come into the Church, soe wee could not see the whoale action but it was thus. There was one Cornett Collins, an Irishman, who was a garrison soldier for the King at Shrawerdine Castle. This Collins made his excursions very often into this parish, and took away Catle, provisions, and bedding and what hee pleased. On the day before this conflict, hee had been at Myddle taking away bedding and when Margaret the wife of Allen Chaloner the smith had brought out and shewed him her best bedd, hee thinking it too course, cast it into the lake before the doore, and trode it under his horses feet. This Cornett on the day that this contest happened came to Myddle, and seaven soldiers with him, and his horse having cast a shooe hee alighted at Allen Chaloner's shop to have a new one putt one. There was one Richard Manning a Garrison soldier att Morton Corbett for the Parliament. This Manning was brought up as a servant under Thomas Jukes of Newton with whom he lived many years, and finding that Nat Owen did trouble this neighbourhood he had a grudge against him and came with seaven more soldiers with him hoping to find Owen at Myddle with his wife. This Maning and his companions came into Mydle at the gate by Mr Gittins house at What time the Cornett's horse was ashoeing. The Cornet hearing the gate clasp, looked by the end of the shop and saw the soldiers comeing and thereupon hee and his men mounted theire horses; and as the Cornett came at the end of the Shop a brisk young fellow shot him through the body with a carbine shott, and he fell down in the lake att Allen Challoner's doore. His men fled, two were taken, and as Maning was pursueing them in Myddle Wood Field, which was then uninclosed, Maning having the best horse overtook them, while his partners were farre behinde, but one of the Cornet's men shot Maning's horse, which fell down dead under him, and Maning had been taken prisoner had not some of his men come to rescue him. Hee tooke the saddle under his arme and the bridle in his hand and went the next day to Wem which was then a garrison for the Parliament.

"The Cornett was carried into Allen Chaloner's house and laid on the floore; he desired to have a bedde laid under him, but Margaret told him she had none but that which hee saw yesterday; hee prayed her to forgive him and lay that under him which shee did. Mr Rodericke was sent for to pray with him. I went with him and saw the Cornet lying on the bedd, and much blood running along the floore. In the night following, a troop of horse came from Shrawardine and prest a teame in Myddle, and so took the Cornett to Shrawardine, where he dyed the next day. Those two soldiers which were taken were Irishmen and when they came to Wem were both hanged—for the Parliament had made an ordinence that all native Irish found in the King's Army, when taken in England should bee hanged."

There is a nineteenth-century edition of Gough's book, but it must be scarce. It deserves a place among the classics of local history and perhaps some day an enterprising publisher will discover it.

Shrawardine has already been mentioned as a Fitzalan castle. Nothing is left of it but the mound and ground courses of masonry. This awkward-looking name has been euphonized into "Shraydon" and is generally so spelt in old documents. And, incidentally, Shavington is properly called "Shenton" by those who have learned the name by ear. But the present generation fear that their scholarship should be impugned if they do not pronounce by eye, and the work of centuries in rounding off a name so that it both sounds beautiful and fits the local idiom is undone. It is sad to see Shropshire place-names, which are particularly beautiful, suffer through this peculiar form of snobbery, and it is high time that someone led a revival movement in these aural amenities or much will be irretrievably lost and even documentary evidence will not reveal, for instance, that Ratlinghope should be "Ratchup."

Moreton Corbet, mentioned in the foregoing, has been the seat of the main branch of the Corbet family since the twelfth century. It was acquired by peaceful penetration and was not one of the manors bestowed on the Corbets by the first Earl of Shrewsbury. At that time it was still in occupation of a Saxon then called Turet, one of the few who had been allowed to retain any vestige of his ancestral heritage. Richard Corbet of Caus and Wattlesborough (great grandson of the original Roger Fitz-Corbet) married a Turet heiress. The family built themselves a castle there which must have been a much more powerful and splendid affair than Wattlesborough, though at that distance they can have had little to fear from the Welsh. Here they lived contentedly until 1606. At that time the then squire, Robert Corbet, being imbued with the contagious Renaissance passion, set about creating a palace in the best approved manner. Even the remains of it are no trifle and find no rival in Shropshire. The work was probably unfinished in the time of Robert's successor, Sir Vincent Corbet. He, unlike his cousin of Adderley, took the King's side, and his house was invested by the Roundheads just before the incident which Gough records. In the following March the garrison burnt it out and left it, and it has never been repaired and occupied. The family now live at Acton Reynold a little distance away.

Elsewhere, a sequel to Gough's story is recorded which gives one a taste of the bitterness of the times. Prince Rupert, who was in quarters at Shrewsbury, infuriated at the news of the hanging of the two Irish soldiers, swore that thirteen of the next batch of prisoners which he took should suffer the same fate. And this threat he carried out, but through the entreaties of Sir Vincent Corbet the thirteenth was spared.

Chapter VII

HOUSES

T H E county lends itself nobly as a background for buildings, providing rich settings for them. At the same time it yields a variety of excellent materials for their construction. There are several sources of good building stones and also of clays. The northern area is situated on the Triassic marls, and the south has a fair supply of red Devonian clays which, in old days, were used for daubing the wattle screens which filled the spaces between the timbers in the wooden houses, and for making bricks and tiles. And timber has never been scarce in Shropshire.

The Triassic sandstone (Keuper beds) makes three conspicuous hills in the northern plain, at Nesscliff, at Grinshill, and at Hawkstone. All three have been quarried extensively for building. The rock at Nesscliff is that full-blooded red which one associates with buildings of the New Red Sandstone. But Grinshill yields both a red and a creamy yellow stone, and the latter is known to have withstood the hard tests of weather for some eighteen hundred years. It is the pick of the sandstones, and the Romans, with their uncanny prescience of judgment, made use of it in their town of Uriconium. The quarry is some ten miles from Wroxeter and the direction does not coincide with any known Roman road or any natural waterway, but there it is! And it is not small stuff cut in those handy cubes typical of Roman building, but huge massive blocks that must weigh more than a ton apiece. Yet those stones must certainly have come from Grinshill, for the nature of the rock is sufficiently distinctive to be indisputable. Even further off is Buildwas Abbey, which evi-

75

dently came from the same source in the twelfth century.

The local sandstone seems to have tempted men into using Cyclopean masonry right down to the nineteenth century. For you see park and garden walls along the roadside in the Nesscliff district (and elsewhere) made with the naïve simplicity of a child's architecture. I took the measurements of an average-sized one at Burlton cross-roads near Loppington and found the blocks to be thirty-nine inches long, nineteen inches deep, and fifteen inches broad. Three of such courses will give you a wall one stone thick, just on five feet high, and you don't need to use mortar.

South Shropshire has a variety of freestones of lower Silurian age. The Hoar Edge grit is yellow with a gay sparkle and is seen at Leebotwood and Cardington. The upper bed of the Soudly Sandstone got at Hope Bowdler is a greenish-yellow with purple bands, the Horderley Stone is a greyish-purple, and the Downton Stone a pleasant yellow; it is seen much used in Ludlow and the neighbourhood. Farm-buildings in Corvedale are made of Devonian conglomerate, warm to the eye, and a smooth red freestone is also got from the same formation.

But not many great stone-built houses of the past, the castles excluded, are left in Shropshire. The most notable ones in a habitable state are Shipton Hall (c. 1587) and Condover Hall (c. 1595). Madely Court has long lain empty and Moreton Corbet is in sad ruin. The latter, of red Grinshill sandstone, is the most pretentiously ornate building in Shropshire and the detail of its carved work has worn wonderfully well in spite of three centuries of neglect.

The mediaeval period is poorly represented in domestic buildings of any kind. Shrewsbury has next to nothing to show previous to the sixteenth century. The most complete building in the county is Stokesay Castle, with its thirteenth-century hall and solar, which was made before the thought of castellation obsessed the owner. Cheney Longueville, now

a farm, has thirteenth-century bits, mostly in the outbuildings, and the old manor house at Aston Eyres, in a similar
state, has work of the fourteenth and fifteenth centuries.

The former home of the Bottrels at Aston Bottrel is a
stone house retaining something of its original character,
though it is engaged in a later building, and is well worth
seeing. The old house now appears as a wing at right angles
to the later main building. Its windows on both floors have
been altered and nothing would lead you to suspect its age
except a lancet light appearing in the gable-end near the back
door. The farmer kindly took me in and showed me his big
parlour and the bedroom above it, which gave no sign of
any earlier date than that of good Queen Anne. Then we
mounted into the attic and found ourselves up against the
veritable roof timbers of the old Bottrel hall. The roof,
which had, of course, in mediaeval days been open to view
from below without the inter-position of the two floors, was
in perfect condition and seemed to be work of the fourteenth
century. There were massive purlin braces cut out in the
form of quatrefoils, a favourite ornamental device in Shropshire church roofs, and the tie-beams of the heavy principals
were embedded in the floor.

There is an interesting and puzzling building at Upper
Millechope. Like Wattlesborough, it consists of a tower
with an annex of much later date which is now a farmhouse.
The tower, now used as a back kitchen, has in its upper
storey two twin-light windows of Early English date, made
by some mason who wrought in the best manner of the
period. One of these windows is blocked and in partial ruin,
but the other is in good condition, complete with nook-shafts,
and is a fine example of its period. It has on the inner side of
its mullion a contrivance I have only seen in two other places
(the castles of Connisborough and Chepstow), a stone loop
through which to pass a draw-bar.

The walls in the lower stage of the tower are six feet

thick with one or two bits of Norman mouldings built into
them, indicating a previous structure. But the doorway is
neither of this earlier period nor of the thirteenth century.
Its semi-circular head is decorated with a well-cut moulding
of the fourteenth century encrusted with the ball-flower ornament. A newel stair gives access to the first floor, now occupied by sacks of potatoes. There are two rooms here and the
partition is evidently of Tudor date. When I went there in
1944 two Italian prisoners and a farm boy in a blue smock
were making a Gargantuan meal in the lower room, which
added a sort of operatic touch of the picturesque to the
whitewashed walls and the huge dark beams; and at once I
had the impression (which still lasts) that the operatic vein
enables the imagination to conjure up the atmosphere of the
dead-and-gone more successfully than the serious academic
mood where preservation pervades and custodians prevail.

In timber work Shropshire is very rich; the half-timbered
or "frame" house, the wooden barn, church roofs. Weather-
boarded barns and outbuildings are a study in themselves.
The largest and most striking examples are in the south of
the county, though the most complete range I have noticed
is north of Shrewsbury at that delightful little village called
Fitz.

Half-timber has been fashionable since mid-Victorian
days, when it emerged from a long eclipse which had lasted
about a century and a half. During that time it was not
thought respectable to live in a wooden house. If indeed you
were so domiciled you must make believe that you were not,
that your house was really made of brick or stone. The
cheapest disguise was plaster, but the most convincing thing
was to put a brick facing on the front, and if necessary on
the ends, too. The old Hundred House at Munslow is a
wonderful example of this kind of faking. Except that it
looks oddly gawky, you would never suspect from the front
or end views that it was not a building of the forties of the

last century: brickwork, windows, doors, chimneys, all complete. But, seen from the back, it is a fine half-timbered house, all three stories of it, with a square tower to match for the staircase. And there is an earlier conversion in Shrewsbury which is even more remarkable. This is the house in Belmont just past old St Chad's church. The gable-end (which has beautifully carved barge-boards) shows that it is a half-timbered edifice. You can see at the same time how a brick front has been put on in the early eighteenth century with correct classic façade and carried up, not to the eaves only, but to the height of the ridge, so as to display a properly impressive cornice.

Shrewsbury and Ludlow are full of half-timbered houses which have not had sufficient confidence in the change of taste to shed their disguises. In Ludlow it seems particularly wanton to retain the camouflage, for if the many excellent timber frontages were exposed the town would probably need to spend no money on publicity. It would be noted as the "best black-and-white place in the United Kingdom" and tourists would flock to see it for that reason alone.

In Shrewsbury, Salopians in authority in the council chamber seem, for a century or more, to have been singularly unenlightened about the values, real and fictitious, of half-timber as well as other objects of artistic and antiquarian interest. Not very long ago they pulled down some of the best and most interesting examples of half-timber in the town in order to make room for a car-park. After the chief aesthetic damage had been done they uncovered the rear portions of the house of the merchant Rowley. It was in a better state than they had expected to find it, but demolition went on. It was then recalled that Rowley had been somebody; so, too, had Dr Adams, who lived there at a later date, for he had been honoured by the friendship of Dr Johnson. In fact Dr Johnson had stayed a night with him—and that was more than could be claimed for any of the other houses which had been pulled down. Queen Elizabeth, Charles I, and Dr Johnson have a sort of guide-book sanctity. It is publicity madness to lay hands on a house where any one of them have stayed the night. There was an outcry. Rowley's Mansion must not go! So it was saved, and that part already demolished was carefully restored.

The result is rather fantastic. The buildings of most antiquarian interest were irretrievably gone. The car-park which had been the cause of the damage was spoilt by the retention of Rowley's Mansion (being only half its projected size). And the appearance of Rowley's Mansion is ruined by the overcrowded and abortive car-park. Furthermore, a public use had to be found for the great empty building which now (restored) encumbered the ground at such great expense to public convenience. Then someone thought of an amenable tenant which would cause no trouble, disarm criticism, and attract funds. It was the collection of Roman finds from Uriconium. Until that time they had been housed in the old school building, where the lighting was good and they could be well seen.

There was really no excuse for these relics not being on show at the appropriate site where they were found, in Wroxeter, except expense, and the fact that they could be so well seen in their show-cases in the old school. If they were moved from there at all they should have gone back to Uriconium, a transfer, however, which would be outside the purview of borough politics. To take the Roman remains out of the old school on the plea of making more room for the free library and to put them in Rowley's Mansion would seem to furnish a plausible excuse for the preservation of that building which already threatened to be a cross between a white elephant and a dog-in-the-manger. So thither they went, out of the way and into the gloom. And now the public has to pay sixpence a time to see them imperfectly.

There are two schools of thought about the colour and treatment of half-timber work. The old idea was to tar the beams and whitewash the plaster, stucco, or brick-nogged intervals, thus producing the "magpie" or "black-and-white" house so much admired at the end of the last century. The modern idea is that old oak should always be exposed, even if discoloured by acids used to take off its former coats of tar or paint, or doped by preservatives (which make it look a dirty brown). The plastered spaces have then obviously to be made a less staring colour and are usually buffed.

In this choice I confess I side with the Philistines. I like the "staring contrasts" of absolute black and white and hold, moreover, that the oak is much better preserved by being kept under a coat of tar or paint than being exposed to sun and rain. You may compare Rowley's Mansion (new style) with the Feathers Inn at Ludlow (old style) and then come to a fair conclusion, if you can rid your mind of the neo-Georgian superstition about the virtue of seeing old oak in the nude.

Frame houses are not so susceptible to local character as buildings of brick and stone, nor are they easy to date if ornament is lacking. The principle is simple and universal. The only masonry which enters into it is the preparation of the stone or brick footings destined to form the foundations of the building. After that, it is a carpentry job, and a carpenter likes to make a thing in pieces and then put it together, having always in the back of his mind that it may be taken to pieces again later on and put together again somewhere else. The half-timbered house was therefore not built up and up, but made on the ground, each piece being duly numbered and marked. So the frame house was really a portable building and could be dismantled and removed if the descendant of the first proprietor chose to go to a more convenient or more fashionable quarter of the town.

There are several good examples of such removals successfully accomplished one or two centuries ago. One is the fine house opposite the old school building in Castle Street. This came from Dogpole. It was built by Sir Francis Newport probably in the latter part of the sixteenth century. His grandson was created Earl of Bradford in 1694. He must then have taken thought that a wooden house was no fit place for a nobleman of earl's rank and holding (as he did) high office under the crown. So the family mansion was removed to its present site, and a new one in fashionable brick and of classical proportions was built in place of it. It is still to be seen in perfect preservation at the corner of Dogpole, bearing the earl's coronet and the date 1696. It houses the mayor's parlour and other municipal offices. The other house was modernized at the time of its removal by having bay windows added to it. That is the best of a frame house. It is easy to add or take away windows, porches, balconies, and other projections.

A case which perhaps demonstrates even better the flexibility of these old buildings is seen at Bridgnorth. During the siege of that town in the Civil War of the seventeenth century the town hall was burnt out, leaving only the stone arches on which it stood. At the Restoration, the authorities, who must have been straitened for funds, looked round for something second-hand to replace their chamber and court-room and picked on a half-timber barn in the neighbourhood of Much Wenlock. This they acquired, took to pieces, and re-erected on the stone arches, where it is still to be seen.

The marks which appear by every joint in a frame house are in a code of their own. Roman figures are used, but in rather unorthodox fashion. Thus IIIX is thirteen and not ten minus three. And they will put one horizontal line through three verticals instead of making three Xs, a short-hand way of writing thirty. These numbers, which give the sequence of the tenoned timbers corresponding with the mortice slots cut to receive them, are accompanied by marks which appear to indicate the face of the building (whether it be front, side, or back). The reader may exercise his own wits on a series at the corner of Hill's Lane and Mardol in Shrewsbury, which are clearly seen from the pavement.*

Mr H. E. Forest was one of those tradesmen who take to antiquarian research with a zest which is quite passionate. He left two valuable records of the Shropshire frame houses in *The Old Houses of Shrewsbury* and *Old Houses of Wenlock*. He was very versatile in his tastes, though inclined to be a little didactic, and his rules for dating half-timber work are not altogether sound. Where he had a bent he followed relentlessly. I met him once, but had great difficulty in drawing him out about matters in which he was really a competent authority. At that time he had gone off half-timber and was developing a theory of the Ice Age which was quite at variance to any held by experienced geologists, and he was eager to make proselytes. There is, perhaps, hardly an old town which does not owe something in the preservation of its lore or its treasures to the drive and pertinacity of some tradesman antiquary long forgotten. I recall an ironmonger at Stafford whose spare time was devoted to raising a fund for the restoration of Izaak Walton's cottage (in half-timber) at Great Bridgeford. When his efforts were finally crowned with success, he insisted, as a last touch, in having the tiled roof taken off and a thatch "as it must have been in Izaak's time" put on. A little while after, a spark from a passing locomotive set the whole cottage ablaze, burning not only the thatch but much of the old timbering. That did not daunt him. He set to work again. And I knew a chemist at Aberdovey who made a life work of restoring the ancient ferry at the mouth of the Dovey River (with rights of way,

*The same system is used in the half-timbered houses in Germany with similar hieroglyphics.

83

watch-tower, boat, and boatman). And a shoemaker who founded a local museum, and many more of the like.

It is a great pity that Mr Forest let the Ice Age spectre distract him from his admirable studies of the sixteenth- and seventeenth-century houses of Shropshire, especially those made in half-timber. If he had covered the whole county (instead of two districts only), his work would have been of very much more value, if only as a record. Mr Forest saw with two eyes, one on the detail of construction, and the other on the family history which clung to the old timbers. And nothing harbours suspected ghosts like a half-timbered building.

Indeed it is very hard to compare the works in black-and-white. The romantic element so often outbalances that of scientific interest. Half-timber is a wonderful mixer. It is hard to say whether it is more beautiful when it stands alone or when it jostles higgledy-piggledy with stone or old red brick. Take Wolverton Hall near Eaton-under-Haywood, an all-frame house of two periods which has never been restored. It is probably one of the few mediaeval half-timbered houses still extant. It has Elizabethan and Jacobean additions, but the purist might give it full marks. Although it has been allowed to decline from a gentleman's house to a farmhouse, and downward again to its present state of cottage tenement, and though it has been stripped of the indigenous furniture which it had preserved until the twentieth century, and its panelling, and other things thought worthy of removal by the auctioneer valuer, its main structure is intact and quite representative of the time when the Prior of Wenlock was lord of the manor. Yet on aesthetic grounds you cannot compare it to its neighbour, New Hall, a mixture of Elizabethan half-timber and Jacobean brick. A delightful rambling old house, that in a setting under Wenlock Edge fits as perfectly as if house and stream and wooded hillside had all been made for one another. This is the house where

West window, Holy Cross, Shrewsbury
Tong Church

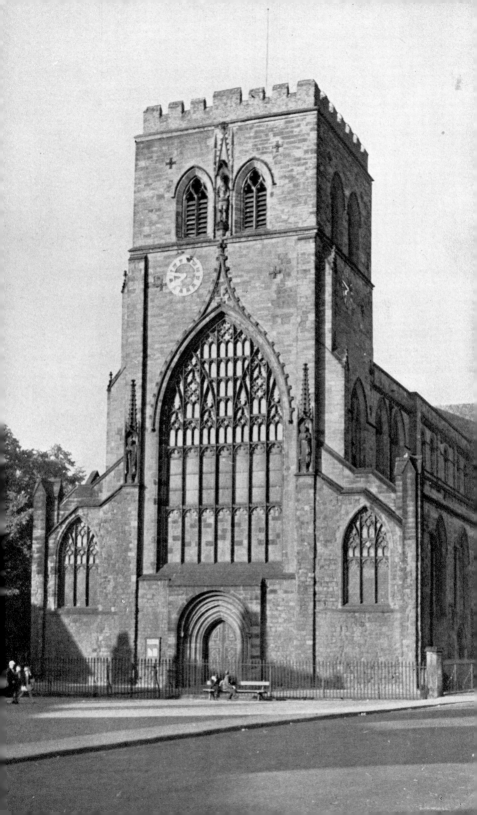

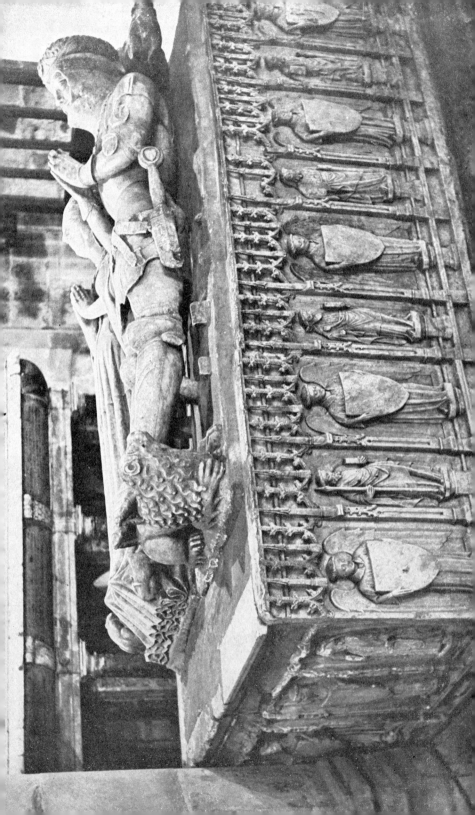

there is a painting more than life-sized in one of the bed-
rooms showing a huntsman jabbing an unfortunate deer in
the neck. It is as fresh as when it was done in Shakespeare's
time. And one can fancy how those drops of blood quiver in
the log firelight of a winter's night.

A terrible loss was Park Hall near Oswestry, made into
an army camp headquarters during the First German War
and burnt to the ground in 1918 through some thoughtless
prank. It was an extraordinarily fine and perfect example of
the normal Elizabethan type of house, with projecting wings
at either end and a prominent porch two stories high in the
middle of the long block. Its simple but effective scheme of
decoration was particularly attractive and in perfect proportion with its seven dormer gables. Perhaps its nearest surviving match, in decorative treatment if not in plan, is
Marrington Hall near Chirbury.

Pitchford Hall is a unique creation. It was built in the
sixteenth century but is reminiscent of the courtyard type
that was popular in the previous century (of which there is
an example at Ludford). Pitchford makes a three-sided
court with a further projection of the hall range beyond one
of the long wings. Unlike Park Hall and Marrington, its
decoration does not depend on the silhouettes of quatrefoils
and balusters which are really an *appliqué* superfluity,
though good to look at. Pitchford is more austere, and yet
nearer to one of the prime canons of architectural art, for its
ornament is structural, depending entirely for its effect on
the appearance of the wooden beams and braces themselves,
which are arranged in diagonals and verticals to form a har-
monic whole. There are, it is admitted, more spars used than
are necessary for the stability of the structure, but the zebra
effect is beautiful and impresses the imagination with the
boldness of truth.

Indeed, Pitchford has never been ashamed of itself and
felt it necessary to adopt a classic veneer. The tyranny of

Tong. Sir Richard and Dame Vernon, Mid 15th Century
The Ciborium, Tong

fashion takes odd turns, and this one of damning half-timber must be explained by something more profound than a craze for academic respectability. One suspects that it may have arisen through a recrudescence of Puritan taste when William of Orange came to power. At any rate wild Tudor and rakish Cavalier "conceits" were put away at that time like childish things and men became solemn and circumspect. So the Gothic Revival was followed by an English Revival, elbowing its way through the decorum of the mid-Victorian period, and the native spirit of jollity as expressed in half-timber was admired once more. But try as they might, the imitators could not quite bring off the old effects. The Crown Hotel at Shrewsbury has made three several attempts to copy the antique manner and bears the dates of the work—1900, 1908, and 1925. All three are admirable in craftsmanship and detail and all three are different in idiom. But all are unmistakably "period pieces" of the early twentieth century.

Among the unusual buildings in half-timber may be mentioned the church at Melverley. This is a special delight, for it shows what the half-timbered hall looked like in early Tudor times, and there must have been a great many of them in Shropshire. Being a church, of course, it has been kept in careful repair and looks as good as new. Then there is the gate-house of Stokesay Castle, and at Cherrington there is a manorial dovecote in half-timber, while the manorhouse itself (an ornate specimen), is reputed to be the veritable House that Jack Built.

Cruck-construction is a simple method of making a main frame for the end of a house out of two timbers instead of four. You must first find a crooked tree which will give you the right vertical height for the wall while the upper part leans at the proper angle for one slope of the roof. You then saw it in twain, turn the faces outwards, secure at the point of the ridge, and you have one gable-end of your house.

Cruck-construction is generally regarded as very ancient and rare. But it was no doubt used for humble dwellings down to the end of the seventeenth century. I was pleasantly surprised in 1942, when motoring down through Frankwell into Shrewsbury, to see a very fine cruck exposed to view at the end of a row of cottages on the left-hand side. I knew that no cruck had been known by the viligant Mr Forest in this area. And indeed, in every other respect—brickwork, doors and windows, and slate roof—the cottages were impeccable examples of the Early Victorian period. The tenant kindly let me see over the house, which was nearly complete with its wooden frames and contemporary floor-boards. She said that the brick facing at the end had only recently been removed.

The brick buildings of Shropshire will, I hope, one day be exemplified in a work devoted to nothing else, written by an author competent to give an authoritative survey of the whole field. It is a subject I can only treat of here very briefly and, I fear, ignorantly. Brick must have come into use in the county in the early sixteenth century, if not before. Probably it was used first of all for chimney breasts and chimneys only as a fire-proof amenity in half-timbered houses. One sees how in cottages of this construction the whole hearth is built externally, its chimney rising to a sufficient height above it to keep flying sparks clear of the thatch. Perhaps such an early and exclusive introduction of brick accounts for the remarkable architectural development of the Shropshire chimney. I don't know any other county—Leicestershire included —where so much has been made of chimneys, whether the construction of the main edifice be half-timber or brick.

In the great houses moulded brick is used only sparingly for wall decoration whereas in chimneys it is sometimes used lavishly. At Upton Cresset Manor House, for instance, there are four tall chimneys in the same stack all made with moulded brick of different patterns. More remarkable,

though, are the chimneys which owe their striking effect to
the skilful use of ordinary cubical bricks set at angular projections giving sometimes the impression of deeply fluted
columns, while others make corkscrew spirals. The classic
example of height for height's sake is Plaish Hall, between
Church Preen and Cardington, but there are many humbler
dwellings where the same passion has ruled.

Queen Anne's period is particularly well represented,
especially in Shrewsbury town and in its neighbourhood. So
are all stages of the Georgian reigns. Some time in the
eighteenth century the Shropshire iron-workers seem to have
turned their close attention to house-fittings. They provided
wonderful filigree fan-lights, of which there are some choice
examples in the houses on Town Walls in Shrewsbury. They
also made a particular kind of iron-framed window which
could be hung on pintle hinges in a wooden frame. It was
perhaps meant in the first instance to replace leaded glass in
mullioned windows, and then became a standard fitting
adaptable for all sorts of openings, especially in farmhouses
and those dwellings where fashion did not demand the presence of a sash frame. One sees these windows in Herefordshire and all over Radnorshire and elsewhere. I have never
been able to find out anything positive about their origin, but
I think they must have come from Shropshire and that their
makers did a roaring trade in the export of them. And where
did all the panes come from? Did they come from the
Shrewsbury glass-houses?

One of the beauties of Shrewsbury is the south quarter of
the town, between old St Chad's and the Wall, where the
streets are all in eighteenth-century brick (at least in outward appearance). There is such an air of complete detachment here both from the lusty brawl of mediaevalism and
the "business is business" of the nineteenth and twentieth
centuries that one can even forgive specious façades.

North Shropshire is largely built of nineteenth-century brick, very neat and trim, with hipped roofs. So often are regular plans repeated that one must suppose that they were inspired by one of those books on ideal farmhouse design once in vogue.

Chapter VIII

CHURCHES

AMONG the Shropshire churches there are no great architectural show-pieces. The two buildings which must have ranked high in this respect, namely, that of the Cluniac priory at Much Wenlock and of the Benedictine abbey at Shrewsbury, are in the one case a ruined fragment and in the other a much depleted remnant of its former self. But to the keen hunter in this field the Shropshire parish churches have a great deal to show, a wide range of variety, and much that is unique. And to the artist they must be endlessly attractive both for their intrinsic charm and for the beauty of their settings in scenery and among old houses. At any rate this is the one branch of Shropshire archaeology which has received a full treatment in book form. Dr D. H. S. Cranage spent eighteen years in compiling *An Architectural Account of the Churches of Shropshire*. The great work is not very portable, but it is an immense advantage to have such a record in being and accessible in a public library.

It is hard for the stranger who is making a tour through the county to choose what to see, as fame and publicity have not been particularly busy with the Shropshire churches. So I take on myself the invidious task of presenting a short list of parish churches (and two chapels-of-ease) based on outstanding architectural features: Shrewsbury (St Mary's), Ludlow, Stottesden, Kinlet, Chelmarsh, Much Wenlock, Acton Burnell, the Langley Chapel, Edstaston, Stanton Lacey, Battlefield, Tong, High Ercal, Melverley, Minsterley, the Heath Chapel.

I have not heard of a single instance of damage to a

Shropshire church during the Second German War, but they had more than their share of suffering in earlier conflicts. The most stable period (after the Normans had settled in and settled down) was the time between Edward I's conquest of Wales in 1283 and the Black Death in 1349 which coincides with the Decorated style of architecture, and that (barring Norman) is the one which is most developed in the county. The Perpendicular period of architecture is very slightly represented as compared with Cheshire, for Shropshire was much more deeply involved in the three great successive turmoils of that time, the Welsh invasions under Glendower, the Battle of Shrewsbury (1403), and the subsequent Wars of the Roses, during the course of which the successful Yorkist claimant to the throne had his headquarters at different times in Shrewsbury and Ludlow. When the country settled down under the Tudor regime no more churches were built until Queen Anne's time, though a great many were ruined during the Civil War of Charles I and restored under Charles II; we owe a great many fine wooden roofs to these restorations.

Of Saxon work there are three interesting examples. Stanton Lacey has most to show. Here there is a perfect north doorway with a cross and "glory" above it and some wonderfully good specimens in the same wall of those curious pilaster strips typical of Saxon external decoration, all carried out carefully in the long-and-short motif.

At Diddlebury (alternatively spelt Delbury, and usually so pronounced by either spelling) there is a door and a window of Saxon date, while inside the church may be seen a carved stone and a small headstone from a Saxon cemetery. But the most remarkable thing is the "herring-bone" masonry revealed on the inner wall. This is no hap-hazard job as in so many examples of the kind. All the stones have been dressed, at both top and bottom, so as to fit flush at the parallel joints. One does not see the structural necessity for such a laborious method of building a wall but the effect is very pleasing. The south door with its curiously carved head seems to be Saxon, too, and is reminiscent of that at Stottesden which is assuredly pre-Norman.

There are not many Shropshire churches which are without some Norman detail, a chancel arch, a doorway, a window, or a font. The Domesday record indicates that the majority already existed, so that the Normans were chiefly occupied in rebuilding or altering. They tackled the restorations with the amazing energy that is fortified by an inferiority complex, destroying no doubt a great deal that was handsomer than the replacement. It is rare to find Norman carved work of a high order in the county. The best specimen, in my humble opinion, is a doorway in Lilleshall Abbey, which owing to the goodness of the stone and some accident of shelter is miraculously preserved. Nothing has ever been done to protect it, though, and when I was there in 1945 the whole of the abbey ruins were in the worst state of neglect imaginable.

The most perfect memento of the Norman regime is the Heath Chapel. This remains as it was built, in the second part of the twelfth century, quite unaltered except for the insertion of a window to light the pulpit. Having always been a chapel-of-ease, it never had a graveyard and stands alone in a field beside the road above the village of Bouldon, still serving a small congregation on alternate Sundays. On the flaked, stratified plaster on its walls dim frescos of both pre- and past-Reformation date show up in a slant of sunlight. Its pewing is Tudor and Georgian, but no structural alterations have been effected since the twelfth century.

The largest Norman work is to be seen in the Church of Holy Cross at Shrewsbury (*c.* 1083), and there is a fine sample within the tower of Wenlock parish church, but the most interesting representative of the period is Edstaston (already mentioned p. 20). A mystery surrounds this church, not only its building date, but the reason for its being here at all. Although quite small, its south door is entered through an arch of four elaborately carved orders. Its north and chancel doors are sumptuously enriched likewise. It must have been undertaken late, for the dog-tooth ornament (an Early English feature) is seen over the south door of the nave. In fact it is a *double* dog-tooth, which is odder still. And the corbel-table is pure Early English in feeling.

There is a great bold chancel arch at Morville where the roll-mould has been made so much of that it seems to have been built as a separate unit, an impression one also gains from the north door at Chelmarsh. Hope Baggot has a small church as wholly Norman in character, though not so free from later intrusions, as the Heath Chapel. Another, even smaller, is at Aston Eyres. It has a carved tympanum showing the entry into Jerusalem, a masterly though not an artistic work. At Uppington there is a Norman chancel arch of a very chaste simplicity and beauty of proportion. By some coincidence (or can it be a craftsman's inspiration?) its qualities fit in with the prospect which surrounds the church. At any rate I always find myself associating them together, as a song with its accompaniment. The church stands (clear of all houses) on that long platform which is the natural plinth to the base of the Wrekin. Westward lies the whole Shropshire Plain with the Roman Watling Street making its last sweep towards its old terminus at Uriconium and then, after all, by-passing it and making for Shrewsbury. I was there on a day in the late summer of 1945 when the Breiddens and the hills of Wales showed themselves in pure azure over miles of ripening corn lands. And I wondered what power this view which could so affect a mere ordinary stranger, as it affected me, might not hold for a poet such as Goronwy Owen (whose ministry is commemorated on a brass tablet inside the church)—or did it merely make him home-sick for those blue distances?

93

Near the east end of the building there is a yew tree of huge girth, and it may very likely be older than that chancel arch. Yews are reputed to live sometimes for over two thousand years. If you could believe such a thing of this tree, it would have seen the buildings of Uriconium before the Saxon raids. If not, no doubt its forbear did. The riddle as to why yews were planted in churchyards has not been satisfactorily solved. A very likely answer is that they perpetuated the sacred grove of pagan worship. That is a third ingredient of the spell which is so palpably felt here. For this was undoubtedly a sacred site in the time of the Caesars; in evidence of which the spade of the grave-digger has unearthed two Roman altars.

The church of the Augustinian Priory at Bromfield has interesting Norman features. Ashford Carbonell I have never succeeded in getting to. But by reports I have read of its unique east end, with a *vesica picis* window over two small rounded-headed Norman lights, I feel sure that the reader ought to have his attention drawn to it.

The transitional period between Norman and Early English has left some interesting things. The abbey church of Buildwas shows just an awareness of the coming change in style, that at Wenlock sees it through. From one point of view the most interesting presentation of the change is St Mary's, Shrewsbury. Here one sees a discriminating conservatism which is most unusual. The nave arcades were built round about 1180, a time when Early English was a complete novelty. Norman was still being built, though "Transitional" was what was really *à la mode*. The bolder spirits who indulged in Transitional used decoration that was very Norman in feeling but they made a point of pointing their arches. But the builders of the arcades of St Mary's have gone clean out of the Norman vein. There is hardly even a cautious Transitional note about their work. It is all pure Early English in manner. Yet they have kept the rounded arch.

And then there is High Ercal. Perhaps I have too personal an attachment to the work here. There are two reasons for this bias. The first is that I made one of those finds here in 1929 which I subsequently lost sight of. During the war years when I often passed through the county on a tour of duty I used to hope that I should rediscover the objects so care‑ fully conserved in memory. But I did not succeed until the autumn of 1945, when I had almost exhausted my process of elimination. The pieces in question were carved capitals of Transitional date, human heads, a ram, and a bull. They seem to me quite outstanding in artistic merit, especially the human heads. I cannot recollect having seen anything of the kind that was better done or more individual in any church in England. Their preservation is nothing short of miracu‑ lous, because in the Civil War of Charles I's time the church was practically ruined and had to be rebuilt from the floor up in the late seventeenth century.

I commend these capitals to the searcher after works of genius by forgotten men. My second bias is more common‑ place. I had always wondered rather vaguely whether the peculiar ornament on the abaci of the Elizabethan classic pillars of the old market house in the Square at Shrewsbury had any pedigree or whether they were the bright idea of the builder. They take the form of a half-sphere—four of them on the underside of each abacus. They look like a neo‑ classic "conceit." Yet on my second visit to High Ercal I noticed the same ornament on the abaci of three capitals in the arcades. I thought that there must be a link of some sort between these two buildings, but one I doubted I should ever find. However, I have learned since that Walter Hancock, who built the old market house (and also Condover Hall) was recommended to the bailiffs of Shrewsbury as the likeli‑ est person by Sir Francis Newport of High Ercal.

There is one very fine example in Shropshire of the tran‑ sition between the Early English and the Decorated styles.

Some authorities call this work late Early English, others
Early Decorated. The famous Angel Choir at Lincoln Cathedral is of that time and so is the small church of Acton
Burnell, whose size is really the only bar to fame as an architectural conception. We shall deal more fully with it later on.
There are a few good details of Early English here and
there, such as the chancel arch at Cleobury Mortimer and
the capital with carved heads at Church Stretton, and two
real Purbeck marble shafts in the very pointed three-light
north window in the chancel of St Mary's at Shrewsbury,
but nothing complete and outstanding. So we may move on
into later developments of the Decorated period with a brief
(and very incomplete) note on two churches which have
some good work in that style to show.

At Stottesden, the centre of the old Saxon hundred of that
name, stands one of the best churches in the county. There
is something about the quiet dignity of its lightsome interior
which sticks in the mind, and one remembers it, as one remembers a house, not only for its architectural merit, but for
its *character*. The Saxon work has been masked by a tower,
added at a slightly later date, and you must therefore enter
the lower story of this to get a view of it. The ornament and
carvings are very arresting and would appear to represent a
deer caught in a net, attended by animals of uncertain species
—an allegorical piece, no doubt. But is it really a deer? Although the foreleg joints of all three animals are drawn the
wrong way round and the first animal has its tail passed between its hind legs before being waved aloft, would the artist
really go so far wrong (living on the fringe of the Forest of
Clee) as to draw a stag with clawed instead of hoofed feet?

The font would appear to be about a century later, done
under Norman tutelage, showing some improvement in design and the execution of a pattern though not in artistic
skill. Its contemporary at Hodnet is much superior in this
respect. But it is carved with great boldness and assurance

and is, if not beautiful, delightfully quaint. So are the square flat capitals in the Norman arcade of the north aisle, with carved foliage on the underside and a sprouting-branch motif on the edge similar to that on the plinth of the font and perhaps by the same hand.

The chancel and south aisle are the richest things in four-teenth-century work I have seen in Shropshire. Indeed they might compare favourably in design and masoncraft with any great work of the Decorated period. All is in indi-vidual taste except the east window. This seems to be a "slavish copy." It is identical with that at Kinlet and also at Chelmarsh. Dr Cranage believes them to have been made in the following order: Kinlet, Stottesden, Chelmarsh; and I feel sure that he is right. The window shows itself to be still in bondage to the rule of geometric tracery, a convention that was quite out of date when the Stottesden restorers were at work. Still more out of date would it be when Chel-marsh was modernized in 1345. Most probably, though, it wasn't the tracery which mattered but the painted glass. There is a hint at Kinlet that this was rather secular than religious—a display of noble benefactors. One can see that that might well have commended itself to other patrons of restoration and why it was flattered by an imitation so exact as to break the very inflexible architectural rule of fashion.

In the south wall of the chancel is one of the most beauti-ful low-side windows in England. There is still no firmly based theory as to the purpose of these openings, though they are found in every county in England and their number runs into hundreds. When attention was first drawn to them in the early part of the nineteenth century they were called lepers' squints, a name still appearing in guide-books though the experts have poured scorn on it for half a century. A great variety of explanations have been offered, now gen-erally narrowed down to two. Apart from its size and posi-tion, a feature of the low-side window is that the lower portion of it was unglazed and made for a shutter which, when removed, gave direct access to the open air. This is well seen at Stottesden, where the shutter bolt-holes also appear. In addition, there is a small aumbrey cupboard immediately below the sill.

The two schools of thought mentioned above hold (1) that it was an opening where the sacring bell could be rung so as to be heard out-of-doors and the parish be advised of the elevation of the Host, (2) that a light (*lanterne des morts*) could be placed there to intimidate evil spirits which were believed to frolic in graveyards during the hours of darkness.

Dr Cranage points to the aumbrey as a possible clue to the angelus theory. The weakness of this theory (and it seems to me a fatal one) is that a few churches which have low-side windows have also got sanctus bell-cotes of contemporary date, a redundancy which would hardly have found favour. And in the second case it is hard to see why it should be better to put a light in a draught than let it shine through plain glass.

Chelmarsh church, already mentioned, is also of the Decorated period and has much architectural distinction. It is an example which is exactly dated to 1345—a great help to the student, and it is first-rate work of the very summit of the period; a summit beyond which the great gulf of the Black Death is fixed (1349). The date is known from the fact that Hugh de Mortimer of Chelmarsh (a branch of the family one does not hear so much about in history) left a sum of money for a chantry chapel to be added to his parish church, wherein daily masses could be said for his soul. It would seem that the terms of the will had been interpreted in a spirit that was either very exclusive or unusually democratic. At any rate instead of an addition to the building a restoration was carried out which left nothing of the old church but a very narrow north aisle. The rest was all the

new Mortimer chantry dedicated to St James which the
ordinary parishioners were at liberty to use for their customary worship. Chelmarsh, like Stottesden, would have been
better off if the master mason who did such an excellent job
had been allowed to put in a window of his own design. As
it is, the interior effect is rather cold, the somewhat mourn-
ful elongated lobes of the geometric favourite seem to con-
tradict the fleshly luxuriance of the other tracery. But the
exterior view of the south side is very striking. Here the
achievement of 1345 is seen in its completeness with its fine
ashlar, its chaste buttresses, and its perfect proportion.

Kinlet lies about half-way between Stottesden and Chelmarsh and, like those places, has a church which must be
reckoned as one of the distinctive ones of Shropshire. Except
for the presence, close by, of the Hall, it stands quite isolated
in the huge park and must be nearly a mile from the house of
any other parishioner save the lord of the manor. In Shropshire, church and manor house are usually found in very
close juxtaposition, though often remote from the present-
day village. One imagines that in most cases that was not
always so, but rather that they were at the centre of the
agricultural community, as elsewhere in England, and that
the detachment is comparatively recent, the settlement having drifted away as feudal ties weakened and times changed.
Perhaps no such thing happened at Kinlet, whose church,
although big, may always have served the primary function
of private chapel and mausoleum.

The hereditary association between the lords of Kinlet
and the land has continued for more than seven hundred
years, for though the present family does not hold it in
direct male succession from Brian de Brampton of the
twelfth century, it has been passed down either by an heiress
or by near kin, and those broad acres of forest and tilth
have never been sold.

The church, although standing high over an open sweep

of the park, is surrounded by an enclosure like a pleasant walled garden that is itself embowered within a thicket of trees and shrubs. So you come upon it suddenly, and the one rare feature about it strikes you at once—it has a half-timbered clerestory. The effect of this glimmer of black and white above the solid stonework is unusual and charming. On the rising ground, beside the winding path through the churchyard, is the base of a churchyard cross (topped by a very poor restoration of the cross itself). It is not the usual plinth standing on a flight of steps, but a massive structure rising to four pediments at the cardinal points. The western end is recessed, containing a niche within it, and there is one above the embrasure.

In Shropshire there are only very few instances of a niche on the base of a churchyard cross; the most elaborate one is at Highley, some five miles away to the east. But in Worcestershire there are quite a number, and some in Herefordshire. Their ceremonial use has been variously guessed at, though the real truth does not seem to have been discovered. Guide-book writers and even ecclesiologists are inclined to pass the mystery over in silence. It has never aroused the violent acrimony of partisans like the low-side window.

With its large tower, its wide stone porch (thirteenth-century, an unusual feature in Shropshire), its cruciform plan and clerestoried nave the church looks every inch a fine parish church and not in the least like a mausoleum. Indeed, only four monumental effigies are to be found within, but they alone are worth the stranger's long digression from the road to see. All are in alabaster. The oldest is of a lady in the dress of the early fifteenth century. She occupies the recess of an earlier figure which has disappeared. It is not certainly known who she is, though probability identifies her with the heiress Isabel Cornwall who took Kinlet to the Lychefield family before it passed to the Blounts. The carving is of a high order.

The English Bridge
Shrewsbury from Laura's Bower

The other three are Blount tombs. Sir Humphrey Blount and his lady lie on the south side of the chancel. He wears a collar with the rose and sun in splendour of the Yorkist faction, true to the Mortimer complexion. He received his knighthood on Tewkesbury field and died in 1477. These figures are in the best manner of the mediaeval alabasterman. Across the pavement are Sir John Blount (the grandson) and his dame. He died in 1531, forty-six years after the Tudors had been established on the throne, and therefore must needs wear the collar of S S, that hated Lancastrian badge so odious to the followers of Edward Earl of March. If the dead turn in their graves, how can Sir Humphrey's bones have rested peaceably these four centuries?

Sir John's tomb was made on the eve of the Reformation when the long tradition of Gothic art fell into sudden decline. Renaissance influence was already at work with a balefully decadent effect. Here we see something exceptional. The little figures surrounding the tomb are grouped in medallion-like Renaissance scrolls instead of the canopy work of the older tradition. And surely there can be no more delightful array of "weepers" anywhere.*

Very different is the tomb of Sir George Blount, made in the greater enlightenment of half a century later. He and his spouse kneel under an elaborate tester with the small figures of a boy and girl between them. The tomb is a very curious mixture of classical Ionic with an unusual hark-back to Gothic trefoils and lancet-heads, and the decoration in heraldry and carved ornament is undoubtedly the best that money could buy. But the general effect of it is the reverse of beautiful. It is rather worse than ugly. It is pompously repulsive.

Moreover, we are told on circumstantial authority that this grim old gentleman (who disinherited the little girl by

*Dr Arthur Gardiner illustrates one panel in his *A Handbook of Mediaeval Sculpture.*

The turn-in to the stable yard at the Lion, Shrewsbury
Grope Lane, Shrewsbury

his side) certainly did not rest under his magnificent façade. I have it on the authority of Georgina Jackson's *Shropshire Folklore* that his spirit haunted a pool in the park. Women who went there to wash clothes were sometimes terrified by seeing the Elizabethan knight emerge from the stagnant depths, mounted on horseback. It was said when thus seen that he was on his way to visit a certain cellar under the old house and make sure that no one had been tampering with his pipes of wine and hogsheads of ale.

Of course a lot of this might be mere fairy tale, but there was no doubt about Sir George's ghost and the trouble it caused, because it had been secured and the actual whereabouts of its prison was known. The clergy had assembled with candle, book, and bell and had first compelled it to appear and then made it crawl into a bottle. And you could see the bottle for yourself, for it was kept on Sir George's tomb. And there it was!

It needs a greater act of faith today to believe the story, because the bottle which so logically proved the reality of the ghost is no longer there. This form of exorcism is no novelty and there are probably several similar receptacles still in existence. I myself have seen the sealed bottle in which a restless and terrifying charioteer called One-handed Boughton of Newbold-on-Avon is said to be imprisoned. That was a triumph of the clergy of Queen Anne's reign operating with a Bible, a bell, and twelve candles.

The Decorated style came to a sudden end at the terrible year 1349 when the Black Death ravaged the country. In most places all building work ceased and some time elapsed before it was put in hand again or new work begun. Meanwhile, at the Benedictine abbey of Gloucester, which was not affected by the plague, a new style was being evolved that is still called by the name invented for it in the early nineteenth century, Perpendicular. Owing to the conditions of paralysis caused by the Black Death, examples of the transition be-

tween these two styles are very rare. A particularly fine one
is seen at Shrewsbury, in the west window of Holy Cross. It
is dated by Dr Cranage (on architectural grounds) between
1360 and 1370. One sees in the tracery an extraordinarily
neat balance struck between the flowing and the rectilinear
motifs. And the figure standing in the canopy above the window would certainly seem to be that of Edward III (d.
1377), for he has the same rolling beard as appears on his
effigy in Westminster Abbey.

As I have said, the fifteenth century hit Shropshire very
hard. There are a number of oddments of Perpendicular
work, notably in the upper stages of towers, but only three
churches in which the style predominates. Two of these were
collegiate churches built early in the century and are of particular interest both architecturally and for other reasons.
The earliest is the church of Battlefield.

The Battle of Shrewsbury was fought in July 1403 and it
is said that afterwards the dead lay thick upon the ground
for a distance of three miles. The clash occurred within the
parish of Albright Hussey, whose rector at the time was one
Robert Ive. When one reads of a famous battle in English
history it does not always occur to one to think of the awful
predicament in which the parish priest must always have
been placed when he found himself suddenly faced with a
mass interment on such a vast scale. His name may survive
in a list of incumbents, but as a rule the thoughts which he
thought perish with him. But Robert Ive was moved to do
more than bury the dead. He bethought him of the fate of
their souls, and it was through his endeavours that a church
was built over the spot where the fighting was fiercest so that
masses for the slain could be constantly said. The church was
for this purpose only. It was served by a master and five
chaplains, Robert Ive becoming the first master.

The church, with its adjoining house for the college of
priests, was completed, except for the tower, by 1410. The

tower was built a hundred years later. Some time after the Reformation when collegiate foundations were dissolved the old parish church of Albright Hussey fell into decay and was not repaired, the chantry at Battlefield being used instead. There was a somewhat rigorous restoration in 1861, but the main architectural features of this interesting building are all preserved. They show a complete work of the Perpendicular period with reminiscent notes of the Decorated style, among which is that long-standing dish, the reticulated window. And the hint has been taken from the great west window just spoken of at Shrewsbury Abbey to place a royal personage in a niche in the gable (instead of a saint). So here, over the east window, we find the victor of Shrewsbury field, Henry IV. In consequence, he usually gets the kudos for having built the church. But no doubt he contributed to the funds; the victory had made him secure on the throne.

Tong church is a little later. The present building represents the conversion of the old parish church into a collegiate foundation of secular canons endowed by the lady of Tong Castle, Elizabeth de Pembruge, in 1410. The most distinctive architectural feature of the church is its steeple, which is in three stages, the first being square, the second octagonal, the third a short spire.

Tong church is one of the prime sights of Shropshire. It narrowly escaped destruction in the Civil War, being actually held by a garrison—the north wall is still pock-marked with musket and cannon-ball—and yet its interior is so perfectly preserved that there must be few churches which can compare with it in this respect. Its screen and stall woodwork, its magnificent effigies, its "golden chantry" have escaped vandalism almost unscathed. The most remarkable survival of all is a ciborium for the reserved sacrament. It is a very beautiful bit of craftsmanship in silver gilt of the early part of the sixteenth century. It used to be kept in the vestry in a safe of very special design. You could get a glimpse of it by placing a shilling in a slot. A panel could then be slid back and the vessel was revealed through a peep-hole of thick glass lit up with electric light. I suppose it is still there, for the safe must be almost as rare as the ciborium. I know nothing like it except the slot-machine at St Mary's Bury St Edmunds, which gives you one minute's floodlighting of the hammer-beam roof for threepence. But on the only two occasions when I have managed to pay the church a flying visit during the war I could find no one who could tell me, and the vestry was kept locked.

This beautiful and well-preserved record of the past has a setting which is eminently suitable to it. Well-kept cottages of the Bradford estate peep from a fringe of woodland on one side of it, and a great green expanse of park land, threaded with water, stretches out towards Tong Castle on the other. More than one romantic story is told of the Vernons of Tong and Haddon Hall and other occupiers of the castle. It is a very muse-worthy place.

The third representative of the Perpendicular period is St Lawrence at Ludlow. This might well claim to be not only the finest church in Shropshire but one of the grandest parish churches in England. It is not really surprising to find such a monument in such a place, for, unlike the more northerly parts of the Shropshire border, Ludlow had been sheltered from both Welsh and faction turmoils since the twelfth century by the protective interests of the Mortimers. The town, in fact, only had its peace shattered once. That was in the winter of 1459 when the Lancastrian party, flushed with their victory at Blore Heath, near Market Drayton, broke into Ludlow and sacked it.

The main part of the church is Perpendicular. Dr Cranage dates the work as between 1450 and 1470, in which year it is known that the tower was completed. When Sir Gilbert Scott carried out restorations in 1859 lumps of melted bell-

metal were discovered, and pieces of charred wood. This is
very definite evidence that the previous tower was burnt
down and it might be thought that it was a result of the
Lancastrian raid on the town. But if the tower had crashed in
flames at that time it would have been expected that the
woodwork of the stalls would also have been consumed.
There is, however, documentary evidence that wood for the
making of these was ordered in 1442. Morever, the stalls
and the bosses in the chancel roof are tactfully balanced
in their reference to both the Yorkist and Lancastrian
powers, displaying emblems and badges of either faction
which suggests that they were carved at a time when Henry
VI was reigning as undisputed monarch. Though there is a
boss of a crowned head with a wildly streaming beard which
might be taken as a reference to the king's madness, an al-
lusion which would not be displeasing to the Mortimers and
their Yorkist friends.

The most striking and unusual architectural features of
the church are the curved internal buttresses which shore up
the tower arch at the crossing and make a not unpleasing
vista from the western end of the aisles. It is the vistas of the
interior of St Lawrence's Church that perhaps strike one
more than anything else. The enormous windows of the
chancel, which occupy with a single range of glass the space
taken up in many cathedrals and "great" churches by the
openings of aisle, triforium, and clerestory, together with
the choice stained glass and its luminous effects on the light
colour of the stone, gives a view towards the altar which
must stir every visitor who enters on a sunny morning.

I use the word "choice" in connection with the stained
glass advisedly, because the great east window depicting the
life of St Lawrence is a restoration of the early nineteenth
century undertaken by David Evans of Shrewsbury between
1828 and 1832, and it is not usual to call any painted windows of that period "choice." But this and certain other

works by Evans are, I maintain, in a category by themselves
and are admirable. I have more to say of this glass-worker
in the next chapter. All accounts of this window I have
seen, including that excellent pamphlet by the late Mr H. T.
Weyman, give the impression that Evans only replaced the
worst bits of the old glass with new. But I have searched
the window with binoculars and I cannot detect a single
old quarry in the whole expanse.

It is easy, however, to distinguish the old from the new in
all the other windows. In them the majority is old and very
beautiful glass. Evans restored those in the north and south
sides of the chancel, which retain a great deal of their fifteenth-century glass. But the most complete windows of that
date are in St John's Chapel. The Lady Chapel has a window
of fourteenth-century glass belonging to the older church
before its Perpendicular reshaping, but there are very few
of the original pieces left in it, and the restorations are not
by Evans.

Nobody has yet guessed what the small chamber behind
the reredos was meant for. The way in is by a door in the
south wall which leads into a passage in the thickness of the
wall, then round the angle into the east wall behind the
reredos. Here in the fairway there is a stone plinth about
three feet high, beyond which is a space lit by a small window. This window is of thirteenth-century form and appears
to have been moved from another part of the church. Many
suggestions have been made as to what it was all for, but
the riddle remains unsolved.

Arthur, Prince of Wales, the eldest son of King Henry
VII and first husband of Catherine of Aragon, died in Ludlow Castle and was buried in Worcester Cathedral. Some
part of his remains, however, is traditionally believed to rest
in Ludlow Church. No one knows where this may be. There
are two features which can be ascribed to his time. One is the
wooden canopy over the altar in St John's Chapel, in the

carving of which the pomegranate appears, the badge of Catherine of Aragon. The other is the carved stonework at the west end of the north aisle. This is, in itself, a puzzle. It is in the form of a double recess with an interval between. The recesses contain slabs as if for tombs. The whole thing might possibly be part of a chantry chapel, and the work is typical of that of the early sixteenth century when Prince Arthur died. A great deal of speculation has for many years centred round this curiosity which many believed to conceal the heart and viscera of Prince Arthur, and an attempt has been made to prise off one of the tomblike slabs. This, however, resulted in a crack opening in the aisle wall. Operations were therefore suspended, but it was always hoped that a more scientific approach would solve the technical difficulty and present the backers of the Arthurian legend with full confirmation of their views.

In 1936 the ashes of A. E. Housman, the author of *The Shropshire Lad,* were brought to Ludlow and it was requested that they should be lodged within the fabric of the church. This was done. The place selected was the north wall of the nave exactly where the enigmatic monument stood. The ashes of the poet were injected through a joint in the masonry on the outside of the wall and sealed in with a grouting of liquid cement. A brass plate marks the site on the outside of the church. Exactly what the symbolic motive of the deposition at that debatable spot was is hard to fathom. But the busybodies who were so deeply concerned about their theories of Prince Arthur's remains will now never be able to confirm them.

In the neo-classic vein there is nothing very distinctive except the little church at Minsterley. It was built in the second year of the reign of William and Mary and (with its cherub heads outside and its interior fittings) is wistfully reminiscent of the end of the seventeenth century. But the sloping buttresses mark it off as something unique and local and surely nowhere else will you find the pomps of a western façade combined with the lowliness of a Border-type wooden bellcote.

As might be expected in a region where as often as not the builder has been the carpenter and not the mason, the church roofs are a feature. There is nothing so rich as the work in East Anglia, but there is a very high average of plain excellence and often engineering problems have been tackled with great ingenuity. An example of this is the roof of Ditton Priors. Here the single aisle is so wide as to divide the nave into two halves, though these halves are not quite equal, so that the arcade is not under the middle of the ridge but a little to one side. The framing adopted is quite original, with a construction like that of a cantilever bridge.

The purlin-brace is very common and is seen in all varieties. At Loppington no two bays are the same. But that, like so many, is a post–Civil War restoration. For the same reason there are an unusual number of late Stuart hammerbeam roofs, the most striking examples being seen at Condover and Bridgnorth (a double hammer-beam roof with a huge span). But these roofs, though efficient and interesting, lack the beauty of the mediaeval hammer-beam construction. For carved work, the small fifteenth-century roof at Cheswardine is probably the best.

CHAPTER IX

SHREWSBURY

IF THERE were a word in our dictionary to express that *something* in a place which is equivalent to personality in a human being, it would be a boon to the topographer. To say that a place, or even a building, has a *personality* gives only a hint of what is meant. A place has neither mobility nor volition. It is a mixture of hard facts, abstracts, and mortal men. The hard facts are geography, topography, and buildings, and the abstracts, history, tradition, and local sentiment. These form a dual environment which has a temporal and a spiritual background against which men live and, by reaction, add to and perpetuate. If one of the abstracts ceases to contribute its quota a loss is immediately felt, as though a supply of nourishment were cut off. That is what is so noticeable in many of the old English towns. History has failed them. They go on but are only half alive. Often they don't seem to have noticed the change. They still have a personality, but that *something* is quite different from what it used to be.

Shrewsbury is a peculiar instance of a town which history has served well at almost every turn. Consequently (times being good or bad) it has nearly always been able to live in the then present moment. The pride of the Salopian is not the vain but the practical sort, equally balanced between consciousness of heritage and confidence in its present powers. It takes its old buildings and ancient things for granted and likes to hear other people admire them, but pulls them down without hesitation if it finds them in the way, replacing them with a fine disregard for anything but its present

needs. Its spirit in this respect reminds me of what someone once said to me about a great railway in the days when
the London and North Western was the premier line in the
whole world of railways: "No one but the London and
North Western would have dared to have a station like
Euston!" And perhaps nobody but Shrewsbury would have
allowed its very historic market square to have been en-
croached on and filled up by a government building of exceedingly banal design in the shape of a post office, or erected
such a *nonpareil* monstrosity of a market house in the place
where it stands, or have county offices designed for its remaining square built to half that design at one period and
finished a few years later on in half someone else's design.

In other respects it has guarded its local amenities more
jealously than other places. In this act of salvation it has been
decidedly helped by both Providence and luck. Its conserva-
tion as a romantic hill-town in the loop of a fair river em-
banked by gardens and greenery is almost miraculous. If you
look out from either its eastern or its western heights you
see only the river below, with broad meadows stretching
out into the distance—no satellite towns or housing schemes
or factories or any of the usual purlieus of a mediaeval town
which still enjoys the full vigour of health. This is where
Providence has helped. It has arranged that regular winter
floods should render all this land unfit for building sites but
very desirable for pasturage, owing to that annual anoint-
ment of good Severn alluvium that will make the grass green
all summer and fatten more generations of red Hereford
kine.

And then if you walk along the Severn side and look up
at the town (well knowing how fabulously valuable every
inch of space is within the embrace of the river), you would
expect the slopes to be terraced with houses, masking hide-
ously all views of the citadel. Instead of that, there are

gardens, orchards, avenues, and huge expanses of grass—
except on a low-lying bit on the west which matters hardly at
all. I have not discovered how far this is fortuitous and how
much owing to the heritage lobe of Salopian pride.

If you stand on the English Bridge and look up at the
lovely spire of St Mary's, you see how it springs from a
cresting of gables and chimneys not unworthy of its grace.
Something has been said about Shropshire chimneys already,
and there is that massive clustered stack of Rocke's House
where Mary Tudor stayed in 1526. And then there is the
carefully proportioned "riverside front" of Newport House
(1696), where the mayor's parlour is now installed, and
then the grave early-nineteenth-century County Hospital in
well-cut free-stone; then follows that curious façade belonging to the more modern end of the Council House that seems
to have at least thirty windows in it. Finally the eye rests on
the earthwork motte built by Roger de Montgomery in the
twelfth century to secure the Norman rule in Shropshire and
threaten the independence of Wales, now topped by Laura's
Bower, a Gothic summer house made by Thomas Telford
for the daughter of his patron. Only gardens and orchards
intervene between all these and the river. And you are told
that the monks of the Abbey* used to have their vineyard
on that slope, and it is a probable guess that private owners
deriving rights from the great spoliation have maintained
them there ever since.

Further round the bend the town has been kept hemmed
in by its mediaeval walls—still to be seen above more
gardens. And then you come to the Quarry, which was established as a public park before the days of the speculative
builder. While, across the river, are the old town pastures
belonging to the freemen of Shrewsbury, formerly used for
grazing and for the arbours of the trades guilds, let on a

---

*The dedication of Montgomery's Benedictine Abbey was to St Peter and
St Paul, that of its church to the Holy Cross.

long lease since many years to the Governors of Shrewsbury
School when it moved out of town.

Although space was not quite so precious in the old days,
Shrewsbury has been short of room ever since the Norman
Conquest. Even the great Roger de Montgomery had to
demolish a number of houses in order to build his castle
(which meant loss of revenue, no light consideration to a
Norman baron). And he had to build his monastery across
the river.

Lack of space has even prohibited the building of a town
hall. It is a strange fact that a county capital which has
succeeded so long in maintaining its influence throughout the
whole shire and holding the reins of government so firmly
should lack an official centre both for its municipal and its
county functionaries. We may indeed be thankful that we
have been spared one of those colossal palaces of local government called a *civic centre* such as were put up in so many
ancient towns before the war, dwarfing all else in their
neighbourhood. Having seen what was done in the matter
of the Market Hall and the General Post Office we may well
be glad that space has balked any plan for a civic centre.

Even the railway has had to accommodate its station in
the most unusual situation of any of its kind in all Britain,
and most passengers do not realize when they tread those
spacious platforms that the greater part of the huge erection is built on a bridge, and that under their feet roll the
broad waters of the Severn. One has to thank the castle for
that. It is the last defensive act in its stormy and illustrious
career. Had it not been acquired from the crown in 1780 by
William Pulteney and turned by his young protégé Thomas
Telford into a private residence, it would certainly have
suffered the fate of those noble strongholds at Northampton
and Berwick-upon-Tweed. And one knows that when those
castles fell the parts of the towns immediately adjoining
were devastated by early Victorian ideas of modernity. If

Shrewsbury Castle had been replaced by the railway station a similar thing would have happened, and the grand old town would wear a very different appearence. Situated where it is, however, the blight has been confined to the north of the old defence-works. Only a mere trickle of infiltration has been able to get past the barbican, and the result is worth careful study (if not a place on the schedule of monuments to be preserved for future reference), for it shows what might have happened. I mean those houses in Castle Gates on the left-hand side, just after you turn out of the station yard. You can see plenty of that sort of thing in Manchester or even in Wellington but not on such a miniature scale. The care that must have gone into the working out of some of that debased architectural detail!

Pulteney's acquisition of the castle was really a momentous event and, like so many others that had taken place there, it was one not only of Salopian but of national importance. Not that Sir William mattered a great deal. Although he had an income of more than £50,000 a year and was reckoned the richest commoner in England, the Editor of the Dictionary of National Biography has passed him over. This seems a little unfair. I have already tried to indicate how he saved Shrewsbury. A more positive contribution to the public weal was his patronage of Telford, who is acknowledged as a great man not only by the D.N.B. but by all and sundry. Those who study the ways of Providence through the details of its working under the headings of "chance" and "luck" will find much matter for thought in the story of Telford.

It happened that in 1786 Pulteney was representing Shrewsbury in Parliament and wanted a house there to go to when his duties as a member required his presence in the town. It occurred to him that if the castle were put into repair it would be the very place to hold receptions in style. And perhaps he was touched by the stirrings of the Romantic

Revival which was already moving certain persons of quality to refurbish mediaeval castles. At all events he knew that Tom Telford was a good stone-mason and full of ideas and he sent for him to convert the ruinous old castle into a residence. In fact he knew all about Tom. Pulteney had really very little to do with Shropshire, though he happened to represent the borough of Shrewsbury. His home was Westerhall in Eskdale just across the Scottish Border, and his baptismal name William Johnstone. It was changed to Pulteney after his marriage to the niece and heiress of the Earl of Bath (an incident which, among other things, made him a Shropshire land owner). Westerhall was the big house in the parish of Westerkirk, and in that parish Telford was born in 1757, in a small thatched cottage.

It is easy to see how the influence of "my ain folk" had brought Telford to Shrewsbury and had further promoted his interests, so that in 1788 he was appointed surveyor of public works in Shropshire. What is not quite so obvious is how the association with Shropshire was really the making of his singularly successful and useful career. He is remembered for his roads, bridges, canals, and harbour-works. But the secret of that fame which brought him into such prominence as to make him the premier civil engineer and consultant of his day was his early grasp of the possibilities of cast iron.

The production of cast iron was revolutionized in the second half of the eighteenth century by John Wilkinson, the greatest of all ironmasters. He came from the Furness District (where he had been brought up to the trade of ironfounding by his father) to Shropshire and set up house at Broseley in Colebrookdale. The time-honoured method of smelting in the old-fashioned bloomery was by charcoal, a product of that very ancient forest tradesman the charcoal-burner. Wilkinson realized that if only coal could be used the output of the smelter would be increased a hundred-

fold. The drawback to this had always been the sulphur
fumes given off by coal which made iron brittle, and the
solution he discovered was to burn limestone at the same
time. Wilkinson found this out after his move south. The
iron, the coal, and the limestone were all to hand in Coalbrookdale. One of the first fruits of his discovery was the
building of a bridge over the Severn, all of cast iron. This
was in 1779. That bridge has had a place called after it—
Ironbridge—and is now preserved as an ancient monument.

The use of cast iron for anything bigger than fire-grates
was deeply distrusted by both the constructor and the public,
but Telford took the novelty up and adapted it to all sorts of
unsuspected purposes. His first trial was in the line of the
new Shropshire Canal which he proposed to carry over the
River Tern in an aqueduct all made of cast iron. It must
have taken great courage for a young man (a non-Salopian)
who was on trial in an important public appointment to take
such a risk in the face of strong expert advice to the contrary.
However, he built this aqueduct at Longdon-upon-Tern in
1793 and it stood not only the stress of weight but also that
of a severe frost (which the prophets had foretold would
certainly crack it, if nothing else did). In 1794 he built the
greatest of all British aqueducts, over the Dee Valley near
Llangollen, using cast-iron troughs in between the stone
piers. In the following year he again spanned the River
Severn with a cast-iron bridge at Buildwas which is still
in use. It was much bigger than the old one at Ironbridge
(now closed to wheel traffic) and made with only half the
weight of metal. He then proposed to replace old London
Bridge with a cast-iron work of single span and drew plans
for it.

The greatest of all Telford's bridges, if not of all his
various works, is the suspension bridge which spans the
Menai Straits. It is true that it was malleable iron which
was used here to make the suspension rods and the huge

116

links of the chains. But it was all Shropshire iron and forg-
ings. The links were tested in Shrewsbury on the way through
on a proving machine, part of which is still to be seen *in situ*
in the workshops of Mr Coles the Decorator at the bottom
of Wyle Cop.

When I went there in 1945 I saw another object which was
of particular interest to me though it does not seem to have
caught the eye of any museum curator. This was a small
iron kiln for firing stained glass, and it was known to have
been used by David Evans. I gather from the records of the
Combretheren of Saddlers, Painters, Glaziers, Curriers, and
Others that Evans was admitted a freeman of the company
in 1819, that he was warden in 1845 and '46, and that he
served his apprenticeship with Sir John Betton, kt. Otherwise I can find out very little about him, except that he became a partner in the firm of his adoption which later on was
known as Betton and Evans.

I think that there is an empty and profitable field here for
a diligent biographer. Among the *chefs d'oeuvre* of the firm
are the restorations of the great east window at Ludlow,
the Jesse window in St Mary's, Shrewsbury, the transepts
of Lichfield Cathedral, and the east window of Winchester
College Chapel. A few windows are signed by Evans, such
as those in St Chad's, Shrewsbury, and there are a great
many windows unsigned and unascribed in Shropshire (including the one I have noted at Hodnet) which show so
much individuality that they can hardly have been the work
of any other man. Apparently, at Evans's death the firm was
taken over by a rival, Davis, who has signed some windows
(one I found in St George's at Llandudno). His work is
very inferior and commonplace, and the business seems to
have been wound up in the eighties or nineties of the last
century. I have not been able to find a trace of the firm's
old books or any proper account of their doings. The com-
pilers of the *Victoria County History*, who ought to have

Corndon Hill
Pontesford Hill

bestirred themselves in the matter, were content with a bare mention of what was already well known. But it is clear that someone in that firm of Betton and Evans had ideas about stained glass that were far ahead of his time, so far as the revival of mediaeval art is concerned. I have heard that they employed a great many artists both English and foreign, but there must have been one inspiring genius, and I think that man was David Evans. The work suffers from the disrepute into which all stained-glass of the nineteenth century has got, so that every window of that period is apt to be dismissed at sight and not examined. It also suffers because quite a number of windows known to have been made by Betton and Evans have had perforce to conform to the prevailing taste of the time and look like the dismal work of other firms. So I invite an enterprising biographer to come forward. He can begin at Mr Coles's workshops, where he will probably find not only the old oven belonging to his hero but several of the original cartoons.

The buildings just mentioned were made by William Hazledine, the Shropshire ironmaster who supplied Telford with most of his ironwork, not only for those bridges already spoken of but for undertakings as far north as the Caledonian Canal. Prowling about the yard and outbuildings there and hearing about the relics of stables where Hazledine kept his huge teams, one catches a flavour of the doings of the coaching days, when the great Holyhead Road was being mooted. That this should be made to pass through Shrewsbury and not through Chester was the last great score in the ancient contest in rivalry between the two towns. The credit for this triumph is given to Robert Lawrence, owner of the Raven and Lion inns and of the famous "Wonder" coach, according to the inscriber of his memorial stone in St Julian's Church. But I think that if Pulteney had not bought the castle, and the castle had not housed Telford, and Telford had not used his influence with the government, it may be doubted whether he would have prevailed.

Every book on Shrewsbury tells how Sam Hayward used to gallop the "Wonder" with its four horses up Wyle Cop, wheel round without a check at the entrance to Dogpole, and dash full speed into the Lion yard. But the best description of those days and a wonderful account of the dinner given to the drivers and guards of the mail and express coaches is to be found in Miss Kenyon's delightful book, *The House that was Loved*.

A street called a street is a rarity in Shrewsbury. Three of the main thoroughfares have their own unsupported proper nouns—Wyle Cop, Dogpole, and Mardol. Elsewhere you will find the Norman reminder, Murivance. Hills have a majority over streets. Pride Hill sounds designedly appropriate for the middle way of the county town, but is in fact called after a family of that name who used to have its town house on that frontage. Ancient passage-ways between houses, like the *lokes* of Norwich, are *shuts* and *gullets*. That so many of these remain for the casual explorer to "find" and that they are so picturesque when discovered is one of the delights of Shrewsbury. There is a series of them leading to the old wall where it crested the escarpment on the northwest side of the town. The wall itself has either disappeared or is engaged in other buildings and no longer available as a public walk. But the passages down to it remain. They take you past the smart frontages of modern shops into the half-timbered world of Elizabethan and Jacobean Shrewsbury and bring you out to where the wall used to be, and where that most ancient view of the river and the water-meadows still is. The first of these turnings off the ascent up Pride Hill brings you to the Old Mint, one of the few pre-Tudor relics of domestic architecture in Shrewsbury. Although money was made in Shrewsbury from the time of the Saxon king Athelstan to that of Henry III, the reference is probably to the mint which was brought from Aberystwyth when the town was garrisoned for King Charles in 1642.

"The Mint is come to our town and one Master Bushell doth coin every day," writes Basil Waring, an officer of the mayor, in a letter preserved among the Ottley Papers, "for abundance of plate is sent in to the King from several counties about us, and a great deal of plate comes out of Wales and Cornwall to be coined here. Also the press for printing is come to this town, and this day they are setting it up in some vacant rooms in my house . . . God of his mercy turn all to good and peace of this Kingdom, and deliver us from the misery of Civil War." Little dreamed Master Waring of the woes to follow! There is a very present reminder of that time to be seen in the great wooden gates of the Castle where the veritable bullets of the Roundhead muskets are still lodged.

Although Telford made the Holyhead Road and supervised the remaking of the road to London throughout the whole of its length, he did not build either of the two main bridges. The English Bridge was finished just before his time, in 1774, and widened with great skill in 1938, all the facings prepared by its original architect, John Gwynne, being replaced stone by stone. Gwynne was a leading spirit in the committee for creating the Royal Academy and one of its original members. His bridge at Atcham still stands, although it has been superseded by a wider structure in concrete, alongside. Here is a case in which the sentiment supporting the preservation of ancient monuments seems to have been overdone. The old bridge when in use gave a beautiful glimpse of Atcham church standing above a bend in the Severn. But now the bridge which is useless obstructs the view, and though it is a good bridge it is not nearly so well worth seeing as that view.

The old Welsh Bridge must have been a very grand and impressive affair with its huge barbican tower bidding defiance to the Welsh marauder, its drawbridge, and its many stone arches. One of these may still be seen by the curious in the cellars of a house in Frankwell some fifty yards from the present river bank. Another relic is the statue of Richard Duke of York, grandson of the last of the Mortimers, which (as already mentioned) stands in a niche of the old Market Hall.

The bottom of Mardol, now a detached alley, led directly onto the bridge, and here you may still see the remains of one of the old Severn quays, reminiscent of a life-line that was once so vital both to Shrewsbury and to the whole county. Telford gives a good picture of this forgotten highway in his account of inland navigations for *Plymley's Survey of Shropshire* (1803) from which I will quote:

"The benefits which the navigation of this river has spread over the county, are numerous and extensive; it has rendered the towns on the banks, storehouses for the surrounding country.

"The county town (chiefly from the advantage of the river) has, for several centuries past, been a sort of metropolis for North Wales; the inhabitants of the county at large experiencing such a ready communication with the lower districts of the country, and also with the sea, have been induced to open mines of iron, stone, lead, lime, and coal, and likewise to establish very extensive manufactures of iron; by means of those mines, and manufactures, much capital has been drawn into the district, a great market has been opened for the agricultural produce of the county; the ready conveyance of fuel and manure has enabled the cultivation to be carried on even beyond the demands of the increasing consumption; and all have so operated together, as to increase the general wealth of the county.

"Notwithstanding the many advantages which have arisen to the county of Salop from the navigation of this river, and the superiority which it has, in times past, given to the products of the mines and manufactures on its banks, when most of the other parts of the kingdom were labouring under the imperfections of land conveyance, over the roads which were scarcely passable, and with machines imperfectly constructed; yet it is equally true, that while the system of land carriage has been completely changed, while artificial canals have been formed in many parts of the country, and the navigation of many of the other rivers in this island have been greatly improved; yet still the navigation of the river Severn has been suffered to remain in its natural and imperfect state; not one obstacle has been removed, nor has one improvement been yet introduced. In consequence of this imperfect state of the navigation, neither the exports nor the imports can be carried on with a facility any way proportioned to those parts of the kingdom which enjoy the benefits of improved water conveyance. From this defect the county of Salop has certainly, of late, been in some measure prevented from reaching that pitch of prosperity at which it would otherwise have arrived.

"The inconveniences attending the navigation of this river, arise chiefly from the following causes, viz.

"*First,* From the fords and shoals . . .

"*Secondly,* From the deficiency of water in drought . . .

"*Thirdly,* From the mode of hauling the barges by men instead of horses . . .

"With regard to adopting the mode of hauling barges by means of horses, instead of the present barbarous and expensive custom of performing this slave-like office by men, it is only necessary that a good towing-path for horses, should be formed along the banks of the river, and which will no doubt take place, if any scheme of general improvements should ever be adopted."

But nothing of the kind ever happened. Canals, roads, and railways followed each other in rapid succession and outmoded this ancient form of transportation with its "slave-

like office" which had no doubt gone on continuously since
the time of the Romans. But it died very hard. Those vessels
mentioned by Telford, properly called trows, continued to
come man-hauled up the Severn to within the memory of
living man.

The Shrewsbury swans seem to be a happy accident, for
though the birds are there in a goodly number there is no
official swanherd on the town's pay-roll and no annual
"upping." In the nesting season you may generally see at
least one mother incubating her eggs so close to a pier of the
English Bridge that you get a plan-view of her from the
parapet. If you watch after dusk you may see her making
angry darts at the rats which have a keen eye to the eggs.
And it is one of the fair sights of the town to see the solemn
procession of swans which usually migrate in the summer
gloaming from one bridge to the other past the great avenue
of limes in the loop of the river.

These lime avenues of the Quarry must be the most splendid of any in the country, perhaps in all Europe. They were
planted in 1719 and have now reached a prodigious height,
so that their tops are even visible from Laura's Bower. The
Quarry is a very remarkable pleasance, as ample in its
space as the rest of the peninsula is congested. Prebendary
Auden, in his *Shrewsbury*, sees it as a parallel to the backs of
the Cambridge colleges, and is not unjustified. There is an
analogy nearer at hand and probably one which influenced
the minds of the Corporation in the days of George I—the
Prospect created by John Kyrle for his fellow townsmen of
Ross-on-Wye a year or two previously, and still in existence.

The actual quarry, after which the park takes it name, and
whence came so much of the stone with which the earlier
town and its defences were built, is, bar the avenues, the only
formal bit of landscape gardening in the whole area. Here
you may see what can be done to romanticize such a bald
memory with trees, shrubs, flowers, and variegated water-

fowl. But here again, as elsewhere in Shrewsbury, we have
no real novelty but something traditional and native, not a
feature which can bear comparison with similar jubilant
horticultural concentrations in other public parks. Perhaps
it is fanciful, but I see a pedigree link with the spirit of this
place in the worn archway peeping from a grotto that actually reveals a bit of the Quarry's bare face. It is called the
Shoemaker's Arch and must have been brought from across
the river when the school was built on the old freeman's
property called Kingsland. But we must go to the end of
the chain to test this link with the Horticultural Society.

The Shrewsbury Show was a perpetuation of the great
procession of Corpus Christi (on Thursday after Trinity
Sunday) inaugurated in the early fourteenth century. Until
late in the last century it was one of three such pageants still
in existence, the other two being in Coventry and Preston
in Lancashire. The procession was formed by the trade
guilds in order of precedence based on the age of their
charters.

In Shrewsbury the guilds were the backbone of its mediaeval life, for it was then an important commercial centre
rather than the governing nucleus of an agricultural county.
And these companies survived the great robbery of the
Reformation, when so many perished elsewhere. They and
their "show" persisted into the last century and are not all
defunct yet.

The Corpus Christi procession appears to have formed
up, after all taking part had heard mass at St Chad's Church,
and then to have marched, carrying the Host, to the weeping cross in the Abbey Foregate. Here the throng not only
bewailed its sins but also prayed for a good harvest. And
Miss Burne in her *Shropshire Folklore* aptly comments,
"If so, they must have transferred the Rogation-tide cere-
monies to this day." Or, to put another construction on it,
there had always been one *big day* for an outing at Whitsun-

tide, and what was done formerly was now done at the feast
of Corpus Christi.

When the procession returned, the wardens and freemen
of the guilds betook themselves to their respective halls and
feasted till sundown, and this they continued to do in spite
of the strictures brought in by the reformed church. However, in 1588, the year of the attempted invasion by the
Spanish Armada, it is recorded, "This yeare in the monthe
of Maye and June was soome contraversie in the towne of
Salop about settinge upp of maye poales and bonyfires
mackinge, and the erection of trees before the Shearnans
haule and other places the which Mr Tomkys publicke
preacher there did preche against and the said precher beinge
present at the perswadinge reformacion was threatenid and
pushid by certen lewde persoonns."

However, these heathen and papistical practices continuing, and the puritan element growing rather stronger in
the town, the "contraversie" was put to a legal test and in
1591, after the usual perambulation, scapegoats were selected in the shape of two young men who were apprehended
and charged before the Recorder for "bringing in the
Shearmen's Tree." They boldly pleaded guilty and were let
off with a caution. Further obstacles and restrictions being
imposed, the trading companies put their heads together
and devised a plan to outwit the municipal authorities. Yet
the Corporation seems to have been quite glad to agree to
it, for it was with its permission that the procession adjourned to Kingsland instead of going back to the guildhalls
in the town.

Here they could put up their may-poles and their boughs
and light their bonfires and erect tents for their feasting.
Soon each company made for itself a stockade like the old
Saxon *burgh,* planting a hedge, round which a ditch was dug.
Within these enclosures permanent buildings of wood and
brick began to take the place of the authorized tentage, an

unauthorized proceeding towards which the Corporation turned a blind eye. Each was called an arbour (not on account of the trees and hedges but from the old word "harbour," signifying a place of shelter and entertainment). After the buildings came gateways, displaying the arms and emblems of each trade, some in wood, others in stone.

The procession (now called the Shrewsbury Show) still went to the Abbey Foregate before proceeding to Kingsland, though even the site of the weeping cross had long since been forgotten, and it marched in the following order.

First the Shearmen with Bishop Blaize in a woollen mitre and full-made shirt (for lawn sleeves).

Next, the Shoemakers with Saints Crispin and Crispian dressed as cavaliers in buff jerkins, jack boots, and high hats.

Next, the Tailors with Adam and Eve girt with leafy aprons.

Next, the Butchers with their Knight of the Cleaver.

Next, the Barber Chirurgeons and Weavers with St Catherine working a spinning-wheel (a mixed metaphor).

Next, the Bricklayers presenting bluff King Hal.

Next, the Hatters with a mounted redskin chief from the land of beavers.

Next, the Smiths and Armourers with a mounted knight.

Next, the Bakers with Cupid and Ceres following a garlanded loaf of bread borne high on a pole.

Next the Flax-dressers with another Adam and Eve, a golden-haired lassie with her hair reaching to the ground.

Next, the Skinners and Glovers with a stuffed stag, and huntsmen winding their horns.

Lastly, the Combretheren of Sadlers, Painters, Glaziers, Curriers, and Others with a richly caparisoned horse led by a groom, and Paul Rubens seated in a cart behind an easel on which he dashed off pictures as he jolted over the cobbled streets.

The Show continued until 1878, by which time the festivities had extended themselves far beyond the bounds of the hedges and ditches of the arbours. The brethren of the mysteries were outnumbered on Kingsland Common by members of the public, show-vanmen, and proprietors of drinking booths. The day of the cheap tripper had come, and the railway disgorged trainloads of them, many of whom got too drunk to avail themselves of their return bargain. So the Home Office stepped in and achieved what the Reformation had failed to do.

But the Shrewsbury Show is not really over. Even the Home Office cannot balk such a high-spirited and conservative community of its long-inherited right to express itself joyously once a year and, at the same time, make its bow to the Lord of the Harvest. There is a spiritual descendant called the Shrewsbury Flower Show. And this is not quite like any other flower show I have ever been to. Its spirit does not reside in the gorgeous flowers and huge fruits and vegetables on display in the Quarry grounds, nor in the acrobatics by firework-light after dark. It is hard to say where it does lie and would come easier from a poet than a prose-writer. But there is something essentially Salopian about the gathering, and the feeling that it is an inevitable old tryst inaugurated long before the Horticultural Society was dreamed of. I have only been to three of these fetes, and each time I have come away with the conviction that such a thing could not have happened anywhere except in Shrewsbury.

That old arch in the Dingle is the sole reminder of the ancient Show. It is the gateway of the arbour of the Shoemakers Company. Here you may make out the weathered figures of St Crispin and St Crispian and the legend which they querulously display to protect them from that Protestant wrath which pursued their Corpus Christi antecedents.

> We are but images of stonne
> Do us no harme we can do nonne

In writing just one chapter on a place like Shrewsbury the task of picking and choosing is unusually solemn and sad. I review the contents of these presents with a truly shocked sense of inadequacy. What, nothing about the churches! not even the Herkenrode glass in St Mary's! Only a bare hint of the great goings on at the Adam assembly room at the Lion! But then there are the guide-books. And this is not a guide-book or I could not have made so free with my picking and choosing. And there are the excellent Transactions of the Shropshire Archaeological Society and the Transactions of the Caradoc Field Club, all to be seen in the Free Library, both series so good yet neither of them exhaustive.

But I cannot wind up this superficial patchwork without paying the tribute of just a thought to what the county through its great town has done for the nation. It has given it a great school. There it still stands by the Severn side, but it is spoken of the world over as a property belonging rather to the map of England. And tucked away in a road off a turning in Frankwell is a prosaic-looking building which is the home of the King's Shropshire Light Infantry, a regiment with one of the most dazzling lists of battle-honours in the British Army. One of its old soldiers stands on top of the tall column at the wide cross-roads in the London approach. It is the first Lord Hill of Hawkstone. His gilded figure is a wonderful landmark, vying in distant views with the spire of St Mary's and the gleaming dome of St Chad's. You see him afar off and say, "That's Shrewsbury!" But how many people know *who* he is—even when they have paid their twopence to climb up the spiral stair and have a close look at him?—even when they have made out that he was one of Wellington's Waterloo veterans? He was a hero in Shropshire before he fought at Waterloo, and the column was already begun before the date of that battle, though it wasn't finished till 1816. Yet there was a time when folk would have looked queerly at you if you had said, "Who is Lord Hill?" Not many, even in this age of stellar adoration, have evoked such spontaneous popularity as the living prototype of that gilded figure, and I hope you won't be bored by yet another quotation, but I should like to convince the passer-by that the column is no more a mere ornament than the one in Trafalgar Square.

"Lord Hill took his seat in the House of Lords on June the 1st (1814) and afterwards received a sword of honour and the freedom of the City of London. So great was his popularity, that at a review in Hyde Park, the mob in their eagerness to obtain some personal memorial of him tore his coat and belt to pieces. He saved his Order of the Bath by snatching it off, and handing it to Major Churchill, who only preserved it by drawing his sword, and threatening to cut off any hand that interfered with it . . . Some kissed his sword, his boots, his spurs, anything they could touch; they pulled hairs out of his horse's tail, and one butcher's boy, who arrived at the happiness of shaking his hand, they chaired, exclaiming, 'This is the man who has shaken hands with Lord Hill.' "

CHAPTER X

SHROPSHIRE LANDSCAPE

LOOKING at Shropshire on a general physical map of
Great Britain it would seem obvious that the reason for its
hilliness was because its boundary overlaps the first foot-
hills of the Welsh mountains and that, in fact, it owes the
best part of its scenic beauty to a borrowed fringe of the
Cambrian highlands. And if the writer were to say, "No!
the hills are as purely Salopian and individual as the people,"
it might seem as though enthusiasm for a theme were being
worked to death. So in speaking of the Shropshire hills I
will not call the poet as my first witness but the geologist.

Incidentally, Shropshire has had a great deal to do with
the first great discoveries in this romantic science of pre-
human history. One of the greatest pioneers of the new
revelation which came at the end of the eighteenth and the
beginning of the nineteenth centuries was Sir Roderick
Murchison. He was the son of a Highland laird and began
life as a soldier, served in the Peninsular Campaign and
was present at the Battle of Corunna. After Waterloo, when
the army offered no further prospects of excitement, Murchison sold his commission and sought relief for his ab-
normally high spirits in fox-hunting. He spent nearly ten
years in doing nothing else and might have died a respected
M.F.H., but otherwise unrenowned, if he had not met Sir
Humphrey Davy in 1823. This acquaintanceship seems to
have drawn out Murchison's powerful and enquiring mind
and shown him how it could be used while satisfying his
appetite for strenuous bodily exertion. More, it showed him
where there were prizes to win in a virgin field, and Murchi-

son had a great weakness for trophies of all sorts. By 1826 he had become one of these new-fangled (but quite genteel) things, a "scientist," and in that year was elected a Fellow of the Royal Society. The new hobby which Murchison had adopted to rouse him out of the ennui engendered by fox-hunting was geology. At that time the young Geological Society was a very humble appanage of the Royal Society. Murchison became its president and at once set himself to raise its prestige and give it an independent life. Meanwhile, he looked for a field in geology where he could not only explore but make a conquest. He found this in Shropshire.

At that time scientific opinion as to the origin of the earth's crust was divided into two opposite and hostile camps. The mineralogists believed that it had been formed under an all-enveloping sea by a process of crystallization. The followers of William Smith held that it had been laid down layer upon layer whilst only temporarily submerged in water. Murchison backed the latter choice. Smith, who had started this idea of deposition in "strata," was still alive, but he and his true-believers had not been able to work out their strata system to a lower base than the Old Red Sandstone. After (or was it before?) this came a great unidentifiable miscellany called the "grauwacke" or "transition" rocks. The answer to the riddle would begin to reveal itself if a place could be found where the grauwacke actually fitted on below (or above) its next existing system, which was suspected to be the Old Red Sandstone. Here was a fox worth running to earth. Murchison mounted a phaeton carriage drawn by two greys and went off from London in pursuit.

This grauwacke does not make one of those hills or ranges which can be claimed as endemic to Shropshire, but there is great plenty of that rock in the county and Murchison began there, driving his greys, striding up every hillside, tapping with his hammer. His fox ran out of Shropshire into Herefordshire and off into Wales, doubled on him, and then, in his own words, "Travelling from Brecon to Builth by the Herefordshire road, the gorge in which the Wye flows first developed what I had not till then seen. Low terrace-shaped ridges of grey rock dipping slightly to the south-east appeared on the opposite bank of the Wye and seemed to rise out quite conformably from beneath the Old Red of Herefordshire. Boating across the river at Cavansham Ferry, I rushed up to these ridges, and to my inexpressible joy found them replete with transition fossils, afterwards identified with those at Ludlow. Here then was the key, and if I could only follow this out on the strike of the beds to the northeast the case would be good."

But Murchison had to get on with his greys to York to attend the first meeting of the British Association. If he had made his discovery in Corvedale instead of the Wye Valley he would, no doubt, have named that series of rock which became the main study of his life "Salopian." But the famous kill was in the old country of the Silures, so he called it "Silurian," though he gave its main components the honour of Shropshire names, and they are still called the Ludlow and Wenlock beds.

Murchison had the most amazing energy, both physical and mental, and a wonderful eye for the lie of the land that was already highly trained by his campaigns in Portugal, Sicily, and Ireland. So quickly did he master the details of structure and position of his newly found Silurian system and its relations to younger and older formations that in 1839 he brought out that huge tome, *The Silurian System,* which gives a minute description of the whole geological structure of Shropshire, a book that is most readable today, and whose judgments have, in the main, stood the test of time. The engravings of the fossils are taken from specimens still preserved in the Ludlow Museum. I have heard that the authorities concerned have had tempting offers to

The Long Mynd, Ashes Hollow
The Long Mynd above Church Stretton

part with them to the larger national collections which they have laudably resisted, and I hope they will continue to do so.

The other geologists I had in mind at the beginning of the chapter were Darwin and Lapworth. The work of the former in this sphere was done outside the county, but he was, of course, a Shropshire lad and went to the old Shrewsbury school, in front of which his effigy in sculpture is to be seen. He was Murchison's junior by seventeen years and they had few contacts. But they made very similar approaches to *la vie scientifique*. Schoolmasters and Examiners please note how we learn from Darwin's autobiography that as a young man he was so madly keen on snipe-shooting he really cared for nothing else. And how orthodox learning was so little to his taste that he did not enter for honours at Cambridge and took his ordinary degree with a tenth place down the list.

Now we return from this digression to where we were at the end of the first paragraph. The Wrekin, of course, is the king hill of the county, though only seventh in height (1335 feet). But he looks every inch a mountain, especially when seen from north or south, when his contours make him a blue pyramid rising from the fertile plain. He is made of an eruptive complex of red lava, called after himself "Uriconian," and his age-group is the basic one of Pre-Cambrian. So that he was made before any of the Welsh hills except that distant toad-like hump called Holyhead Mountain.

I cannot claim that hills made of Uriconian rock are exclusively Salopian products, as the Malverns are made of the same stuff. But Shropshire has the lion's share as it musters the kindred trio above Church Stretton, the Lawley, Caer Caradoc, and Ragleth. Probably the Breiddens (p. 57) are about the same age together with the other two related lacolites of Pontesford Hill, whose rounded

Stiperstones, the Devil's Chair
The Ancient Portway on the Ridge of the Long Mynd

hump is such a striking feature among the hills which deck the southern fringe of the Shropshire Plain, and Corndon Hill, at the other end of the same group (the Stiperstones Ridge), standing just across the county boundary, in Montgomeryshire.

But though we must venerate the great age of these hills, the nature of lava cannot engage our historical sentiment in the same way as sedimentary rock. That is a thing which when we see and touch we can feel that it is a body retaining association with the past in the same way as an ancient monument made with human hands. For the very grains of sand and slabs of mud are there that were washed down by primaeval waters. What we see and touch are the veritable fragments of a still older world in which those primaeval waters moved. Although the period is immeasurably removed from any conception the mind can grasp as an "epoch," the remains are there in hard fact for us to try our imaginations on. And so hills of sedimentary rock seem to me more moving than those of the igneous sort. And Shropshire has two hills of that earliest known geological period, the Pre-Cambrian—Haughmond Hill and the Long Mynd.

Haughmond Hill is only a modest reminder of the dawn days, of more interest to the scientist than the artist or poet or (shall we dare to say?) the general reader. But the Long Mynd is otherwise. There it stands, our most ancient ancient monument, a thing that has watched out not merely the reigns of kings and the turmoils of peoples but all the known ages of the world. It is not spectacular. It is notable for its completely uneventful outline and its smoothness. In this very featurelessness it looks the part of untold antiquity to perfection. And the valleys leading up into it are unusual. Those best known to the Church Stretton visitor are the Cardingmill Valley and the Ashes Hollow, and they are typical of the others. The hillsides come down so steeply that you think the stream which flows along the bottom must lead you up into a gorge. But the gorging has all been done long ago. Even the huge and everlasting forces of denudation have almost exhausted their powers over this sublime mountain. The bottoms of the valleys are flat platforms, deserted arenas where the old fury of the elements has been spent and in which the stream now loiters, its enfeebled hydraulic energies devoid of power to excavate. So you go on, traverse after traverse, and the distinctive charm lies not in dynamic excitements but in the sort of serenity that dwells in a ruined castle.

The Pre-Cambrian theme is one that, while it may move the poet to awe, must fill the cynic with delight, for it is barren of any signs of life. Our remote Darwinian antecedents do not show up until the Cambrian times, with that hideous crustacean the trilobite. There are some horrifying specimens of these in the Ludlow Museum. And the places in Shropshire where they and their kind may be located may be found in J. D. de la Touch's *Handbook to the Geology of Shropshire*. I confess I have not had sufficient luck as a fossil-hunter to guide the reader.

This period has not left any outstanding topographical features in Shropshire. It is otherwise, though, with the next, the Ordovician. But here I am tempted to return for a moment to the authors of our knowledge of the essential make-up of Shropshire scenery.

Murchison's greatest friend and co-worker was Adam Sedgwick. He also worked on the grauwacke or transitional rocks, but in the deeper strata and in Wales. It was known that these rocks were definitely older than Murchison's which he had called Silurian, and therefore Sedgwick called his Cambrian. Their spheres of operations were carefully divided up and the boundary of each was near the old time-honoured one of Shropshire and Wales. It was always taken for granted that there would be one of those sharply defined divisions between the two series of rocks that geologists have based their time epochs on, and this cleavage-line was sought for year after year. But it was not discovered, and at length it became obvious to the younger disciples who were not blinded by the name-prejudice that the fossil evidence showed that both series belonged to the same geological epoch. For the Silurian trilobites went down into the Cambrian, and the Cambrian trilobites came up into the Silurian. There was, in fact, no dividing line. Thereupon the two friends became protagonists, each protesting before the world that both series should be known henceforth only by his own pet name. Murchison said that the Welsh rocks were obviously Lower Silurian, and Sedgwick as stoutly protested that the "so-called" Silurian rocks should properly be known as Upper Cambrian. But Murchison was not the man to lose a trophy. Presently they were the bitterest of enemies. And when they died the embarrassed faculty of geology, thinking it unseemly to dim the splendid memory of either great pioneer, let matters rest, as well as the original nomenclature. But this naturally caused endless confusion and the combat was now waged not between geologists and geologists but between paleontologists and stratigraphers. It was Lapworth who found a solution. He invented a *new* name for a sort of no-man's-land between the old kingdoms, calling it Ordovician (after the neighbour Celtic tribe to the Silures). Of Lapworth's more positive contribution to Shropshire we shall hear later.

The Stiperstones Ridge and the Shelve District are all Ordovician and form one of the most remarkable features in the Shropshire landscape, about which so many of those delightful legends which enrich Shropshire folklore have sprung. The crest of the ridge is formed by a hard white quartzite which has weathered into strange tors which fringe the sky-line like ruined castles. The largest and highest is called the Devil's Chair (1731 feet). Mary Webb in her

Golden Arrow has described it much better than I could, so
I give you her picture:

"On the highest point of the bare, opposite ridge, now
curtained in driving storm-cloud, towered in gigantic aloof-
ness a mass of quartzite, blackened and hardened by un-
countable ages. In the plain this pile of rock and the rise
on which it stood above the rest of the hill-tops would have
constituted a hill in itself. The scattered rocks, the rugged
holly-brakes on the lower slopes were like small carved
lions beside the black marble steps of a stupendous throne.
Nothing ever altered its look. Dawn quickened over it in
pearl and emerald; summer sent the armies of heather to
its very foot; snow rested there as doves nest in cliffs. It
remained inviolable, taciturn, evil. It glowered darkly on
the dawn; it came through the snow like jagged bones
through flesh; before its hardness even the venturesome
cranberries were discouraged. For miles around in the
plains, the valleys, the mountain-dwellings it was feared. It
drew the thunder, people said. Storms broke round it suddenly out of a clear sky; it seemed almost as if it created
storm. No one cared to cross the range near it after dark—
when the black grouse laughed sardonically and the cry of
a passing curlew shivered like broken glass. The sheep that
inhabited these hills would, so the shepherds said, cluster
suddenly and stampede for no reason, if they had grazed too
near it in the night. So the throne stood—black, massive,
untenanted, yet with a well-worn air. It had the look of a
chair from which the occupant has just risen, to which he
will shortly return. It was understood that only when vacant
could the throne be seen. Whenever rain or driving sleet or
mist made a grey shechinah there people said, 'There's harm
brewing.' 'He is in his chair.' Not that they talked of it
much; they simply felt it, as sheep feel the coming of
snow."

A bleak stony moorland rolls down from the Stiperstones to the Shelve District. Below the next crest the Mytton beds come near the surface. They are full of metalliferous veins bearing lead and zinc with accompanying barytes and blue-john (fluorspar). The white spoil-heaps from the old mines gleam from afar. Lead has been worked here continuously from the time of the Romans until the beginning of the present century, when the industry was killed by foreign competition.

This "Ordovician patch" between the Long Mynd and the Long Mountain is a very strange and rather fascinating country (for those who can tolerate eyesores) for what they mean in scenic reality and historical sequence. It is full of contrasts. At the southern end are miles of wild grass-moor scarred with the ruins of mining enterprise and dominated by the distant bulk of Corndon Hill. Here are the only two stone circles in Shropshire, Mitchel's Fold (where they say St Michael kept his cow) and another without a name. In the high midst of this bleak but picturesque wilderness stands the tiny church of Shelve with nothing to give you a clue to its age but a font which seems to belong to the twelfth century.

At the more northerly end of the Shelve District is the largest and most recently worked of the lead mines, called Snailbeach. Here are spoilbanks, ruined engine-houses, and smelting-sheds. Perched up above is the Lord's Hill Chapel, built for the mining community and still frequented. It formed the centre-piece of Mary Webb's eerie novel (or is it a prose-poem?), *Gone to Earth,* and you would think that there could not be such magical scenery as she describes so near such a scarified region. But there is, and immediately, if you follow the green track through the woods towards Habberley. This is a relic of the Stiperstones Forest where some old holly trees stand which are reckoned to be as much as a thousand years old.

Snailbeach is on the eastern slope of the Hope Valley which passes into a narrow and tortuous defile up which the road from Minsterley to Bishop's Castle goes, rising six hundred feet in a few miles. It has long been a favourite drive out of Shrewsbury, even in the horse-drawn days, one of Shropshire's most "noted beauty-spots," for there was no blight of industrialism here and the woodlands were a main feature of the gorge. When I went up that road in 1944 the whole of those beautiful woods on the western side had been cut—not a tree left. Even the exigencies of the war did not demand such a wholesale slaughter in one place. Of course, this is only part of the sad tale of what Shropshire has suffered in one of her most characteristic scenic assets, and one might have thought that a place with such a long-established reputation as the Hope Valley would, if not spared, at least have been treated with consideration. The Cotswolds have not suffered in like manner. Salopians, you cannot any longer take your scenery for granted! If you can let Atcham bridge Stand and half Hope Valley fall something is amiss—*Floreat Salopia* is belied!

But let us return to basic structures. We rise now into Murchison's own jealously guarded territory of Siluria and confront Wenlock Edge. It is an extraordinarily fine scenic feature. Standing in a straight unbroken front between the Church Stretton Gap and the Severn Gorge at Iron Bridge this escarpment of blue-grey Silurian limestone may be compared to a huge wave about to break. The north-western face is a cliff, but seen from the other side where the back of the wave rises up from Corvedale you see how its crest undulates along the whole of its length.

Towards the steep front of Wenlock the Severn advances and the cliff wall divides, as if by magic, letting the river pass on from the Shropshire Plain into that of Worcestershire. And the mystery of the penetration of this great barrier linking the Edge with the foot of the Wrekin was unsolved by Murchison, who, to the end of his life, remained sceptical of theories about an Ice Age which had grown up after he had learned and propounded his geology. And it was left for Lapworth to demonstrate the answer.

But now, if you look at an Ice Age map of this part of the country, you will see a huge sheet of water extending from the Wrekin right up into Cheshire, covering all those fenny places we visited earlier. And it is named Lake Lapworth in honour of the man who guessed this riddle. His theory was that the upper Severn originally found its way not to the Bristol Channel but to the Irish Sea and, in fact, excavated that estuary now occupied by the River Dee; that on the advance of the Irish Sea ice-sheet its waters were impounded between this barrier and Wenlock Edge until they overflowed, finding the most convenient escape-route to the south. When milder times returned they had cut so deep a channel along the new route that the Severn did not return to its old exit, and the Dee waters from Bala Lake were left in sole occupation.

Similar contingencies through damming-up by glaciers from Central Wales and Clun Forest are believed to have caused that spectacular gorge called Marrington Dingle near Chirbury, and the Plowden Gorge, and to have opened a way for the Teme through Brindwood Chase and enabled it to make its dramatic entry into the Vale of Ludlow.

This last gorge is cut through the uppermost member of the Silurian series, the Downton sandstone. The river goes on to expose the Upper Ludlow beds in the Whitecliff opposite the weir. It is the top layer of this where the "bone bed" lies, being a solid mass of the bones of fishes which swam in the latter-day tides of the Silurian sea. It is only an inch or two thick, but it may be mentioned that its presence has caused diversion not only to modern fossil-hunters but to saints and philosophers of the Middle Ages. There is a well near the old church at Richard's Castle which, after heavy rains, becomes loaded with the spiny wrack of this fossiliferous layer. What sort of miracle this signified in pre-Reformation days has not come down to us, and Camden in his *Britannia* is the first to call attention to the phenomenon. By then it was roundly declared that they were merely the bones of frogs, though why frogs should only appear here (and in such quantities) in skeletal form only must have puzzled many thoughtful minds.

The Old Red Sandstone (Devonian) which makes such imposing mountains in Herefordshire and Brecon is only seen in Shropshire as a rich colour enriching the floor of Corvedale and the lower slopes of the Clee Hills.

But the Carboniferous system is scenic and makes a very unusual display of itself. The limestone is seen in the north-west at Llanymynech (p. 56) cutting a typical figure. It is next seen in the south-east, limestone, coal, and all, high in air, forming the Clee Hills. I cannot think of anywhere else where folk go to a mountain summit to get coal. The coal, however, is very poor stuff and has never been systematically mined. Moreover these are the highest hills in Shropshire, Brown Clee being 1792 feet (only eight short of the official status of a mountain) and Titterstone Clee 1749 feet. Volcanic action caused the elevation of this isolated fragment of a coalfield. The congealed lava spouts are still there within the heart of the hills and their outpourings remain on the tops protecting the rest from the erosion of the elements. Titterstone is crested with a thick sheet of this basalt (dhu-stone dialectified into jew-stone), whence the sharp characteristic outline of its summit which is as great a landmark as the Wrekin and even more striking. Diorite, dolerite, and kindred hard igneous rocks are accountable for some of our finest bits of scenery. But since the era of good roads and railways they have been ruthlessly and indiscriminately attacked. In this way we have lost the whole grand profile of Penmaenmawr, and the fine aquiline peaks of the Rival Mountains are rapidly being reduced to road-metal and ballast. The great Whin Sill where Hadrian's Wall is magnificently perched has only been saved by a fluke. The Breidden is already beginning to lose its shape and beauty. But some effective check has been placed on the destruction of Titterstone Clee from its most sightly angle, for although it has been worked for a long while the owner stipulated that his view of it from Downton Hall must not be in any way marred. And as this happens to be the best view you can get of the hill it is still preserved to us.

No such check was placed on the depradators of Brown Clee, and the whole of the top has been cleared, including the Iron Age fort described in the *Victoria County History* (1908). The periphery of the summit of this Clee, outside the jew-stone area, is pitted with slight depressions which are the remains of the small surface mines that were sunk by individuals or small parties of men in the old days for coal.

The New Red Sandstone (Triassic) hills of Hawkstone, Grinshill, and Nesscliff have already been mentioned. This attractive setting puts in another appearance at Bridgnorth, enhanced by the rugged chiselling of the cataract which rushed out of Lake Lapworth. All the more recent formations have disappeared from the face of Shropshire, though the Jurassic just breaks the surface in the neighbourhood of Prees church.

So there appears to be nothing more for an amateur geologist to notify the "general reader" of, except to point out the historical importance of the fault which has opened a way through the hill barrier and made an easy north-and-south route between the Long Mynd and the fantastic jaggedness of Caer Caradoc, a geological accident which first determined the boundary between the anti-Roman Ordovices and the collaborating Cornavii, gave the Romans a main route from Uriconium to Magnis, the Georgians a coach road from Shrewsbury to Hereford, and the steam engine its main west link to Bristol.

CHAPTER XI

MARCH BEER AND
SHROPSHIRE CIDER

G O O D home-brewed ale is far better than the beverage
of the commercial brewers, and in the thirties there were
quite a few farms in Shropshire which still used their brew-
houses for the proper purpose and one or two inns which
brewed their own beer. The one I remembered particularly
well was at Cleobury Mortimer. I revisited it in 1945. But
it had changed hands and there was no more home-brewed.
I had to drink the usual war-time product of the commercial
brewer and listen to a lecture from the bar-tender, who was
a South Walian, on the wickedness of the Conservative
party.

Cleobury Mortimer used to be a good spot for teetotalers
as well as topers, for it has a noted spring of pure water
which gushes straight out of the hill-side in miraculous
volume like the ebullition at St Winefrede's Well. But I
was told, on this visit, that the fountain has been tampered
with, and the bulk of the flow intercepted and piped to
houses in the town—not in its native purity (which was
justly celebrated both for drinking and healing in the Middle
Ages) but impregnated with chloride of lime. This information I have no official confirmation of. It was a spinster lady
who told me, one who knew how to make a good pot of tea.
She complained that the chlorination had spoilt the good
taste of the water both for drinking and tea-making. I am
inclined to believe that what she said is true, because one
knows what the urban routinist is capable of doing.

Home-brewing has fallen off in Shropshire as elsewhere,
but I had been told of the location of one inn which still

practised the royal and ancient art, and I set out to find it on one of those autumn days that seem made for Shropshire, when the colours in the March land are so vivid and the air so sweet.

On this quest I was loitering in Westbury when a large herd of Hereford bullocks came crowding along and, after them, a farmer mounted on a spirited Shropshire cob. Seeing a stranger standing aside to let his bullocks go by, he doffed his wide-awake hat in a most engaging manner. I enquired who he was and heard that he farmed the land about Caus Castle, that he was one of the keenest farmers in that part, that he was making a great success with his stock-feeding, and that he usually moved his herds from one pasture to another mounted on horseback.

I suppose there are still any number of places where you might see a farmer driving cattle in this fashion, but they might not be red-and-white Herefords, all in such good fettle, barging along between tawny yellow ragstone walls in mellow sunlight. And the man might not give you such a grand and gracious salute, and it might not all happen in such lively air and rich colouring as you get about the Long Mountain.

The Long Mountain itself is in Wales, but if the name is used for the whole of this isolated hill group then it is half in Shropshire and half in Montgomeryshire, a position more favourable to the Welsh than in the time of King Offa, who built his dyke on the far western slope, above the Severn, a line still observed by place and farm names, which are English. This conservative retention is probably due to the establishment of Caus Castle. I now went to see that old ruin which I hadn't visited for some fifteen years, and was even more amazed than formerly at the massive strength of its earthworks. And what a charming bit of country it is perched in!

Here are high-hedged twisting lanes which give you choice

foreground peeps of meadow dells (old pastures with hazel hedgerows looking as long established as the Norman banks) and then sudden openings-out to the Shelve Hills with the distant ridge of the Stiperstones and the blue knob of Corndon Hill. There is something altogether old-fashioned about the pastoral scenery of the Long Mountain, a Morland landscape. No wonder Old Parr lived to such a great age here—150 years—and his cottage is still to be seen.

The Long Mountain has the same significance as the Long Mynd, for the latter half of this name is evidently from the Welsh *mynydd,* a mountain. And it is rather a typical Shropshire paradox that the further you get into England the more Welsh do the hill names become—Long Mountain, half in Wales, is all English, Long Mynd, all in England, is half Welsh, Caer Caradoc, still further east, is all Welsh.

The more westerly of the two Roman roads which went from Uriconium down into South Wales must have passed near Caus Castle to reach the spine of the Long Mountain which it followed on its way to the fort now called Caer Ffoss (or Y Gaer) whose ramparts show plainly through the ploughland.

The Romans must have chosen that devious route over the high ground to avoid the forest and swamps lying in the Rea Valley between the Long Mountain and the Shelve Hills. But the Mercians evidently cleared the woods, for a road has gone that way from Westbury to Chirbury since early Norman times and that is where the succession of mottes I spoke of earlier (p. 42) is to be found. A main road has grown up there since the Hundred of Chirbury was taken from the March and put into Shropshire.

On the day I am talking about I found my way down to it from the Wallops. It is odd to find an Upper and Lower Wallop here, reminiscent of the Over and Nether Wallops in Wiltshire. The former, however, would appear to be no sort of imitation but of true Shropshire origin and quite local in reference, *hope* being a name in these parts for a valley and *Wall* meaning of Wales.

So I went down into the Valley of the Rea Brook towards Marton Mere, which figured in the direction I had been given for locating the site I was in quest of. And there, sure enough, stood the little unpretentious house with a faded sign setting forth the golden legend "Licenced brewer." The innkeeper was having his mid-day repast in the bar parlour with his daughter and another. I asked if there was any home-brewed on tap and received a comfortable assurance that there was. The daughter rose and led me up two steps into the little bar beyond and served me. On my way out her father asked if I wouldn't join them at their dinner. Now this (like the incident of the mounted farmer) was another hark-back to the Shropshire of pre-war days I have always remembered so fondly. Nothing loath, I sat down to a very noble helping of a savoury Irish stew, and we discussed the good home-brewed in both senses of the verb.

Mine host tole me that when war broke out he had had a notice from the authorities saying that he must reduce the gravity of his beer. He wrote in reply pointing out that he brewed in the old traditional way and could use no other, and that if he reduced the gravity of his brew the beer wouldn't keep at all. He stated at the same time what was implied by his traditional method, and a very comprehensive process it was. To begin with, he grew his own barley on his own land. Then he was his own maltster. He germinated the grain on the stone floor of his malting-house and killed it in his own kiln. These were part of the inn building, and the traditional wooden cowl with its wind-vane was perched on the roof. Thus, having produced his raw material and malted his malt, he brewed his beer.

His letter was addressed to a higher authority than the local excise officer, but that official presently informed him that he was at liberty to continue brewing as heretofore. The innkeeper emphasized that he had not been told *why* this was. His actual plea had been that the beer would not keep if he made it less potent. He did not think, however, that that won him his case. He believed that a technical point was involved, that because he grew the barley on his own land and did all the processes himself they *couldn't stop him*. He said he was the only man in Shropshire who did all this and surmised that he must be the sole survivor. Anyone who has read the eighteenth-century drama by George Farquhar, *The Recruiting Officer,* in which March beer and its effects play such a strong part will take particular and solemn note of this solitary survival.

It will be remembered that another Marton Pool has been mentioned (p. 26), the relic of a great lake which once surrounded that island settlement whose earthworks and causeways, now high and dry, are called the Berth. But it was the near-by Marton Mere that I associated with a dugout canoe I had seen in a museum years ago. I asked my host if he had heard of it. "Oh yes," said he, "it was took up on my land. I'll show you the place where it lay."

We went to the northern fringe of the mere, where the water gradually melts into the firmer element by easy stages —sedge and rush, marsh, water-meadow. He pointed out the very spot. They had been opening a dyke and they came across this old shipwreck of the Iron Age lying athwart the cut, about two feet below the present level of the ground. Then he took me to see a platform raised above the marsh flat, roughly circular, where he said he believed that people must have lived when the lake overflowed his meadows. That was *his* idea, and it looked likely enough, though whether it has caught the antiquary's eye I do not know.

Shropshire is still a cider county, though not so great in this respect as it used to be. Not so long ago every big farm in South Shropshire had a cider orchard, a mill, and a press.

148

The old cider-mill is a picturesque machine worked by a horse. The millstone, set in the vertical plane, travels round in a circular trough crushing the apples.

A number of things have happened to restrict the home-brewing of farm cider. To begin with, horses are scarcer. And the motor lorry has invaded this province, as that of the milk-yield. The cider manufacturers of Herefordshire will now buy crops from the farm orchards, and the farmer finds it simpler and probably more profitable (since cider is no longer an important part of the farm labourer's wage bargain) to sell his apples than to ferment them. But the petrol engine has also come into the picture in another way, this time perhaps as a blessing. It has taken on a similar role to that of the steam thrashing-machine which a hundred years ago began to oust the flail and threshing-floor. There are now a number of mobile motor cider-presses which go from farm to farm in the autumn. This has conserved a good deal of farm cider-making which would have otherwise have died out. But I think it is doubtful if the beverage thus produced by half-proxy can be so carefully prepared and of such individual flavour.

Tree summer house in half-timber, Pitchford Hall
Daffodil fields under Wenlock Edge

CHAPTER XII

THE SHROPSHIRE DALES

GOING south from Shrewsbury, the road to Ludlow and the Wenlock Road form two sides of a triangle whose base is Wenlock Edge. The area is intersected by lanes, mostly tortuous. There is nothing which could really be called a main road anywhere. Yet four of the most famous houses of Shropshire are located here, and their isolation from main traffic routes adds to their charm. They are the halls of Pitchford, Condover, and Plaish, and Acton Burnell Castle.

Pitchford has already been spoken of as the finest half-timbered house in Shropshire. The church is in the park and an early member of the Pytchford family, carved in wood, seven feet from top to toe, lies within it. The old hall of the Pytchfords must have stood close by. The estate was bought in 1473 by Thomas Oteley, a merchant of the staple of the mart of Calais. He was not only a great man in the wool trade but also a dyed-in-the-wool Shropshire man, a descendant of William Oteley of Oteley (displaying three oaken leaves on a bend azure), who took part in Edward I's siege of Carlaverock Castle. Oteley still stands on the map near Ellesmere, though it is represented by but a single house.

The Ottley family held Pitchford for thirteen generations in direct male descent, the last of them dying in 1807. The property then went to an adopted heir who was a son of the first Earl of Liverpool.

An extraordinarily interesting collection of documents relating to the Ottley family remained in Pitchford Hall until quite recently—the Ottley Papers, to which I have referred more than once. The present owner, General Sir Charles Grant, has presented them to the National Library of Wales, a migration which seems a little odd in view of the old Border prejudice, and one hopes that no political turn of fortune will make these very English records even less accessible. Aberystwyth is something of a pilgrimage for the English student, so it is to be hoped that the recipients of this gift will justify their trust by publishing a well-annotated full text of the papers. All that has been done in this direction so far appeared in the Transactions of the Shropshire Archaeological Society. It was only a small part of the whole and dealt with the period of the Civil War when Sir Francis Ottley was Governor of Shrewsbury and the most prominent moving spirit of the King's party in Shropshire. The able compiler of the four instalments was William Phillips, and anyone who has access to these Transactions will find the vivid presentation of this chapter of history well worth reading.

Pitchford is an apt name which even yet does not belie its meaning. The ford is across a tributary of the Cound Brook (which gives its name to Cound and Condover) and the pitch infiltrates into a well by the very brink of the stream. The source of this unusual ingredient is a thin bituminous layer in the coal-measures—for this is the margin of the Shropshire coalfield though not in the mining area. The well itself is dry, except after heavy rains, when both water and pitch reappear. In the eighteenth century a famous medicine was concocted with the bitumen of Pitchford and sold as Betton's British Oil.

South of Pitchford comes the first of the three hill groups which contain the Shropshire Dales—Ape Dale and Corvedale. These hills are very dissimilar in shape and in geological structure. The first is called Hoar Edge and is structurally classed in the Ordovician family, though it did not receive a mention in Chapter Ten, partly because the author did not feel competent to discuss its very complex nature and partly because he did not wish to confuse the geology-shy reader. The other two are successively Wenlock Edge and the Clee Hills. It is interesting to find the word *dale* in these parts as a sort of southely outlier (Coalbrookdale and Hope Dale are in the same region). It chiefly belongs to the northern counties and is not elsewhere found in force south of Derbyshire. It smacks of the Norseman who, so far as I know, has left no other trace of his very small influence in Shropshire. And these dales are not at all the same kind as the Cumbrian and Yorkshire sort which are first and foremost river valleys. Here they are valleys in which a small stream happens to flow because in such wide catchment areas it can hardly avoid doing so. One may therefore look for unusual configurations not present in the standard type of dale, and they are certainly there.

Acton Burnell Castle stands at the beginning of this scenery, on the north-west slope of Hoar Edge. It must always have been a beautiful place, and its blend of woodland and pastoral charm has been preserved by its comparative privacy within the grounds of Acton Hall, possessed since the seventeenth century by the Catholic family of Smyth, and now a convent.

The castle and the church were both built by Robert Burnell, Bishop of Bath and Wells, and chancellor to Edward I. He was, however, a Shropshire man, a Burnell of Acton, and he built this castle before that much more fortified one at Wells, which is also standing at the present time. Indeed, the Shropshire house is not a military work of any significance, and though the ambitious man was duly granted a licence to crenelate in 1283 he evidently had no serious fears of the peril of the Border reaching so far. Also, 1283 was the year of the Edwardian conquest of Wales. The King had his headquarters at Rhuddlan and was prospecting a site for the castle at Conway. But the new house cannot have been finished when, in the same year, Edward came to Acton Burnell and held one of the first parliaments, a historical event marked by the passing of the statute *de Mercatoribus,* of great significance to the early commercial world. In a field close by the castle stand two gable-ends of a building that might quite well have been a hall of the early thirteenth century. Local tradition connects it with the earlier Burnell hall in which that parliament was held, and though the experts have sown the usual doubts I don't think they have been able to debunk the gables.

The church is a very complete and beautiful "period piece" of the end of the thirteenth century, contemporary with the Angel choir at Lincoln. Both have an east window of similar geometric design. The carved work is exceedingly good, and it has been suggested, with great probability, that the crowned head which appears three times in different places is that of Edward I. It has not got that aquiline refinement of feature which one associates with the Plantagenet type. On the contrary, it is a burly head, a head without any nonsense in it, a hammer head. And perhaps that is, in fact, what the Hammer of the Scots looked like.

Bishop Burnell had something of the genius and temperament of Wolsey, though he was more trusted and better requited by his king. His ambition took the form of wishing to found a great family in his native county, but his clerical calling forbade the usual short cut to the acquisition of land by marriage, nor could he leave a direct heir. The first problem he solved by the purchase of manors, not an easy market in those days, but he managed to buy up twenty-one within the county. For heir, he had a younger brother. He also had a nephew and a sister. He took the greatest pains to ensure the aggrandizement and perpetuation of his name, and he surely could not have found a more favourable soil than Shropshire in which to plant for posterity, for the longevity of a family name is proverbial there. But his plans quickly went agley. His male next-of-kin wasted the patrimony and produced no successors. His sister, Maud, had a son by her second marriage. To mend matters this man took his mother's name and confronts us from the splendid brass within the church as Sir Nicholas Burnell, but within half a century after his death the name vanished and the estate was broken up.

The Ministry of Works was given custody of the castle in 1933; it is also guardian of the Langley Chapel not far away. This pretty bit of country has, in fact, quite a collection of those things tourists enjoy looking at. Near the chapel is the early sixteenth-century gatehouse of Langley Hall, and about a mile and a half to the west is Causeway Wood with the Roman bridge and the Roman bath. The causeway thus named is paved in stone and has always been attributed to the Romans. It is so long since I saw it that I cannot form an opinion on the matter. The bridge (a culvert through the causeway) and the bath I have never seen. But I have seen other stretches of the same old road at Rushbury and on the slope of Brown Clee, where (in both cases) it is called Roman Bank. The older authorities who were so certain about the Roman date assume that it went to the great entrenched work at Nordy Bank which they always believed to be a Roman fort. In the light of present knowledge, however, I do not think that this ascription is justified, for Nordy Bank is a typical work of the Iron Age Celt.

There is no doubt, however, about the Roman road just north of Acton Burnell which crosses the present road near Pitchford village, a narrow green lane which peters out in about a quarter of a mile. It reappears near Frodesley and is identified with the present thoroughfare, which is very narrow. It used to continue like this for several miles, just missing every Saxon settlement till it came to Little Stretton, but the Church Stretton by-pass was built on top of two miles of it during the war. This is the road that went from Uriconium to Magnis and Isca Silurum (Caerleon).

It is this route whose making is believed to be connected with the campaign of Ostorius Scapula and his defeat of Caractacus (Caradoc), and, therefore, Caer Caradoc (Caradoc's Fort) has been assumed to have been the site of the last struggle of this picturesque British prince whose bearing and captivity are still a theme of school history books. The learned, however, comparing the present topography with the story as told by Tacitus, are generally in agreement in denying the honour of the battle to the rugged Church Stretton mountain but are in complete disagreement about an alternative site. Some name the Breidden as certain, others plump for Pileth Hill, near Knighton.

So far as names go, there is actually a competitor Caer Caradoc in the county, near Clun, and if strength of Iron Age fortifications counted for anything, the position at Clun ought to win, for the fosse and rampart there are vast and infinitely stronger than the works at Church Stretton. But perhaps for obvious reasons this out-of-the-way monument has never had the publicity of the other. Yet it is the lack of a river at Church Stretton which the debunkers of the traditional site always point to as failing to comply with the picture of Tacitus, and there is a river at the Clun site which in the Roman times might have been just as nasty to cross as Tacitus describes.

Elsewhere, there is yet a third Caer Caradoc. For my part I have no preference. But I would like to add a note to the confusion by observing that Caradoc's backers were the Silures who were assuredly a Goidelic-speaking tribe. And therefore the name Caer Caradoc, which is Brythonic (Welsh) must have been given some time after Gaelic had ceased to be spoken in these parts, which might be the fifth or sixth century, shortly before the coming of the Saxons.

Ragleth, Caer Caradoc, and Lawley abut on Hoar Edge

to form one side of Ape Dale. But so little like the Northern conception of this word is it that it has a watershed in the middle of it, giving a stream southward to the Onney, and another northward to the Severn. The way into it from the south is by the road from Church Stretton, over the saddle between Ragleth and Caer Caradoc down to Hope Bowdler. A lover of old things would turn off here to see the little church at Eaton-under-Heywood, the fine half-timbered houses of New Hall and Wolverton, and perhaps go on to see the two neighbours at Harton Bank. Further along the Dale is Rushbury, the most beautiful village under Wenlock Edge. The main road to the crest goes up at Longville, but by narrow lanes you can pass Plaish with its famous tall chimneys and see the little church at Hughley which has one of the few rood screens in Shropshire, and then get on top at Five Chimneys.

The view from the highest point of the Edge is very fine indeed, the cliff is so sheer as to be a "dizzy height," and at one of the dizziest points there is marked on the one-inch ordnance map in old English letters the Major's Leap. There are "leaps" in many different parts of the country, each with its tale. Shropshire has two, Douglas's Leap on Haughmond Hill, where it is told how the horse carrying the Black Douglas in flight from the Battlefield of Shrewsbury fell and the rider was captured. Most leap stories are unauthenticated, but I believe that relating to the major would bear scrutiny. He was Major Thomas Smallwood of Wilderhope Hall, some three and a half miles away to the south-west, now a youth-hostel. He was a very ardent cavalier, but his near neighbours were hostile. He came home one night to find that some Parliamentary troopers had been there and made themselves rather free. He guessed the way that they had gone and took another route full tilt in the dark so as to cut them off and confront them. This he succeeded in doing at the bend of one of those deep, narrow lanes. All unaided, he attacked forthwith and slew two of the troopers. This called for revenge and, not long after, a much stronger force surrounded his house. He escaped and, mounting his horse, rode off towards Wenlock, hotly pursued, but not by all. Some imitated his own tactics and managed to head him off right by the brink of the Edge. The major did not hesitate, but put his horse to the cliff and sprang over it. The poor animal was killed, but Major Smallwood lived to see the Restoration.

Exactly how he was saved and what broke his fall we are not told, but then Smallwood had no biographer. He may have had a dash of the same Border pluck which informed Jack Mytton, who took equal risks with less provocation. And though we are now far from Halston Hall it would almost be unseemly not to make at least one mention of Jack Mytton in a book about Shropshire. He is usually spoken of as the prize example of a wealthy dare-devil, a prodigy of animal spirits. But he had fine and rare qualities which seem to me typical of the Border race, the tempered blend of Saxon and Celt. Given less money and more opportunity to display his parts he would have been remembered very differently. Here is just one incident to give him his due in this work and to illustrate the parallel with Thomas Smallwood. I quote from Jack's biographer, Nimrod:

"As he was one day driving one of his friends in a gig, who expressed a strong regard for his neck, with a hint that he considered it in some danger, Mytton addressed him thus: 'Was you ever much hurt then, by being upset in a gig?' 'No, thank God,' said his companion, 'for I never was upset in one.' 'What!' replied Mytton—'*never* upset in a gig? What a d———d slow fellow you must have been all your life;' and, running his near wheel up the bank, over they both went, fortunately without being much injured!"

Corvedale is more individual than Ape Dale, and though it has been formed by upheavals of the earth's crust rather than the denuding action of a river it lies between two definite slopes, and the Corve runs in its midst throughout its length. It is so different from the rest of Shropshire as to be almost a "country," and yet it conserves elements of rustic life that must be more typical of old Shropshire than elsewhere. The dialect is still alive; in this respect the younger generation is bilingual and can use both old talk and school talk. There is a Celtic sprinkling—"grig" for heather, for instance, but the bedrock is plain English—"luggin' muck" (carting manure).

Although the head of Corvedale is so near the industrial region of Coalbrookdale (which was one of the chief centres of energy and progress that raised England as a great power among the nations), its activities have left Corvedale undisturbed. The Coalbrookdale cult of trade and housing has spread to the north only; to Wellington, Oakengates, Lilleshall, Shifnal. Corvedale is as much detached from all that as if it were a hundred miles away. Its two chief towns, the one at the head and the other the foot, Much Wenlock and Ludlow, abiding in a settled mediaevalism which has lost its driving power and never been able to renew it from the springs of modernity, seem to have guarded the dale like the sentinels in a fairy tale.

To a student of topography there is nothing more surprising than the stubborn inertia of traditionalism. A place which has thriven for centuries on one particular regime will not perish and disappear from the map when that rule is over. But it is seldom that it can be made to adopt another mode of life, preferring to live on its memories of the past than to rouse itself and set about a constructive programme of revival.

Much Wenlock has had a great and prosperous past which came to it entirely through an accident of religious enthusiasm. We see it as a small picturesque market-town. But geography has not favoured it as a natural centre for a market, nor as the site of a strong feudal power. Its market has come there because *it* was there, and has so remained. And its high road has been established for the same reason. St Milburge, a Mercian princess who lived at the end of the seventh century, built a small convent at Wenlock and laid her bones there, and it happened that the legend of her sanctity was a popular one. But her cult had almost been forgotten by the eleventh century when Earl Leofric of Mercia took it into his head to build a monastery on the site of the nunnery ruined (they say) in a Viking foray. Leofric's monastery does not seem to have survived for more than thirty years, for at the time of the Norman Conquest it was deserted. But the saint's name must have been of great repute in the neighbourhood, for after Roger de Montgomery had been settled at Shrewsbury nine years he began to build yet a third religious house at Wenlock in honour of St Milburge (three years before he founded his abbey at Shrewsbury). He gave the Wenlock house to the new order of Cluniac monks, and one sees an obvious link here, for Roger was also Earl of Arundel (and Count of Sussex) and it was at Lewes that the first great Cluniac monastery in England was established (1077).

The Cluniac priories were exempt from visitations of the bishop of the diocese; they took their instructions and bore rebuke only from the Abbot of Cluny, and to him was paid an annual revenue from all the houses, until the time of Edward III, who put a stop to this money going abroad. The Prior of Wenlock held his own court and owed no obligations to either the hundred court or the sheriff's court, and the lands which constituted his domain were carved out of the old hundreds and made a separate area of jurisdiction which is still called the Franchise of Wenlock. It coincides with the greater part of Corvedale and a strip of the fat lands lying at the foot of Wenlock Edge.

Wenlock Priory was dissolved in 1539, but its fame had

dwindled, and its popularity, for at the sequestration only the prior, the sub-prior, and eleven monks were there, a sparse company for so great a choir. Monastic rule had not been popular for a century or more. But by a strange turn of events the town and franchise, though it got rid of its civil government by a high-ranking ecclesiastic, exchanged its government in church matters for that of a much greater prelate, no less a man than the mitred abbot of Shrewsbury. The great abbey of St Peter and St Paul was dissolved in the same year and its ruler, Thomas Butler, was retired on a pension and at the same time offered the vicarage of Much Wenlock, which cure he saw fit to accept.

Abbot Butler was Vicar of Much Wenlock from 1539 to 1562, a period which covered eight years of the reign of Henry VIII, the whole of the reigns of Edward VI and Mary Tudor, and four years of Queen Elizabeth's. During the whole of this time he kept a register of events connected with the church and the many chapels attached to it very fully annotated and drawn up more in the spirit of a diary than a church register. This rare and (to the student) invaluable manuscript vanished from Wenlock, but was discovered in the eighteenth century in the muniment room at Longleat by an antiquary, James Bowen. He copied out certain bits which amused him and then the owner, Lord Weymouth, thought it might be of more interest to Sir Watkin Williams Wynn of Wynnstay and made him a present of it. A few years later, some curious person asked to see it, but it could not be found. It came to light again in the nineteenth century in a lumber room of Stafford Pryse the Bookseller in Shrewsbury. It was sent back to Wynnstay and another extract made by the Rev C. H. Hartshorne. In 1859 Wynnstay Hall was burned to the ground. So all we have are the two extracts, the earlier one in the Bodleian Library, and the later published in the *Cambrian Journal* of 1861.

From these we have a unique picture of the doings in a country parish during the extreme fluctuations of the state's interpretation of the Christian faith, by one who had ruled a great community as a mitred abbot and then ministered as a country vicar. Thomas Butler must have been something of a trimmer, but at heart he remained entirely in sympathy with the old persuasion. The relics of St Milburge had evidently been protected by him after the dissolution of the priory and deposited in the parish church, and he would no doubt be very familiar with the account by William of Malmsbury, who wrote in the mid-twelfth century of how they were found after their first eclipse; "St Milburgh's tomb was discovered by a boy running over the grave. A fragrant odour of balsam breathed through the church, and her body raised high wrought so many miracles that floods of people poured in thither. Scarcely could the broad fields contain the crowds, whilst rich and poor together, fired by a common faith, hastened on their way. None came to return without the cure or mitigation of his malady, and even the king's evil, hopeless in the hands of the leech, departed before the merits of the Virgin."

But then on Nov. 7, 1547, Abbot Butler has to record the public burning of these precious bones in a common bonfire, together with the images of St John the Baptist from Hope Bowdler, St Blaise from Stanton Long, and two images of the Virgin Mary. Usually he writes in English, but these he notes grimly in terse Latin, so that the vulgar may not read.

He keeps in touch with the monks and officials of the priory and has something special to say about each that died during his ministry. And thus we hear who and what manner of man was the organist who once led the choir in that stately ruin: "Augst 1st here was buried before the Chancell door of our lady's Chancell wthout in the Ch yard, John Morgan sometime Organ player of the Monasterie of St Milburge, (surrendered) in his time an experte and full conynge man in Musicke and did set many a swete and sol'ne song to the lawde of Almighty God whoo take his sowle to his m'cy Amen."

He stood very stoutly by every ancient privilege of his church in the matters of licences and burial fees. Parishioners of the chapels-of-ease, some of them a great way off, thought that under the new dispensation they ought to be allowed to bury their dead in their own grounds and sent him constant petitions, to all of which he returned a peremptory negative. The dead must continue to make their last journey to Wenlock, and the mourners bring their fee to the mother church.

We hear much incidental news; how one funeral party was stopped from taking a short cut, evidently from a fear of the old unwritten rule that the passage of a corpse over your land opened a right of way. "Mr Thomas Lawley stoped a Corpse coming from Wyke at the way at the Brook at the grene Myll coming the way thro the Barnesfold in a cart where the Body remained 'til next day he was buryed." He mentions that felons were hanged on the highest point on Wenlock Edge overlooking Ape Dale, in one case a little girl of eleven years old. And he records a super-centenarian who certainly ought not to be forgotten, seeing how much sentiment has been lavished on Old Parr of Wollaston.

"1543. "1st Feb. bur'd out of the Almshouse John Trussingh'm on Saterday before he died he said unto me S'r Tho's Butlar Vicar of this Church that he was of the age of 7 score and I said it could not be, he said he was 4 score at the Battle of Blowre heath and that sens he was 3 score years and rad'r more, and that he had been Serv't to thold S'r Gilbert Talbot kn't of Blakemer." This sounds convincing, though erring on the side of understatement. The battle of Blore Heath (p. 65) happened in 1459, eighty-four years before John's death. If he was then indeed four score years old, his life must have lasted one hundred and sixty-four years, thus having a clear win over Old Parr of fourteen years. But if his first computation was as modest as his second he beat Old Parr hollow.

Perhaps the reader will think that Abbot Butler is taking up too much of the room which ought to be given to a description of Much Wenlock. Even so I am tempted to detain him with one more entry which gives a pretty peep at a stirrup-cup in Tudor times.

"16th July, 1554. Memorandum. That the same day last above written my Lord the Bishop of Worcester Dr Nicholas Heath, Lord President of the Marches of Wales coming with Justice Townesynde in company with him from Salop, and riding towards Bridgenorth, about two of the clock in the afternoon, was desired by the Burgesses of this Borough of Wenlock to drink, and so they did alight and drank, sitting in the house of Richard Lawley Gent. at the Ash, hanged and decked in the best manner the said Burgesses could, with clothes of Arras, Covering of Beds, Bancards, Carpets, Cushions, Chairs, Forms, and a Cupboard covered with Carpet and a cloth, whereon stood the silver plate whereof they drank, borrowed for the time of Mrs Agnes the wife of Mr Thomas Rydley, sometime wife of Mr Richard Lakyn of Willey; the table covered with Carpet Cloth of diaper and napkins of the same, three dishes of Pears and a dish of old apples, Cakes, fine wafers, wyne white, and claret, and sack, and bread and ale for the waiters and servants without, at their pleasure, where my said Lord and Mr Justice sat the space of half an hour, and then arose, giving the said Burgesses great and gentle thanks for their cost and chear, and so departed towards Bridgenorth."

Mr H. E. Forest's book, *The Old Houses of Wenlock*, is, I think, still available in spite of war-time paper shortages, and gives a very good and full account of the town and neighbourhood.* I have spent perhaps more time than I should in saying what Wenlock *was* rather than what it *is* because I feel (is it in my bones or in my spirit?) that, together with the other outpost of Ludlow, some power of the past has survived into the present time and casts an indefinable spell of detachment throughout the intervening territory of Corvedale. It would not be difficult to cite parallels elsewhere—West Suffolk, for instance, where the pre-Reformation influence of St Edmundsbury still broods, and, again, the triangle formed by Rivaulx, Helmsley, and Byland in Yorkshire. But we are not concerned with other parts.

Looking across Corvedale from the grey undulating crest of Wenlock Edge, you see through breaks in the greenery how the floor of the valley is made of the rich red clays and earths of the Old Red Sandstone. Beyond, the great bluff hill of Brown Clee is set on a wide plinth of the same rock, its scars showing at intervals where the thick woods have been cut, an operation which is, alas! still proceeding as aftermath of the war. The Clee is a mass of flaming gorse in spring and deep orange in the autumn from the sere bracken, but one would hardly look to these for the compromise which calls it *brown*. There are similar hills (to look at) in Cornwall called Brown Willie and Brown Gilly. The explanation here offered is that brown is from the old Cornish (therefore Welsh) of *bryn* meaning a hill. But then the Welsh, who are very particular indeed about the shade of meaning attaching to their hill names, would not use *bryn* for anything but an insignificant rise. *Bron* (breast) would be a more likely root. The word might even be pre-Celtic, or it might be, after all, plain English and mean just what it says. At any rate Clee would seem to be Anglo-Saxon, cog-

*Mr Forest says in this book that there must have been two Thomas Butlers, that the Vicar of Wenlock was not the same as the late Abbot of Shrewsbury. He bases this on an entry in the Register, but I feel sure he has misconstrued the rather crabbed text.

Shropshire green lane with hedgerow timber
Chapter-house and Prior's lodging, Wenlock

nate with cliff, and related to that other hill name in the north, at Clive. It has wriggled down to us through a good many spellings which the lawyers of the seventeenth century took care to muster in a body when mentioning the place—"Soe that this is the true Boundary of Lesclives, alias Cleys, alias Cley, alias Clees, alias Clee, alias Brown Clee . . ."

Brown Clee is the highest hill in Shropshire (or was). The map shows it as some forty-four feet superior to Titter-stone Clee, beyond, which cuts such a startling figure against the sky and *looks* so much higher. But the basalt top of Brown Clee has been blasted away and it is doubtful whether its old pre-eminence, as given on the map, is still preserved.

There are two roads down Corvedale, the main, through Shipton and Munslow, and the ancient and higgledy-piggledy through Holdgate and Tugford. Along this way there are three castles, that of Helgot the Norman (whose name is embodied in Holdgate), Broncroft Castle, and Corfham Castle. Of the last only the motte and moat are left in a marshy wood and not easy to find. Less difficult to locate (if you can read your map) is Rosamond's Well in a field on the left bank of the Corve, below the bridge. This is the very Fair Rosamond of romance, mistress of Henry II, supposed daughter of Walter de Clifford, to whom it is said the King gave Corfham Castle as a sop.

Broncroft Castle, built of the local red sandstone, cuts a very picturesque and Border-like figure. A good deal of its original self remains, with additions, chiefly of the nineteenth century, but it played no important part in historical events. The oldest work is late fourteenth century, and its builder is thought to have been the nephew of Sir Simon Burley, companion-in-arms of the Black Prince and tutor to Richard II. Its longest connection was with the Lutely family. It was held by small garrisons on either side during the Civil War. When the castle was built there can have been even less threat of a Welsh inroad than at Stokesay and the

Upper Corvedale
Clun sheep at the mart, Craven Arms

embattling must have been more a matter of pride than security.

Castle Holdgate is much less of a castle to look at, but when I first saw it in 1930 it stirred my imagination profoundly. It was then a farmhouse and preserved without any violent contrasts the links which took one back to the days of Helgot, its first owner. I took tea in the great kitchen where a Tudor fireplace seemed to be the most modern of the fittings. Then I was shown a way from this room into a half-round tower of the thirteenth century with long oillet loops. Just outside was the high and well-preserved motte which Helgot himself had raised in the eleventh century when he came to take possession of the many manors of which he was lord. And at the very foot of the mound on the side remote from the newer castle, though doubtless within the enclosure of the original baily, stood the church, a foundation that was probably of much greater age.

Since then, the house has been carefully modernized and I do not think any of the essential archaeological features have been disturbed. Such an evolution tends to preserve what might otherwise decay, though it is bound to disturb that magical atmosphere of continuity with old ancientness which transported me when Holdgate was an old-fashioned farmhouse, and I hope the present owners will not think I am saying anything disparaging.

As to the antiquity of the church as a hallowed site long antedating its architectural evidence, I took note on that first visit of a strange figure projecting from the south wall of the chancel. It was what the antiquaries call a Shiela-na-gig, that I can only describe as a female in a very indelicate and uncompromising attitude, known by another euphemism as a "fertility figure." When I went on to Tugford, the next village, I found two more, one on either side of the south door, within the church. Dr Cranage in his work on Shropshire churches mentions the Holdgate figure without speci-

fying its character, and discreetly passes over those at
Tugford, so that when I reported these ladies to a prominent member of the Faculty of Archaeology I was hailed in
an official journal as their discoverer, an honour which I am
sure is not due to my powers of observation so much as the
nicer-mindedness of an earlier generation.

But what are these strange figures (now we are so
frank)? There are three next-of-kin not so very far away,
one over the north door of Church Stretton church, not a
very clear example, and two other quite shameless ones, respectively at Kilpeck in Herefordshire and at Llandrindod
Wells (at present kept under lock and key in the vault with
the heating apparatus). Others are in places far remote
from the Shropshire Border—I "discovered" one at Auster-
field in Yorkshire. So far as can be gathered, they have all
been carved in the post-Conquest times, but they must be
symbols of an early cult which have survived. It is not clear
whether they are marks of condonement or opprobrium. But
it is striking to find two examples so close together as in
Corvedale carefully preserved from the vengeance wreaked
on the images of saints and angels. But that they should
have remained fortifies that feeling of the old, old, very old,
which remains throughout the Dale.

The Brown Clee ascends from Corvedale by two stages.
The first rise has a wide platform above its escarpment and
Clee Hill (which a little while back I called the plinth),
densely wooded on the steeper part, while on the platform
are fine pastures and good arable land of stiff red loam.
Where this country joins the wild open moorland of the hill
a small rough road wanders along from Ditton Priors to
Clee St Margaret and then (even smaller and rougher) to
Stoke St Milborough. These are the two principal villages
of "The Clee," as the district styles itself (leaving all other
sorts of Clee out of account). It is another world within the
outer one of Corvedale, as much concerned with its own

affairs as if it were an island, having some regard for what
they do in Ludlow, hearing the voice of Shrewsbury afar off,
not thinking much of what they do elsewhere, but very proud
of its Shropshire birthright.

The two villages, with their houses of red conglomerate
and half-timber, their gardens and orchards and old
churches, are as pretty rural centres as you might find anywhere in England. When looked down on from the heights
above they seem inevitable decorations of the landscape as if
they had just grown there to improve the view. And the
roads don't seem to lead into them so much as lead out of
them—a grudging concession to men's weakness to leave
good homes.

But this part is full of ways, other than roads, in the
shape of bridle-paths and "parish roads." The latter are
green lanes going between high hedges, in some cases for
miles together, one of which being the Roman Bank I have
already mentioned. The destinations of several of these are
obscure and no one seems to know what business they were
supposed to take a man on and why they persist. I think one
answer may be found in the grazing rules for the old Clee
Forest between the time when it was disafforested and the
land inclosures of the eighteenth century. These are laid
down in an ancient document, "A Description of the Clee the
Lordships, Commoners and Strakers adjoined made about
1612, 10 Jac." According to this, twenty-eight townships on
both sides of Brown Clee have rights on the common (the
more distant commoners being spoken of as strakers). To
facilitate the passages of the strakers and their beasts with
a minimum of trespass, these green roads were provided and
in time made as fool-proof as railways, though guarded
jealously with regulations, as witness: "And the Strakers
Inhabiting in the Townships of the Heath, Norncott and
Tugford are and have used to drive up their Cattle along a
way between the said Waste Soile of St Margaret's Clee and

the Waste Soile of Abdon, near unto a place called the Kings Shield, and there are to put of their cattle in the s'd place called the Hay Meadow being parcell of the said Clives alias Brown Clee as aforesaid, and if they Staff drive or put them off before they come to that place they have been used to be fined and amerced (at the Swanimott Court)."

It is at the Heath, above named, where that complete little Norman chapel-of-ease stands which I spoke of (p. 92). It retains its old limitations and no right of burial has ever been granted. But it is an odd comment on the forgotten strictness of these old rules to find a grave at the very outskirt of that field in which the chapel stands. A bridle-path crosses the present road going along the hedge of the chapel ground to Tugford. The old four-cross is just through the field gate and there, in the midst, barely projecting from the mire are the tops of two stones. They mark the implementing of a coroner's verdict on a suicide. Who the deceased was has long been forgotten, and so would the grave have been if it had not become traditional to point out the site when handing over the farm to a new tenant.

It would seem that since the time of the inclosure acts the "strakers" have lost their right of free pasture on Brown Clee, but the freeholders of Clee St Margaret still preserve theirs and are very jealous of the common rights. About thirty or forty years ago other cottagers who were not freeholders began to turn out an odd beast on the hillside. Nothing was said or done, so they grew bolder. After a while they managed to collect small flocks of sheep and a bullock or two. But the freeholders of the Clee are a close and watchful corporation and do not lack leadership. The two ancient families of Duce and Heighway have for long supplied an uncrowned monarch of the Clee. They only waited now until the non-freeholders had collected a sufficient stock to be a real embarrassment to them if their food supply was cut off. The eviction was carried out late on a moonlight night.

The welkin suddenly rang with shouts, view-halloos on a hunting horn, whistle signals, blasts on a bugle. Shadowy figures galloping on horseback scoured the hillside. Animals were rounded up, herded in groups, sorted, driven off through the guarded gates, sheep, cattle, donkeys, ponies; some driven down to Bouldon, others seen off as far as Tugford and then left for their owners to find, claim, and feed or dispose of.

In this part of Corvedale the heavy red lands are hard to work, though rewarding to the industrious farmer. But from the same cause the visitor is beguiled with a wonderful display in the spring-time. Between Bouldon and Delbury the wild snowdrop grows abundantly by the streamside, and the lanes of the Clee are full of primroses and the dark-blue scented violet (as well as the white one). The hedgerows have not yet been robbed of the great timber trees (whose planting found so much favour long ago for both shade and the naval dockyards), and here the birds make merry in the early mornings, as in the ample cider orchards. Hedges are good, as in most parts of Shropshire, for the Salopian has always prided himself on his pleaching. The Radnorshire man believes himself to be a thought better in the art, and sometimes transfers himself to this part of Shropshire. He is almost bound to be a good man with sheep, and that is a big asset in Corvedale farming.

The breed seen everywhere here is native to Clun Forest. With their black faces and tubby yet agile toy-baa-lamb bodies and their bouncing young families they add another liveliness to the spring setting and the solemn background of the great farms whose outbuildings are like the courtyards of castles.

CHAPTER XIII

CRAVEN ARMS AND CLUN FOREST

CRAVEN ARMS is a "centre" rather than a place of
normal growth, and this process, being of modern and not
historic origin, has not so far exercised the ingenuity of any
local topographer. Indeed, so far as a casual enquiry (which
is all I have been able to make) is concerned, the history of
Craven Arms is as little documented as though it had grown
up in the Dark Ages. One would think that some help could
be had from the substantial Georgian hotel by whose sign
one guesses that it must have been the first house there. But
the Manager told me that he has tried many times to find
out when it was built and can't get a clue of any kind. The
obelisk in front of it has no date on it, but it is obvious
from the distance given to Holyhead that it was erected before Telford's new road was opened via the Pass of Nant
Ffrancon. I have found a mention of the hotel in Cary's
Road Book for 1825.

The railway station, which took its name from the hotel,
was built as a junction for the London and North Western
line to Swansea, and to this accident of railway engineering
is due the establishment of the *place.* Although it had always been at a junction of roads out of productive agricultural centres, its distance from all of them was too great
in the horse-drawn days to attract an ancient market. But
the coming of the two railways with subsequent branches to
Much Wenlock and Bishop's Castle promoted the formation of an auction mart. An "auction mart" is a funda-
mentally different creation from a chartered or manorial
market. It is without lordly or holy prestige, without asso-

ciation of the pomps and executions of justice, and without those social contacts realistically grounded in the system of striking bargains. Consequently it demands different and less picturesque buildings. And Craven Arms is a mart-town, not a market-town, with the most important beast-mart in Shropshire. And now its history has moved on again, for the coming of the large petrol vehicle has made it independent of the railway and given it a much wider sphere of influence.

Compared with a town of mediaeval beginnings and development it is a dreary place to look at. But whereas the former has had many centuries to become what it is and has been moulded in its slow evolution by cultural influences, Craven Arms has barely had a century. Better things will come, of which the post office is a harbinger. The department has done here exactly the reverse of what it did at Shrewsbury. It has erected a large building of such irreproachable taste as to make its shabby neighbours look shabbier than ever. And you must not criticize the amenities of the place until you have inspected its main shopping street, not easy to find by guess-work, but it gives a clue to the upside-down planning of this farmers' town.

Craven Arms is not only a centre for beef and mutton but for the best scenery in Shropshire, and I imagine that it is on this account rather than the custom of the mart that the two excellent hotels thrive so well. The Dales, the Long Mynd, Bishop's Castle, Clun Forest, the Vale of Wigmore, and Ludlow are all at about equal distances. There is, close to (I have read) some of the best fossil-hunting in the county, and I know that there is some good trout-fishing to be had (if you can get permission).

The little Bishop's Castle Railway which ran up the lovely Plowden Gorge is defunct, killed by that ugly levelling monopoly the Railways Amalgamation, a beautiful and tragic victim which always seems to have had the odds against it. This I judge from a story I was once told by a barber, in a place remote from Shropshire, who had at one time been a porter on the line. It smacks of the Border way and sounds likely but I have not attempted to corroborate it. He said that when the Company was in a *particularly* bad way their creditors put a bailiff in. This man acted with resolution. He had one of the rails removed and carried bodily into the garden of the premises where he was lodging, announcing that no more trains should run until the ransom was paid. But the company had secret agents and the bailiff was not a teetotaler. The leading-up process took a little while, during which time Bishop's Castle was isolated (no motor traction then) and the supplies mounted up in the goods yard at Craven Arms till the sidings were chock-a-block. In due time the planned bout came off, the bailiff was carried to bed incapable and the rail taken out of the garden and replaced. *Sub rosa,* officials of the Bishop's Castle Railway Company prevailed on the local authority of the Joint Railways to lend them all available locomotives standing under steam in the Craven Arms yard. With these they made up one immensely long train of all the delayed waggons and drew them into the beleaguered borough.

A mile away from Craven Arms is Stokesay Castle, whose name commemorates the De Say family of Clun, a long memory, for the last of this family died out early in the thirteenth century, before any of the existing work was put in hand. The half-timbered Elizabethan gatehouse is a picturesque but wholly indefensible feature, yet it weathered the only siege the castle is reputed to have stood (1645), when the Royalist garrison made a descent on the Roundheads who had taken possession of Stokesay. At that time the church was so badly damaged it had to be rebuilt, but the little gatehouse remained intact, though, after the war, the curtain walls connecting it with the main building were blown up by the Parliamentarians. On the wooded hill above the Onny gap, where the Celts built a fort now called Norton Camp, I have heard that that rare umbellifer *Astrantia major* grows.

The picturesque little ruin at Hopton Castle is also associated with the De Says, who probably made the motte mound on which the ruined peel tower stands. It is associated with the name of Walter de Clifford (p. 165) in the mid-twelfth century, but the main architectural features which appear are of the Decorated period. In 1644 it was owned by one Master Wallop, a Puritan, and a Parliamentary garrison of twenty-six men were put into it. Sir Michael Woodhouse, in command of the royalist force at Ludlow, beleaguered it for five weeks, its stout commander refusing all terms of surrender. There was no Geneva Convention in those days, but there was a rule of war (intended to prevent unnecessary bloodshed) that an untenable position must not be held; to do so the besieged forfeited any right to quarter. This was brought to the notice of the captain of Hopton Castle. But he was no collaborator. In the end the castle was taken by assault and the garrison judged liable to the penalty prescribed for their breach of the humane rule. Accordingly they were put to death by the expedient of tying them back-to-back and casting them into the pond which fed the moat. This was no way to advertise the royal clemency. But the other side who made a boast of religious motive acted no better. It was the Roundheads who enforced the same letter of the rule at the fall of Basing House, and when the Parliamentary general Mitton took Conway Castle (by treachery) he had not even the excuse of the rule to wreak vengeance. Yet he had the Irish members of the garrison tied back-to-back and thrown into the estuary.

The bus from Craven Arms to Clun turns off to touch at Clunbury, and the walk from here along the old green road under Clunbury Hill is the prettiest approach to Hopton Castle. When I went that way in 1945 the apple orchards were in bloom and, looking down on Clunbury from the hill, the church tower and the gables of its old houses stood out from a square of blossom, nothing new appearing anywhere; a rare view.

At Clun you are again in another world quite different in scenery and in feeling and atmosphere from anything else in Shropshire, and not quite like anything in Wales. The character of the scenery and the small farms in the hills, and a certain baldness in the look of the buildings in the town one associates inevitably with Wales, but Clun has not been in Wales since the eighth century. Yet there are indications in its ecclesiastical history that before that time it may have been an important religious centre when the Celtic church was flourishing. Perhaps that is the very thing about the Clun "atmosphere," a hint to the inner consciousness that it is not English, Norman, or Welsh. The name has completely stumped the etymologist. But Gaelic *Clon* equals Welsh *llan* and Irish Christians were doubltess here before the seventh century.

If the site of the church had had a mere Saxon reputation of sanctity the De Says would probably have re-established it near the castle. But not only did they let it remain at that inconvenient distance, but they spent a lot in giving it that solid, if sober, grandeur which it still presents. At the close of the twelfth century Isabella, the last of the De Say owners (p. 38) presented the advowson of the church to the priory of St Milburge at Much Wenlock, with all its chapels-of-ease, an astonishing and far-flung group, among them Clunbury, Clunton, Edgton, Hopton Castle, Llanfair Waterdine, and Sibdon.

Clun Castle deserves preservation. It is a very majestic relic and, of its kind, unique. But in spite of our enlightened outlook on ancient monuments it is allowed to go on crumbling. At any time one of its most interesting features, the solid wall-bastion, hanging on to the last remnant of the huge curtain, might fall. If the tourist were better up in these matters he would go to Clun to see that even more readily than Henry Howard's Hospital, so the work should be undertaken even on the less elevated plea of preserving an attraction for visitors.

In passing, let me harp on one Border note which illustrates the extraordinary punctilio that was observed in the Custom of the March. By an Inquest of 1272 William Kempe is seen to hold a messuage and croft on the tenure of carrying to Shrewsbury the heads of felons. For a criminal captured on the land of the lord of Clun but tried and condemned at Shrewsbury had to be sent for to Clun for execution and then have his head carried back to Shrewsbury for identification. By this insalubrious service the heirs of William Kempe held their lands.

The whole area of Clun Forest, amounting to more than twelve thousand acres, was still unenclosed in the early part of the nineteenth century. No doubt it is largely owing to this that the finest remnant of Offa's Dyke is to be seen there. Anyone who cares to be impressed by the grandeur of this earthwork of our Saxon ancestors should follow the line of it from Newcastle (three miles from Clun) over the hills of the forest to Mainstone. Westward of this section, where Clun Forest joins Kerry Hill, at the Shropshire-Montgomeryshire boundary may be seen one of the most remarkable features of Offa's system, now shown on the ordnance map as the Upper and Lower Short Ditches. These were evidently outpost works of the main line, and the military-minded will wonder how on earth they were held and maintained in a country which lent itself to the old tactics of the Welsh. But of the Dyke itself the most imposing relic is found by going south from Newcastle, starting at Lower Spoad Farm. Between Springhill and Llanfair Hill, for a mile or more, the parapet maintains its old level and is broad enough to walk on. But you should ask in passing by to see the chimney-piece at Lower Spoad Farm where a hunting scene is carved with great vigour of imagination. It looks like a work of the early sixteenth century and bears some resemblance in technique to the lively creatures (and plan-view rabbits) on the remains of the rood-screen at Llanfair-Waterdine Church, over the hill.

There is a rough road all the way to Llanfair-Waterdine which goes near the best bit of the Dyke, though I would not like to say how a car would take it. For the walker, it has the sweets of mountain air and long views over the Radnorshire hills. Llanfair-Waterdine Church attracts the tourist because there is in the church-yard a gipsy's grave with a Romany inscription on it. But there is a much more intriguing inscription inside the church, for nobody has ever been able to read it. English, Welsh, Latin, and Hebrew scholars have all had a go at it without success. Yet it does not seem to be mutilated or defaced and it cannot be older than a few years on this or that side of A.D. 1500. One cannot help wondering whether it might not be the work of an unlettered wood-carver who thought he ought to put in a little reading-matter among his decorations, and went to work in the spirit with which one imitates the sound of a foreign language, knowing that the local congregation would be sufficiently edified by the result. Whatever was his weakness in this respect he made a very fine rood-screen with animals displayed which have the same natural bold liveliness that remind one of the paleolithic artists of Altamira. Only a sad relic of this fine piece of unconventional art remains made up into communion-rails.

The pew-ends have the names of farms in the parish painted on them, as at Bettws-y-Crwyn, rousing speculative reflections in those who have read Richard Gough's *History of Myddle* (p. 70). But Bettws-y-Crwyn retains its rood-screen. This church is right on the watershed between the valleys of the Teme and the Clun at the end of an almost impassable green road, an offshoot of which wanders on for miles over high and picturesque but desolate country to end by that cheery and hospitable inn, the Anchor, on the Clun-Kerry road, just within the Shropshire border.

The "competitor" Caer Caradoc I spoke of in the last chapter is near the eastern end of this range of hills, above Chapel Lawn. There is a good and a bad road to that point from Clun, and I naturally took the bad one when I went that way in 1945;—for Border scenery and air I can recommend it. Only by that route can you pass a stone circle marked on the map. I asked about it in Clun. "Oh yes," they said, "the Druid's Circle, but somebody's taken the stones away." When I got near I called at one of the small farms that are typical of these uplands, much more like the Welsh than the Shropshire idea of a farm, and the farmer, though he hadn't a word of Welsh and would not have liked to have been suspected of one, spoke a brisk dialect which had a distinct Celtic ring about it. No, he said, the stones weren't all gone. The last big one that was "took off" was dropped in the hedge a couple of hundred yards away. He gave me careful instructions how to find it.

The site of the circle (if it ever was one) was planted with fir trees about a hundred years ago. It has an unusual appearance, being somewhat mounded up in the centre as if a large round barrow had once stood there. On this matter I have not been able to find any guidance. Having speculated, and admired the view, I began to follow the farmer's directions to find the stone which had been carelessly dropped in the hedge. Measuring off the paces in the oblique line recommended, I came to the hedge and peered in. There I saw not a prehistoric stone, but a very old motor-car without wheels. It was the most curious vehicle of its kind I have ever seen, and looked like a motorized growler cab. It was so odd that I felt quite grateful to the farmer, for I should never have seen it but for his formula of oblique line and exact number of paces. The stone I had to look for (it was by the next gate, if he had only thought to tell me so) was a very fine monolith. It lay on its side and must, I think, have fallen or have been uprooted at that very spot. What its relation was to the "Druid's circle" I should like to know, and also how the wheel-less car got into the hedge on that hill-top.

It was late when I got up to the prehistoric battlements of that lesser known Caer Caradoc; clouds over the western hills were lighting up with the fires of sunset and on the crisp sweet-smelling greensward just within the entrance of the huge empty stockade I found patches of the large yellow mountain pansy. I suppose that pansy faces, low vibrations of the spectrum, and romantic dusk light over the Welsh Border have nothing to do with the question of whether Caractacus was ever there or not. But there are moments when the imagination becomes suddenly resonant, and it is better then to listen for a message than to ask questions.

CHAPTER XIV

LUDLOW AND BRIDGNORTH

L U D L O W , like Stonehenge, ought to be seen for the first time from one particular approach, the road coming from Wales through Wigmore (or Leintwardine) and over Whitecliffe Hill. Here you see, first of all, a most wonderful picture. The castle presents all its features to view, the early Norman keep, the embattled curtain embracing both wards; in the outer one the slender tower built by Roger Mortimer, in the inner one the great buildings where the Council for the Marches of Wales held its court. From this aspect that yellow-grey shell looks weathered and softened by time into a shape of romance, its hollow desolation hidden from the eye, which glances delightedly downward to the wooded scarp and the flashing Teme below, and upward to the roofs and chimneys of the town, the tall stages of St Lawrence's tower, and the sharp-featured profile of Titterstone Clee in the background.

And you see not only a wonderful picture, but a sort of concrete diagram whose lay-out can be studied in relation to history. There are the walls, the halls, the thoroughfares which moulded at so many junctures the fortunes of the race! You do not see the vacuities, the rotting timbers, mouldering brickwork, and incongruous clap-traps from here. So if you are a stranger to Ludlow and have the philosophy to take pains in your methods of sightseeing, you will come this way for a first sight of the place.

The traveller Leland, who took such useful stock of our antiquities for his master King Henry VIII, ferreted out a very interesting particular with regard to Ludlow. He was

Ludlow, western approach
Ludlow, southern approach

looking through the muniments of the recently dissolved monastery at Cleobury Mortimer when he came across a document which had an entry under 1199. In that year, it said, the church at Ludlow was enlarged to the west, a renovation which entailed the removal of a large mound in which were found stone cists containing three human skeletons. These, says the report, were immediately claimed by the churchmen as the relics of Irish saints, and they were transferred to the interior of the new building, where no doubt they were put to a profitable use. This supports the common experience that where the word "low," "hlow," or "howe" occurs the reference is not to a mere hill but a hill crowned by a burial mound. Examples are plentiful, and there is at Bleddfa in Radnorshire a large mound so near the west end of the church that the gable-wall is built into it —perhaps an exact parallel of what Ludlow's state used to be. Occasionally the tradition of sanctity is very deeply rooted.

At Knightlow Hill near Rugby there used to be a gathering an hour before sunrise on the morning of November the eleventh at which the steward of the manor presided and demanded that tenants of his lord (the Duke of Buccleugh) should place two pence each in the hollow stone on the hilltop, following which the party adjourned to the local inn and drank a breakfast toast to his grace in punch, after which clay churchwarden pipes were handed round and plates of shag tobacco placed on the table. I was present at this rite in 1928 and genially fined half-a-crown as a "spied stranger" for my pains. The point of this stray-away story is that the hollow stone where the money was deposited was actually the base of a mediaeval cross sunk into a rather depressed mound which had no doubt been a Bronze Age tumulus, its pagan sanctity tolerantly endorsed by Christian reconsecration. And so, exceptional sanctity of site and not strategic

181

considerations, would seem to have settled the beginning of the fame and power of Ludlow.

It was first of all an ecclesiastical centre, its fame probably noised abroad before the coming of the Saxon and then renewed in strength by the foundation of the Palmers' Guild of which that legend of Edward the Confessor and the ring is related in the east window of St John's Chapel in the parish church. Its power also had a two-fold blossoming. First as the headquarters of the Mortimer family, and next as that of the Council of the Marches of Wales.

This had a very brilliant and distinguished career and was, more than anything else, "the making" of Ludlow as it appears today. But its story is obscure, many documentary links being missing.

I believe that some idea of the kind must have been in the mind of Edward I when he passed the plans for Carnarvon Castle, which is so roomy and sumptuous as to suggest a palace as much as a fortress. The heir apparent, Edward of Carnarvon, was not created Prince of Wales when a baby in arms as the story goes, but when he was seventeen years old. It would have seemed a policy in keeping with the King's love of good government to give the Prince some substance to his title and to charge him with the holding of a high court in the heart of the newly conquered country to keep order and redress abuses. It was very necessary. But what with the unexpectedly long and stubborn campaign in Scotland and the indolent character of the Prince, such a scheme, if it ever existed, did not take shape and the *soi disant* successors of Llewelyn held an empty title until well on into the fifteenth century.

But Edward Earl of March, knew all about Wales and its needs, and he knew a thing or two about the Lords Marchers and their ways and means, for he was descended from the greatest and most dangerous of them. The heir of the Mortimers, his accession to the throne as Edward IV

automatically brought the greater part of the marcher lordships to the English crown without more argument. But a
great many were still left with their old privileges and im-
munities from the justice of the King's courts. Naturally
(and County Durham was in like case) they were becoming
sanctuaries for rascals. Edward had this matter in mind
when he created his son Prince of Wales at the age of one
year. He was, however, provided with a real council who
could not only look after the boy if his father were removed
but also set about the composition of a court to manage
matters in Wales and in the Marches, which sadly needed
attention. So the babe and the officials were sent down to
the old Mortimer home at Ludlow. Those who visit Ely
Cathedral and see that very elaborate chantry raised by
Bishop Alcock may bear in mind that this man was the first
President of the Prince's "Counsail of the Domynion and
Pryncipallitie of Wales and the Marches of the same."

When the Prince of Wales turned thirteen he was still at
Ludlow Castle with his Council, and in that year he became
King Edward V. His younger brother Richard of York was
with him there. The coronation was to take place in London
in the forthcoming summer, and Uncle Gloucester arranged
that the boys should come up to town to prepare for this
event. They set forth, therefore, on a spring morning, in
high spirits, with a body-guard of two hundred armed men.
But the bodyguard was waylaid and the princes were taken
by an unknown party for "protective custody" to the Tower
where they were pitilessly done to death.

Exactly what the Council did when it lost its titular head
is not known, though there is evidence that Bishop Alcock
continued to act as Lord President. When Richard III, who
had seized the royal power so ruthlessly, was killed at Bos-
worth by Henry Tudor the problem of government in
Wales and the Marches came to the fore again. For Henry
was Welsh on his father's side and the Welsh adherents of

183

Sir Rhys ap Thomas had been the mainstay of his force when he landed at Milford Haven. Through his mother he was the surviving champion of the old Lancastrian faction and by his marriage with Elizabeth of York he united the long contested badges of the red and white rose. The son of this union, Prince Arthur (named after the legendary champion of the ancient British race), must have seemed a symbolic figure appearing in a world tinged with the early dawn of Renaissance. And he and his sixteen-year-old bride, Catherine of Aragon, were sent down to Ludlow Castle immediately after their marriage in St Paul's Cathedral to take charge of the Prince's Council. With them went the new President of the Court of the Marches, Bishop Smyth of Lincoln, the founder of Brasenose College, Oxford.

Great were the preparations over the coming of this Arthur. He made a triumphal entry into the grim old Border fortress of the Mortimers. But there was an enemy in the gate whom no one saw. Within five months this boy of fifteen was dead. The room is still pointed out to the visitor who peers skyward through the floorless and roofless building of the north-western tower.

No royal governor was sent down again for twenty-four years, when Henry VIII made his daughter, Mary, Princess of Wales and she (then ten years old) went to Ludlow with a huge retinue. But the work of the court was continued unbroken and grew in importance. Mary Tudor remained only a year in the Marches, perhaps the happiest in her life. Her absence was no doubt convenient to the King, who was already beginning to think about his first divorce. She was the last of the child governors. But the great days of the Council were yet to come. They began in 1534 with the appointment of Rowland Lee Bishop of Coventry and Lichfield as President of the Council of the Marches. He was one of Wolsey's men who stood no nonsense—a hanging judge. In the second year of his office (1535) Henry VIII achieved his Act of

Union with Wales, whereby new counties were created in Wales and the whole of the March was absorbed into the shires of one or other of the two countries, and the ancient and embarrassing anomaly of petty states vanished over-night. Now indeed there was work to do at Ludlow.

As an organizer and a viceroy, Rowland Lee was prob-ably the greatest of the Lords Presidents. But the best and kindliest memories are those of Sir Henry Sidney, father of the more famous Philip. He was President from 1559 to 1586 and made those extensive Elizabethan additions to the castle. His arms appear over the gate to the inner ward.

Ludlow was the headquarters of the council, but it held sessions at several other towns within its jurisdiction and the presidents had an official residence at Shrewsbury, still called the Council House, opposite the old school, at which Philip Sidney was a pupil. The Council of the Marches is an even more interesting experiment in jurisprudence and deputed government than the Court of the Star Chamber and it is curious to find that only one competent person has ever made a careful study and written a book on the whole subject: Miss Caroline Skeel. Her work, *The Council in the Marches of Wales,* published by Hugh Rees, appeared in 1904 and has long been out of print. That a study of such vital interest should be unobtainable is one more reminder of our heedless-ness of the lessons of the past.

But nowhere does the contrast between the present en-thusiasm for political experiment of all sorts and the refusal to learn from recorded experience appear so sharply as in Ludlow itself. Here you will be told incessantly of its pride in its ancient heritage but find no active curiosity in the matter, and very little real concern about the visible relics which remain. It has a very much finer market square than Shrewsbury ever had, with the castle gateway at one end, and the finest houses in the town on either side. Into this set-ting it inserted a market hall in the nineteenth century which looks rather like a railway station designed for a manufacturing town.

In Shrewsbury one can almost forgive their casual treatment of old buildings, because the springs of life are so robust that the place has a perpetual youth, and youth is always Philistine. But in Ludlow the guilds have gone and the trade and craft fraternities which followed them. The Mortimers have gone. The Council of the Marches has gone. Quality Court is a slum. Even the museum is dead. The attention of the townspeople and their local governors is wholly concentrated on what alone seems to be left, the shops. They talk of their "heritage," but what it is they prefer to ignore.

Yet Ludlow has an asset. It is the most complete mediaeval town in England. If the half-timbered houses had their original fronts and ends exposed, if the muniment room were tidied up and a trained archivist put into it, if a local historian were found who could make a proper inventory of all the old buildings and collate his discoveries with those of the archivist, and if the local authority would prepare to receive visitors by subsidizing (if necessary) an ample provision of good and cheap accommodation, life might return in spite of that resistance to changed conditions which an ancient place of decayed fame always puts up. There are no imitation Ludlows anywhere else. There is only this one. If it revealed itself all the world would come and see.

Quite a lot might be done by persuasion if local pride began to smoulder. The Earl of Powys might be persuaded to hand over the castle to the Ministry of Works. Apart from its historical associations it has two unique features, an eleventh-century entrance on the ground-floor of the keep, the like of which is to be seen in no other castle, and its round chapel which resembles the churches of the Knights Templars but has no connection with the order. The Ministry of Transport might be prevailed on to build a by-pass road so that more room is made for those who come to stay and pay, and the crooked ways and ancient bridge and the last of the gatehouses not be threatened. And some kind friend might restore the museum. It would be far better to restore than to modernize it, for with its collection of stuffed birds and the Murchison fossils it is in itself with its proper academic design and all, a period piece.

Perhaps I shall be neither heeded nor applauded for this exhortation, but I would like to show two glimpses of what Ludlow used to be. The Hon John Byng writing in his diary for 1784 says "Ludlow is one of the best, retiring-to towns I ever saw, having that gaiety that cannot be expressed, and compensates (in part) for want of fortune; and confinement in any place." This was but thirty years after the castle had had the lead stripped off its roofs and had been left to the vengeance of the weather. And here is another glimpse a century and a half earlier, "a true Relation of the solemnity held at Ludlow in the Countie of Salop, upon the fourth of November last past. Anno Domini 1616. Being the day of the Creation of the high and mighty Charles, Prince of Wales, and Earle of Chester, In his Majesties Palace of White-Hall."

There follows a list of persons of distinction present at the ceremonial parade. The Lord President (Lord Eure) is away on attendance to the Prince at the London investiture and is therefore represented by the Chief Justice of Chester, Sir Thomas Chamberlaine. The high sheriff of Shropshire, Sir Thomas Cornewall of Burford (where we shall presently pass by) is here, various functionaries of the Council and the Castle, and "many other worthy Gentlemen and persons of good account."

First of all, printed notices setting forth the styles and titles of the Prince are set up under the pulpit in the parish church, in the chapel and court-room of the castle, on the high cross, and on all the principal posts and pillars in the market place.

"Afterwards, about nine of the clocke in the fore-noone of the said fourth of November, William Gregory, and Thomas Blashfield Esquires, Bailiffes of the said Towne of Ludlow, accompanied with the Magistrates and Bretheren, and all the chiefe Burgesses of the said Towne, very richly clad and apparelled, attended by their Officers with their Maces before them, and all the Quire of the Church there, singing of Hymnes and Psalmes of thankesgiving and praise of our sayd Prince, bringing with them sixe yong Youths, being Schollers of the Kings free Schoole of the saide Towne, well and richly decked and adorned, who did beare in their hands severall Penons and Bannerolls of the Arms and Atchivements of our said Prince Charles, that is to say:

"The foremost Scholler bore in his hand the Armes of England and Scotland.

"The second carried the Armes of the Brittains and Saxons.

"The third France and Ireland.

"The forth Nothwales and Southwales.

"The fift, Cornewall and Chester.

"The sixt and last, carried the Armes of York and Lancaster, with the Plume of feathers and the Prince his Name;

"Having before them the Towne Waites and other lowd Instruments of Musicke, and before the Musicke marched along the number of two hundred souldiers, being well appointed and furnished with Halberds, Pikes, Corslets, Muskets, and Calivers, under the conduct and leading of Leonard Lloyd their then Captaine, who in good order had his Lieutenants and Sergeants bravely arrayed, having four Drums and two Trumpets sounding before them, besides Fifes and other winde Instruments, all of them, thus appointed, came up to the Castle to attend and bring the said Iustice and Counsell to the Church:

"And having repayred to the Castle Greene there, and meeting Maister Justice in his Scarlet Robes, with the rest of the Counsell before named in decent manner, upon the Castle bridge, accompanied with all the worshipful Councellors of Law, Atturneis and Clarks belonging to that Court, with sundry Esquires and Gentlemen, having before them Richard Jones Esquier, Sergeant at Armes, carrying his Majesties Mace, William Gooderick Esquier, Gentleman Porter, Richard Collins, one of the Ushers of his Maiesties Chamber, and the two Messengers of the Court, viz Piers Gruffith and Thomas Pringle gentlemen, in rich coates; Francis Trollop gentleman, Marshall of the said Court, Thomas Stevens gentleman, Yeoman of the Kings Wardrobe there, Griffith Jones, Constable of the Castle, together with all the chiefe Officers of the said Castle (being all of them very richly apparrelled, and having another company of Waits and good consorts of Musicke, as Cornets, Sagbuts, and other winde Instruments, playing and sounding all along the way before them) a great Volley of shot was discharged by the said Muskettiers and Calivers, which so pierced the Ayre with great noyse of Drummes, and sound of Trumpets, Fifes, Flutes, and other Instruments as the like in these parts hath not been seene, to the great admiration and much rejoycing of all the Spectators.

"And thereupon marshalling themselves in good array, they all went through the Towne Streets, to the Church, singing and rejoycing all the way they went, where was another Volley of shotte discharged.

"After Prayers said, and Psalms sung, one M. Thomas Pierson, a grave reverend divine and worthy Preacher, made a very learned Sermon of an houre and half long, upon the first verse of the 72 Psalme, viz.

"Give the King thy Judgments, O God, and thy Righteousness to the Kings sonne.

"Which Sermon being ended, and Psalmes sung by the

Singing-men and Quiristers, to and with the great Organs there, all the whole Company returned.

"And as they issued out of the Church and Church-yard into the Market place, there was a new Scaffolde purposely erected neare unto the high Crosse (with a great Bonefire not farre distant) upon which Scaffolde the said Schollers with their Penons and Banerols of Armes in their hands, as aforesaid, ascended; and as the said Justice and Counsell passed by, *alternatim* uttered and pronounced these severall Speeches following: [and here we are treated to the usual stilted exercises of the Neo-classic school of poetic adulation, concocted by the "painful industrie" of the headmaster of the Free School, followed by an exhortation on the part of the Chief Justice].

"Whereunto all the people with a loud voyce prayed and cryed *Amen, Amen.*

"And thereupon all the Musick played, Drums were strucke, Flutes whistled, Trumpets sounded, people showted, and another piercing and thundering Volley of shot was let flie, the echo and report whereof resounded admirably, to the great solace and comfort of all present.

"And then, being full one of the clocke in the afternoone, the said Justice, and Counsell, with the Knights, Esquiers, and best sort of Gentlemen returned into the Castle to dinner (where was a great feast provided, with excellent Musicke) the Bailiffes also with their Bretheren and Burgesses went down to the Towne, to spend the rest of the day in all joyfull and joviall manner, having all of them, before departure thence, in the presence and by the appointment of Ralph Mansfield Esquier, chiefe Steward to the Kings Household there, drunke plentifully of wine, to the happie health of our said gracious Prince of Wales.

"Dinner being scarce ended in the Castle, the aforesaid Bailiffes in like pompe, being againe accompanied with the whole Quire of the Church, and the Penon-bearers with their

Banerols of Armes in their hands, and their Musicke playing before them, came up in great solemnitie into the Castle,
where Maister Justice joyfully receiving them, brought
them straight into the Chapell there to offer their Evening
Sacrifice, where much rejoycing was without doores and excellent Musicke of Voyces in singing many Psalmes and new
Anthemes, within the saide Chapell.

"Which being finished, the aforesaid Schollers very
humbly prostrating themselves with low obeisance, delivered
up their sayd severall Banerolls into the hands of the said
Justice who willed Richard Adams Gentleman, being skil-
full in heraldrie, there present, to see them orderly placed
in the said Chapell, where they now remaine as remarkable
Trophies of that Solemnitie.

"And after Prayers ended, the Bailiffes with their Company humbly taking their leave of the Counsell, Maister
Justice required them still to continue their Ringing, as well
for the full solemnizing of the said day of our Prince his
sayd creation, as also to expresse their joy and thanksgiving
unto Almightie God for our said dread Soveraignes most admirable Deliverance, with the royall Queene, illustrious
Prince, all the Lords Spirituall and Temporall, and Commons of this Realme assembled together in Parliament, from
the Papists treasonable conspiracie, and unmatchable intended Practise of the Gunne-powder Treason, in the yeare
of oure Lord God one thousand six hundred and five, and
to be in readinesse with the said Justice and Counsell the next
morning to praise God for the same.

"Which accordingly was performed the next day, and a
very learned sermon preached . . . Which sermon being
ended, every man returned to their home, the Musicke, Ringing, and Bonefires continuing to the great comfort of all his
Majesties said loving and faithful Subjects all the said day."

It was for a pageant such as this that eighteen years later
John Milton wrote *Comus* for his pupils, the children of the

Lord President, to perform at a masque in the great hall of the Castle. Richard Baxter, that level-headed and tolerant divine who served as a chaplain to the Roundhead forces and also as a chaplain royal to Charles II, without ever modifying his candid opinions or concealing them, was here about the same time and gives a picture of the seamier side in his autobiography, saying that "the town was full of temptations, through the multitude of persons (counsellors, attorneys, officers and clerks) and much given to tippling and excess." His house at Eaton Constantine remains, much as he knew it.

It is not always that the scene of a poet's muse can inspire the same feelings of beauty and mystery in the common beholder when he goes on pilgrimage to view the spot. But those woods where the Earl of Bridgwater's children got lost (prompting the argument of *Comus*) have that peculiar ethereal quality which breathes from the poem and mercifully are still spared to us, though not on Milton's account I suspect. The veritable Sunny Gutter dingle is on the way from Ludlow to Richard's Castle.

Le Scrob's pre-Conquest Norman castle and the curious Bone Well have already been spoken of (p. 140). The *Comus* magic extends thus far, and if you go there as I did recently on a Sunday morning without first looking at the guide-book, you would probably have the same eerie feeling about the old church that I did. Eleven-thirty on a Sabbath morn is not a propitious time to visit a church for secular antiquarian purposes. I crept towards it with the profane design of finding out how far the service had advanced. But no sound came out of it. I tried the door, which yielded, and I found myself in an ample building whose architectural features were mediaeval, and the pews and pulpit of eighteenth-century woodwork. Not only was there no service there today, but it did not look or smell or *feel* as if one had been held there for years and years. Yet it was a large church for so small a place, very well appointed and of much archaeological interest.

The answer is easy. A rich parishioner built another church at a lower stage of the hill in 1891. One wonders whether this came of an urge to build or whether the situation was easier for carriage horses. But it seems a sad pity as well as an insoluble embarrassment.

The Hon John Byng, quoted above, compares Bridgnorth with Ludlow unfavourably. He says "There is an upper, a side hill, and a lower town beyond the Severn, but not the all can compare with Ludlow, (as we were taught to believe it would) ; as it can neither boast the buildings streets, situation or chearfulness of Ludlow." This shows in the first place that he hadn't read his history. Taken all round, Shropshire probably suffered more damage in the Civil War than any other county in Britain. And, of Shropshire towns, Bridgnorth came off worst of all. It was defended to the last ditch by its Royalist garrison, and before the castle yielded the church had been wrecked and the whole town gutted by fire. Afterwards the whole of the castle was demolished with gunpowder except the Governor's House and the Norman keep which stuck together in one piece and, like that other tower at Caerphilly, leaned over but refused to fall. As to situation, it is hard to guess what he is thinking about, though we know he had a marked prejudice against dizzy heights.

The situation of Bridgnorth is the most striking thing about it, whether you see it from beyond the river with its great red rock, red-tiled buildings, towers and dome silhouetted against the sky, or whether you look out from its cliff promenade below the old walls to the Severn pouring down to the bridge under steep red cliffs topped with dark pines.

As to cheerfulness, perhaps the last war has helped it more than it has Ludlow, for at the present time it gives a distinct impression of keenness and briskness that is altogether lacking in Ludlow. But to suggest that Bridgnorth hadn't got a street to match anything in Ludlow was the unkindest cut. "What about East Castle Street?" they would have exclaimed in shocked incredulity. That, indeed, was a great matter of pride with the townsfolk in the eighteenth century, so much so that Telford (who here tried his skill on church architecture) was prevailed on, when he rebuilt St Mary Magdalene's, to mis-orientate it so that its classical façade might form a suitable terminal vista to East Castle Street.

The prestige is older than eighteenth-century elegance. It is a case like that of Oswestry where the castle has melted into the town. The baily has lost its embattled isolation, and the Governor's House (with its Charles I bedroom) has become just one of the other houses.

Bridgnorth has some surprising features. As at Knaresborough and Nottingham, it was often found cheaper and quicker to cut the back rooms of your house out of the rock and only use brick for the front part. A few of these parti-fabric houses are still standing and lived in on the "side hill" part of the town and across the water. In one of them, now gone to pieces, Francis Moore, the astrologer and founder of *Old Moore's Almanac* was born in 1657. He published his first almanac when only twenty-two years old. Its predictions took the form of weather forecasts, but it was in fact a publicity venture to advertise certain astrological pills prepared by himself. One of the diverting features of the place is the many approaches to and descents from the rock top. The most picturesque is a long flight of steps cut in the Triassic sandstone itself, edging between and under houses like the postern of a Corsican hill town. Or there is a funicular railway called the "lift." On the other side, the railway station, proper, is linked by a foot-viaduct of extraordinary length.

But the lift is not so new in Bridgnorth as all that. One

was installed in Master Forster's house built in 1580, a very fine half-timbered building down by the river side with its own quay on that once busy highway. Here in 1729 was born Thomas Percy, Bishop of Dromore, whose *Reliques* brought in the revival of old romance verse. The house, one of the very few on the Upper Town side of the river which survived the fury of the siege, is now a boys' club and can be inspected at any time. It is little altered, so the accessibility of all its parts and its assured preservation make it of particular interest to the student of the frame house. The lift (only a food lift, after all) is arranged in the square well of the stairway.

Among the exterior decorations is a sort of staggered fleur-de-lis, a convention, I think, for the Prince of Wales's feathers. It is found in many places in Shropshire and is well seen at Deuxhill, a fine black-and-white house a few miles out on the road to Cleobury Mortimer. It is (if I am right about the plume of feathers badge) a touching reminder of the attachment of Shropshire to its intimate association with princes of the blood, from Edward Plantagenet to Charles Stuart, so singularly ill starred.

There is no way over the Severn except by ferry between Bridgnorth and Bewdley in Worcestershire, though a narrow strip of Shropshire lies all along the left bank. Just here is the only firm evidence we have of Norse contacts. The *Anglo-Saxon Chronicle* for 895 says that the Danes "took their way towards Wales and came to Quadruge near to the River Severn where upon the borders thereof they builded them a castle." A mound is pointed out as the very spot. Whether it is not rather a Norman motte I leave you to decide. But the reference must be to Quatford. There are a Danesford, a Danford, and an Upper Danford a little further down stream. It is believed that on this visit they forayed as far as Wenlock and destroyed the first convent which enshrined St Milburge's bones (p. 103). They are said to have moved on when the next spring came. Such a brief visit would hardly account for the naming of the Dales.

Northward across the river between Bridgnorth and the Watling Street is a part of Shropshire we have not touched on except to mention Tong (p. 158). It is average pretty country but there is not much to attract the stranger. Boscobel House, where the Pendrel family sheltered Charles II after the Battle of Worcester, is still an unspoilt farmhouse, though the old furniture which used to lend atmosphere to the rooms has been sold—the Royal Oak has long been replaced by a scion.

North of Bridgnorth on the road to Shrewsbury are Morville and, over the hill behind the church, Upton Cresset, with its old hall of Tudor brick whose chimneys I noted (p. 87), and its perfectly preserved gatehouse. It stands detached in byways in a sweet bit of country. I was there at cowslip time in the spring of last year and, wandering along the stream below the house, I found to my great joy four well-grown morel funguses (a great dainty for the venturesome).

Two roads go to Ludlow. The more direct passes between the Clees and goes through Bitterley, where there is a perfect churchyard cross, complete with its tabernacle head, and a rood-loft which was restored by Francis Bond, the author of the greatest of all books on English church architecture. The other and longer way takes you over the shoulder of Titterstone Clee, rendered bleak not only for its height but for the usual accompaniments of a quarrying neighbourhood. But there is a charming interlude at Hopton Wafers where manorial ties still keep a pretty village intact within the fringe of the jew-stone industry. And when you descend on the far side an unrivalled view over Herefordshire towards the Black Mountains and the Brecon Beacons.

If you do not take the Ludlow turn at Cleobury Mortimer but go on to Tenbury and follow the road along the southern

border of the county you come to Burford, the ancient manor of the Cornewalls, whence came Thomas Cornewall, who was named at the Ludlow celebrations (p. 187). Here are some family monuments of extraordinary interest. One is a triptych painted in 1558 and signed by the artist, Melchior Salabuss. It is a first-class work of art in all its parts, besides being the only one of its kind in the country. It was made to take the usual place of such a furnishing, which is behind the altar, though more recent ideas of Protestant reverence have caused its removal to a place on the north side of the chancel. Perhaps that is not surprising, for although the twelve apostles in the wings and the heavenly host on the pediment give it a religious sanction, the large central panel is occupied by a Cornewall family group, and there is such a wealth of heraldry in all its parts as hardly to save the faces and Christian humility of the apostles. But it is a grand thing.

The most interesting of the other memorials is the effigy of Princess Elizabeth of Lancaster, daughter of John of Gaunt and sister of Henry IV. She took for her second husband Sir John Cornewall, who fought at Agincourt and was the champion tilter of his day.

Nave arcade, Buildwas Abbey
New power plant, Buildwas

CHAPTER XV

THE SEVERN GORGE

THERE was one corner of Shropshire to which none of my war-time missions took me, the neighbourhood of the Severn Gorge, where the river breaks through the great wall-like barrier which in pre-glacial days linked Wenlock Edge to the foot of the Wrekin. That defile through which the waters swirled between steep banks (where grey and buff crags jutted from hanging woods, for either shore formed the fringe of a great forest) must have afforded one of the grandest scenes in Shropshire at the end of the seventeenth century. But a little later on it became one of the main centres of industrial production, indeed the actual starting-point from which the ideas came, and where the principal actors were stationed who ordered the prologue of that strange melodrama in which Britannia is seen to rise to supremacy in world trade and commerce.

So I went there a little while ago to seek enlightenment for this last chapter. I could only spare four days to enjoy the hospitality of the Tontine Hotel at Iron Bridge and in that time I had as many surprises as a hardened topographer can expect, and came away with the certain knowledge that I had seen and understood but a fraction of what there is to be learned in that locality.

The surprises were pleasant ones. In the first place Nature is having a decided come-back here without any artificial aids. The huge blast-furnaces and iron-foundries of John Wilkinson, the greatest of all the ironmasters, in the neighbourhood of Broseley, which must have darkened the heights of the right bank with their fume, are not merely closed and derelict but have entirely disappeared. At Willey, where the main works stood, nothing is to be seen but certain inequalities in a huge meadow of rich grass where cattle graze. On one side of it a green undulation sweeps up. An avenue of trees crest the top of this, sheltering a little lane. It looks like a Roman causeway in the grand manner. That is the great dam which Wilkinson built to impound the water for driving the bellows of his forges and furnaces before the steam engine came to power. And now the artificial lake is gone with all the rest.

A historic site, this. It was John Wilkinson who enabled James Watt to perfect his steam engine. The cylinder had ever been the weak point of the machine. The earlier experimenters (including James Brindley) had made their cylinders of hooped staves of wood, but the damp heat always warped them. Watt made his of iron but could not cast one in which the piston fitted steam-tight. Wilkinson devised a method of boring a cast-iron cylinder true,* and then ordered the first engine for himself from the new partnership— Boulton and Watt—which was setting up shop in Soho that very year, 1775. It was erected at Willey. Even Wilkinson had not been bold enough to think of working the bellows by steam, so the engine was set to work vicariously, pumping the expended water back into the great pool behind the dam.

The coal-pits and workings have also gone from round Broseley village and the cliff side overhanging the Severn. Across the river, too, they have closed and those still operating are well back out of sight beyond the crest of the hill. But in spite of these removals the lovely gorge would still have appeared derelict and scarified if the material of the endless tips and spoil-banks had not proved to be of a nature kindly to vegetation. Now there is some fifty years' growth

*The actual operation was performed in Wilkinson's works at Bersham. A working model of the machine is exhibited at the Science Museum, South Kensington.

of trees over most of them, large enough to make tall and bosky woodlands but not so sturdy as to have tempted the eager woodcutter during the war. So although the old contours of Nature's carving can never be replaced, the Severn Gorge is once more a beautiful place, and the nightingale sings above the toll-house of the iron bridge.

And there have been other clearances, helped, no doubt, by the demands of the war. The slag-heaps which earlier processes only half exploited have vanished, and so has the scrap iron. The greatest surprise, though, is the condition of the villages themselves. They show none of the signs of an industrial interlude. Hardly one but has its Tudor, Queen Anne, and Georgian houses. The mid-Victorian house is rare and where it appears is generally built entirely in local character and not in the manufacturing-town style such as imparts that impenetrable gloom to Wellington. The bricks and tiles, of course, are local, for that was one of the main industries, but in general they are pleasant to look at.

The explanation for this would seem to lie in the particular phase of the industrial boom and in the local character of the district invaded. It was the very beginning of the new era—the second half of the eighteenth century—when the master was still a master-craftsman and there was no real social gulf between him and his men; though it was expected of him to live in a good house and keep servants and horses and sit in one of the best pews in church. So the Tudor and Stuart and Queen Anne houses in Madeley, Broseley, and Jackfield have twofold histories of interest, a "costume" background of the old Shropshire families who built and lived in them and a "personality" background of those iron-masters and master-potters who occupied them later. And the great tradesmen did not go in for modernizing. They took over most of the furniture as it stood, and left the panelling and the fireplaces alone. Decay and depredations set in only when their days were over.

Where all the workmen lived when the many and various works were going full blast I did not discover. Large numbers must have been housed in very temporary dwellings which have vanished as completely as the ruins of the works. It is one of the things which the local historian does not tell us. Surely Coalport must have had a large population? Now it is hardly a village, though it has two railway stations, one a terminus. There are a great many things the local historian does not tell us, taking it for granted that his readers will know all that, or that such things could never be forgotten, but it is more than half a century since John Randall published his last book, and it is frequently easier to get at mediaeval facts and figures than recent ones. Parchment is more permanent than paper, which goes indiscriminately to the pulping mill in war-time. But Randall had enough material to write five fairly substantial books about the district, and yet he left out a great deal. Unfortunately all his work has been out of print for some time. A re-edited single volume giving Randall's main facts and character sketches and supplemented with the many missing links (if they could be found) would be of great service. For this is likely to prove a new country to the tourist, if he can be told what to see and what the story is. Meanwhile, I will supply the reader with an account of my own short visit and what I was able to learn from it.

I knew that Mr D. was a man learned in local lore and that his wife had a copy of Randall's *History of Broseley* which she was not disposed to lend to anyone. I would have liked to have read this before looking about me, but as they had no copy of the work in the London Library I felt that I must go and throw myself on the mercy of Mrs D. My mother had brought me up to believe in the saying that "Everything comes to the man who waits" which I have always found to be very true, and in the present case fulfilment came after ten months when I found myself in a train bound from London to Worcester and on the same evening alighted with bicycle and rucksack at Iron Bridge station.

The iron bridge (after which the small town was named) has been closed for some time to wheeled traffic and is scheduled as an ancient monument. The foot-passenger still uses it, paying a halfpenny toll between 6 A.M. and 10 P.M. About half a mile down stream there is a free bridge, but no doubt they will, in time, make another on the old site. If so, I venture to hope that the authorities will use more discrimination than they did at Atcham. A derelict bridge is an unsightly embarrassment and spoils the view. It would be better to take it down (as could quite easily be done in this case) and re-erect it at some place like Whipsnade where it could be both used and well seen. And so far as being seen for its own sake is concerned, the iron bridge is much more worthy of attention than Gwynne's bridge at Atcham, for it is a thing which marks a critical turning-point in the development of the New Iron Age.

The bridge was designed to replace an ancient ferry, and its construction must have first been mooted about 1775. The proposal was to build in wood, and a company was formed for the purpose. John Wilkinson said it should be in iron, and *cast* iron. This suggestion was treated at first as an absolute chimera. Wilkinson had already been described as iron-mad. It was said that he never wrote a letter to anyone without mentioning the word "iron" in it—just as in later times Mr Derning Lawrence never put pen to paper without mentioning in set terms, "Bacon is Shakespeare." But John had a sound reputation of being a very practical man, and he had, moreover, the most dominating personality of any of the ironmasters, and so the promoters were eventually browbeaten into assent. It was arranged that Mr Darby's foundry at Coalbrookdale should undertake this gigantic experiment and make the necessary castings of an unheard-of size.

It is rather remarkable that in spite of the confidence of Wilkinson and Abraham Darby (III) and his very capable and eminent manager Richard Reynolds it was thought necessary to consult an architect for the design of the bridge. The man chosen was Thomas Farnolls Pritchard of Shrewsbury. He certainly deserves great credit for his original contribution in the new medium but has not gained a place with the other principals in the D.N.B. His plans were ready by 1777, when the work was put in hand, but he did not live to see the triumphant opening day.

I went down to the foundations of the bridge before supper to have a close look at it. The arrangement is very simple and logical, almost like a Chinese conception for building in bamboo. The outer arch is formed of five separate bars of cast iron, square in section, each seventy feet long, whose feet are secured mortice-wise into an iron plate on the bank. Five similar bars arch over from the other side, and where each set meets in the middle of the bridge they are fastened. These are reinforced by two inner arches, each shorter in arc than the other. They fit into the same iron bed-plates and are strutted at intervals, and steadied by vertical iron posts at either end. The masonry which forms the abutment on each bank is the most architectural feature and is reminiscent of work of the late seventeenth century.

When the bridge was completed and opened in 1779 it attracted so much attention that it was thought the Seven Wonders of the World ought to be revised so as to include it. Indeed, as an advertisement of what could be done with iron its function was probably even more important than that of being a bridge, if only because it caught Telford's eye— with far-reaching results, as explained in Chapter Nine. It is interesting to note from the subsequent history how perspicacious that eye was. Telford looked, and immediately spotted the one weakness which all the other experts had missed. What if the abutments on either bank were to move towards each other? Why, the bridge would *crack*. He bore this in mind when he himself was called upon to span the Severn a little higher up after the flood of 1795, which washed away the old bridge at Buildwas. Telford's design was very much more scientific that that of the other, and though the span was thirty feet greater, the iron involved amounted to only 173 tons as compared with 378 of the one at Iron Bridge. This time, however, the ironmasters were not so venturesome. They regarded their first essay (which had been designed by a real architect) as the final and unalterable pattern for all iron bridges. But Telford was never uncertain of his powers, and he got his way. Recently the Buildwas Bridge has been altered to suit modern requirements of traffic. It was then found to be in a perfectly good condition and the main iron arches of the old work have been incorporated in the new. But the other has amply fulfilled Telford's prediction. It has cracked, and gone on cracking, and still cracks.

After supper I made my way up to Broseley and melted Mrs D. sufficiently to allow me to borrow Randall's volume, provided I took it no further afield than Iron Bridge. I spent the greater part of the next day reading it and had only one interlude when I went to see Harry Rogers in his shed on the river bank.

I knew that Harry was a descendant of the ancient race of coracle-fishers and that he had, and still made, these craft which are now so rare. But I also knew that he had made a number of broadcasts on the art of poaching, so I was rather shy of approaching such a celebrated person. But I found him not only quite as picturesque as he ought to be, but also extremely natural and unspoilt. It is rather typical of the Severn Gorge that the coracle should have survived the coming and going of the coal-and-iron impulse which made us all so up-to-date, and that Harry Rogers should be there talking and thinking like a proud Salopian of the seventeenth century.

It was just across the water, so Harry said, where John Wilkinson launched his iron barge in 1787 which proved to be an even more spectacular event than the opening of the iron bridge. I had often heard of this occasion when the first non-wooden hull ever to be attempted was put to the crucial test, had been reading accounts of it in Randall during the day, and now heard Harry's version, which he had received by oral tradition from original eye-witnesses. It seems that people would *not* believe that anything made of iron could possibly float, and they came from enormous distances in Shropshire and the neighbouring counties in the certain hope of seeing it go straight to the bottom. Nothing contributed so much to the wizard legend of the iron-mad man than the success of that launch. But Wilkinson's idea was not to astonish the neighbourhood with a feat of magic but to find a quick means of augmenting his fleet of barges, as he could not get wooden vessels built fast enough for his expanding trade. He was at that time casting cannon for our war with France. Also he was making iron pipes which were to be consigned to Paris, and purported to be for the new water works there, that Wilkinson himself had engineered. But it was presently discovered that these were really cannon in disguise to shoot back at us, and that Wilkinson had supplied boring and other tools to the French for making the necessary conversion. By his black arts, however, Wilkinson got off with just the stoppage of this branch of his extensive business.

The coracle, of course, has a respectable antiquity of two, three, or even four thousand years and on all those of our rivers where it persists slight modifications have crept in. The Severn coracle is a roundish basinlike boat with a frame of ash laths and a skin of tarred canvas. Its particular variant is that on the bottom the laths are interlaced. Harry had a new one on the stocks—which was just the floor of his workshop. But I think what I admired about him more than his rabbit-catching, his salmon-tickling, and his boat-building was the way he had withstood the slum-clearance enthusiasts who had tried to move him from his ancient family seat on the river bank to a prepared position a mile inland. He had gone doggedly on resisting (and manoeuvring) till his case was raised in the House of Commons. I gathered from him that what the authorities were really after was not so much to give him a more sanitary house to live in but to tidy up the water-front by razing all the small houses on the bank. If this were so, Harry put the kybosh on the plan by taking active steps while matters were pending. He pulled down the ancestral cot and built another house in the same place out of the same bricks, but all in the modern style. He put in new floors on new joists and made new doors, all without spending a penny, for, as he explained, the wood "was all ketched out of the river."

I have referred earlier to Plymley's *Survey of Shropshire,* a publication of 1803, in which Telford wrote an essay on the Severn navigation and the canals. He gives diagrams of a method of taking canal-boats from one level to another by using an inclined plane instead of locks. He adopted this system on his Shrewsbury Canal but gives the credit for the invention "to Mr William Reynolds (whose character is too well known to need any eulogium)." I was anxious to find out if there was anything left of one of those neat contrivances of pre-Telfordian days and my principal objective was to look for any ruins of Reynolds's own Ketley Canal and especially the great inclined plane which brought boats down from the cliff-top overlooking Coalport to the river level, a drop of 207 feet. If this descent were done by the usual method of locks it would need at least twenty stages, take over an hour to go up or down, and waste a vast amount of water. Reynolds's plan was very much quicker. The boat was floated onto a cradle which ran on a railway. The cradle was hitched onto winding-gear which pulled it up a short incline until it was clear of the water. It was then at the summit of the descending incline, down which it proceeded by gravity, its weight bringing up an empty boat from the dock below.

I set off immediately after breakfast and, as Coalport was little more than a mile away, I thought I should get to the incline quickly. That was a mistake because I found that Iron Bridge was not as I had thought, an entirely new place made after the bridge was built. I came across several half-timbered houses. The first seemed to me to have merited the attention of the slum-clearers more than Harry's old abode. It was small and exceedingly picturesque within and without, but quite at the end of its tether, which must have reached back to the hand of an Elizabethan. The most imposing of the houses was a mansion dated 1642. They told me that from time out of mind it had been four cottages. If I had read my Randall on Madeley then, I should have recognized it as the Lloyds. But I had not at that time been able to lay hands on the book. In its only remaining gable it had a decoration which was new to me, that was an obvious attempt to copy in wood what is usually only seen in stone and called "strap-work." If this is a good guess, it will also explain the meaning of the pattern (less pronounced) in the gables of the market-house at Bridgnorth.

Taking my way again, I looked across the river to Jackfield and thought of William Hazledine, Telford's contractor, who I think had his forge there, and of all the ironwork for the Menai Bridge stipulated to be of "the best Shropshire hammered iron" that went from there. The two great tile-works of Dunhills and Maws must stand on or near the site. I had read a good deal about both these manufactories in Randall and elsewhere, but had not been able to ascertain whether or not there was work going on at either. I now saw, however, that the chimney of Messrs Maw was smoking, a hint which I could not resist, especially as there was a foot-bridge over the river at Coalport, just by the bottom of the old inclined plane. I therefore postponed the inspection of the latter and crossed over. They received me kindly in the office, although it was getting very near the dinner hour.

Before going on, I feel that the reader must be told a little more of the ground-work and general structure of this story of the Severn Gorge. It is more complex, more complete, and, in its way, more romantic than the story of the March, and I think when another century has gone by it will be considered (with its world-wide implications) more historical. But it is the very devil to tackle in a single chapter! It makes me envy the art of the pre-Norman stone-carver who discovered a more adequate means of putting over his message in visual symbols. He began at ground level with monsters of the underworld, next above were men, and then came gods and other figures of the spirit world. All these he was able to relate and reconcile with each other by a convention called "interlace." Flowing ribbons, like the spiritualists' ectoplasm, emanated from the monsters and involved the men. They ascended from the men and involved the gods and spirits. The labyrinthine twining and intertwining of the tendrils demonstrated a mystery that would be hard to unravel in detail; but then at a single glance you could grasp the whole purposeful picture.

The story of the Severn Gorge is very much like that. You have the raw materials all gathered together in a rich hoard by monstrous forces of the antedeluvian world, and then the men who found this treasure-trove and exploited it, and then the social and spiritual influences of these men on each other and on their several acts of exploitation, all connected up (by more tendrils) with the England of yesterday and the world of today.

The hoard is the special endowment of that geological epoch called in general the Carboniferous period, and in particular the Coal Measures. Its treasures lie directly on the Wenlock limestone (Murchison's famous Silurian) without the usual interposition of the Old Red Sandstone. The river, cleaving the gorge in its post-glacial adventure, and certain faults of an earlier date cracking open Coalbrookdale at right angles to it, showed the world what was there—coal, ironstone, and several sorts of the best kinds of clay (a) for bricks, (b) for pottery, and (c) for fire-resisting vessels. The whole hoard was covered by a thick forest, ready to the hand of the charcoal-burner.

Part of the story of the iron has been told—more is to come. When I entered the office of Messrs Maw and confronted the fire-grate in their own majolica (a ceramic masterpiece encrusted with masks, swags, and garlands) I was conscious of being out of the iron and into the clay. A memory came back to me of the refreshment room in the Victoria and Albert Museum in London with its frieze all done in this ware and I asked if that had come from the Severn side. They turned up an old pattern-book going back to the time when Walter Crane had designed for them; but the quest was soon lost in a maze of other trails in mosaic tesserae and encaustic tiles.

Formerly there were tileries at Coalbrookdale, Benthall, and Broseley, as well as Jackfield, and one or other of them (I don't know which) can claim the honour of having resuscitated the mediaeval encaustic tile, but the well-known restoration examples in the chancels of Chester and Christ Church cathedrals came from Jackfield. The revived Shropshire product was a far more perfect work of craftsmanship than the mediaeval one, but it does not make the same appeal—though it did to the Victorian eye. The care and ingenuity expended on its production were incredible, but have I not more than once heard the highbrow sightseer dismiss the modern encaustic with "Oh yes!—sanitary tiles"?

This branch of ceramics was a native growth of its own,

descending from the roof-top to the drawing-room. But the interlace (above mentioned) connects it indissolubly with a flourishing of the more rarefied realm of porcelain, also local, and now much prized by collectors. A little way down stream from Jackfield is the site of the Caughley (pronounced "Cuffley") pottery owned by a Mr Turner towards the end of the eighteenth century. From fragments dug up in the course of various excavations it would seem that there had been earthenware potteries both here and at Jackfield from time immemorial, working the local clays. But in 1772 Caughley started making porcelain in the new fashion from imported materials.

This small pottery was the nursery of two great figures in the ceramic world, both Shropshire lads. One was Thomas Minton, who later on founded the great Staffordshire firm which bears his name. He learned the designer's craft under Turner. The other was John Rose. He and his brother Thomas were sons of a farmer at Sweeney near by. John was a clerk at the Caughley pottery and he left in 1780 to set up in partnership with another at an ancient earthenware works in Jackfield which had been in operation for over a century. John brought in great improvements here, probably to the detriment of the trade of his old master. Meanwhile Thomas Rose, who must also have been initiated by Turner, joined a company which built a new pottery across the river at Coalport. It would seem that the aforesaid William Reynolds financed this venture. He was lord of the manor and his name appears as one of the promoters. The works were placed between the river bank and the new canal which Reynolds had made (from the bottom of the inclined plane to Stourport). Next we hear that the old kiln at Jackfield is being given up and that John Rose is forming a company to build a new works across the river, adjacent to those of his brother. In 1799 the good Mr Turner seems to have been beaten by the rivalry of his former employees who had the improved facilities of the new canal at their back doors to bring coal and take the goods to market, for in that year he not only retired from business but sold the Caughley pottery to John Rose, who presently pulled down both it and the one at Jackfield, and carried the material across the river to build his new ovens at Coalport; and now the name Caughley no longer appears on the map.

In 1804 the two Coalport potteries were amalgamated, but Thomas Rose seems to have dropped out, as his name does not occur again on the board. Reynolds had died the year before, but collectors should honour his memory, for if it had not been for him and his canal there would probably never have been any Coalport pottery. In 1820 John Rose made his next bold move. He found that he was losing custom, for one of his best buyers in London was giving preference to wares coming out of South Wales made by one William Billingsley. Billingsley was a great artist of real genius and with the temperament to match. As a painter of china he has probably never been excelled. But it was as a potter that he valued himself. He was in possession of a recipe for making the paste for a fret body which he insisted on following wherever he worked. It gave very fine results when it came off, but more often than not it failed in the kiln and was only fit for destruction. Billingsley wandered from one great firm to another, but they all found him too expensive a luxury. At length he gravitated to Nant Garw in Glamorganshire and set up on his own. Here he was saved from financial disaster by a near neighbour, Mr Dillwyn, who had started a new pottery at Swansea. He invited Billingsley to join him. Mr Dillwyn had now to bear the brunt of Billingsley's idealistic extravagance, which he did with fortitude for three years, buoyed up by the fact that the occasional successes of his tame genius had caught the eye of connoisseurs and they were calling eagerly for more. However, in 1817 Billingsley was back again at Nant Garw, where he remained till 1819 (no doubt reduced to great straits), when John Rose appeared in person and spirited him away to Coalport. In 1822 Rose bought both Nant Garw and Swansea potteries, shut them down, and had all the moulds and patterns sent to Shropshire.

The Coalport pottery has only been closed within recent years. Up to the end of its long and romantic career it was noted for a standard of production as high and rigidly enforced as that of old Josiah Wedgwood. At the same time owners, artists, and workmen prided themselves on being a corporate body bound together by the family spirit rather than that of business. There was a happy measure of indulgence, loyalty, and concern for each other that was reminiscent of the mediaeval guild rather than the modern commercial concern. But two great strikes interrupted this bond of union. The first occurred in 1833. The masters stood out the men and, when work was resumed, John Rose's neighbouring industrialists presented him with a large silver cup which was engraved as a "Tribute of respect to his Public and Private Character and to the uncompromising firmness with which he has recently resisted the demands of an illegal conspiracy." The other strike was not long before the war. Once again the masters stood out the men. But times had changed and rifts of this sort were not so easy to heal. There were no applauding friends and neighbours now. The guild spirit had gone and had been replaced by trades-unionism, which was quite another matter. The owners lost interest and sold out, and "Coalport" is now made at Worcester. The old bottle-kilns remain standing, but what part of the works is still used is divided up into a number of petty industries which have no connection with each other or with the making of china.

It may be observed that Billingsley did not move on again. He continued to perpetrate his occasional masterpieces at the expense of enormous waste and died in Coalport nine

Severn coracle at Iron Bridge

years after he had been kidnapped by the energetic John Rose, having made the fame of three potteries but never a fortune for himself. I could not find out where he is buried, though heaven knows what pilgrimages are not made to many lesser shrines!

And so I returned over the foot-bridge and found the bottom of Reynolds's inclined plane. The old canal at its foot is entirely silted up and overgrown, but the track where the barges came down on trucks is clear enough, though the rails have long since been taken up. I began pushing my bicycle up the steep ascent, about 1 in 5, which goes for 350 yards to the summit, 207 feet above. Telford mentions the date 1788 in connection with this work. It seems strange that except for his own copies of Reynolds's invention it does not appear to have been used elsewhere in the vast system of waterways that were made in the Canal Era. Nothing like it was tried again until the early twenties of the present century when the lift at Anderton was constructed to take boats down from the Trent and Mersey Canal to the Weaver Navigation. That is a very much more elaborate affair and the boat is lowered vertically, afloat in a watertight compartment.

Up the steep green track I went, through the thick woodlands that have grown up on either side, and came at last to the thing I wanted to see, the remains of the old dock from which the boats commenced their overland journey. The sturdy masonry stood up through briars and nettles like a Roman relic. I suppose no one will think of scheduling it as an ancient monument till it is much further gone in decay. The old Ketley Canal which terminates at the dock is not so dilapidated as its continuation on the lower level. It still holds water and supports a succulent jungle of aquatic plants. Any roads or tracks which used to come to this point in the old busy days have vanished. I found myself and bicycle isolated in a huge meadow. On the sky-line above stood a large

Making a clay pipe at Broseley

ancient house surrounded by high walls. A herd of cattle grazed or lay at ease chewing the cud. It was more like the idyllic scene on a piece of early Coalport than an old stamping-ground of the Industrial Revolution. I turned my binoculars onto the house and noted the large brick chimneys in which that attention so customary in old Shropshire houses had been paid to decorative detail, but in quite an unusual way, the upper part of the stacks being faced with arcading in the Stuart manner. It turned out that the house was the Haye, a name dating from the particular year 1260 in which the priors of Wenlock were given permission to enclose part of the royal forest of the Wrekin and empark it within a haye (or hedge) for the benefit of the monastic larder. This is one of the houses I spoke of as having an interest relating to people of both the old and the newer days. In the latter connection it was the home of John Rose.

I had a hasty look at the place and went on to Madeley. Although the surroundings continued to present an absolutely unbroken rural simplicity, I felt sure I should soon find myself in the outskirts of industrial squalor. It was really the fear of this which had kept me so long from seeking out Madeley Court, which I had always heard was one of the oldest and finest stone houses in Shropshire. It was written in 1880, "Ugly pit-mounds are seen surrounding the building; the place is illumined by the blaze of blast-furnaces, the screech of machinery is heard around it, the snort of the iron horse sounds across the park where hounds were wont to cry." At a much later date Forrest in his *Old Houses of Wenlock* writes that "it is shorn of all majesty by its sordid surroundings." Nothing is more depressing than such a contrast. But now that I was in Madeley I felt bound to go.

The village itself bore none of these sordid signs. I passed through it and came to the screen of post-World-War-No-1 council houses; there was a sudden steep hill down and Madely Court appeared—not by itself, but surrounded by a little cluster of buildings, barns, and farmhouses in black and white, all of Stuart or Tudor date, or earlier. The whole of this charming old-world group lay between two great woods. An ample pool (last relic of the manorial fish-ponds) flashed back the blue of the sky. It was surrounded by some of the noblest bulrushes I have ever seen. A new discovery in an old country!—the biggest surprise of all. Not only was there a clean sweep of the industrial taint and a replacement of it by fresh timber and grass, but a complete air of rustic detachment prevailed. There was not a single modern thing in view except a distant and inoffensive railway embankment. Nowhere would I have liked better to have stayed and explored, but I had promised Mr D. to go to Broseley that afternoon, and it was already well past two o'clock. So I had to retire. I even had to miss seeing the Upper House and its adjacent barn where Charles II hid after the Battle of Worcester, the day before his adventure in the oak at Boscobel.

I paid a hurried visit to the church. There is a very curious and rather moving exhibit here. In a glass case a number of things are collected. There are two folded papers. The curious may read in faded hand-writing that they contain "Mr Fletcher's hair" and "Mrs Fletcher's hair" respectively; a plain glass bottle labelled "Mr Fletcher's water-bottle"; part of Mrs Fletcher's wedding-dress, her black dress and cap; a sword in its scabbard; an open printed tract in which one reads: "At Lisbon he had made arrangements to go further abroad on a Portuguese man-of-war but the carelessness of a servant-maid who upset a kettle of boiling water over him upset his plans." I confess the collection struck me as both inexplicable and ludicrous at that hasty glance. But I was quite wrong, unless relics of the saints can be called ludicrous. It was merely a faulty presentation of such things to the uninstructed.

The story relates to Jean Guilhaume de la Flécherè, a

Swiss, born at Noyon in 1729. He entered the French Army (hence the sword) and was on his way to take up some appointment on a foreign station when the incident so baldly stated in the tract "upset his plans." We are told that he desired to learn English, and he is next discovered at Tern Hall near Atcham engaged as tutor to the family of Mr Hill, the member for Shrewsbury. While still there he was ordained in 1757 and in due course Hill presented him with a living that was in his gift. The parish was a small one but the stipend good. But Fletcher (as he now called himself) had an ardent desire to work among the population of the coal and iron district which had been growing in ever increasing numbers during all the first part of the century. He had preached at Madely and he felt an irresistible call to go there. It was an immense parish in those days and included Coalbrookdale, but the stipend was much more modest than the one in Mr Hill's gift and quite inadequate for a worker among the vast new population. Still Fletcher was bent on going to Madeley, and he persuaded Hill (much against his inclination) to ask the incumbent to exchange that living for the better one, which he did with alacrity.

Fletcher was certainly of the stuff that saints are made of. The workmen who within a generation had flocked there from all parts were ignorant and hardened sinners, depraved by the conditions under which they lived and worked, and much besotted with drink. They were exceedingly hostile, so were the well-to-do and the newly made rich. So, even, were his own brethren of the church. But nothing turned him aside. His ministry at Madeley began in 1759, and not the least astonishing incident in his extraordinary career was his marriage in 1782 to a Yorkshire woman of good social position and gentle birth who was scarcely less self-sacrificing and single-minded than himself. He died in 1785 broken in health and worn out with the arduous fatigues of his self-imposed task. John Wesley wrote of him "So unblamable a character, in every respect, I have not found, and I scarcely expect to find such another on this side of eternity." He accomplished what he set out to do, though, and when he died the people must have thought that no one could ever forget such a man. That is what that pathetic little collection of relics seems to say.

Mr D. was full of stories about John Wilkinson. He lived at the Lawns, the big house opposite Broseley church. It seems to have been built in the time of George II, for it has a rain-water-head dated 1727. The house next door was his office where he paid the men in his own tokens. These, Mr D. said, he minted in the cellars of his own house, for which he had iron shutters made to baffle the burglar. He used to come out late at nights and stand on top of his steps to observe the sky over Staffordshire where he also had large furnaces. And he could tell by the glow whether or not "the iron was coming properly." If he was doubtful, he would send for his horse, no matter what the time, and ride off to see to it that things were put right at once.

The tale of the coffins was one I knew better than Mr D., as the Randall scriptures only give the first part. It is the best of the Wilkinson saga if only because it is most typical of the man and truly ironic (in the dual sense). He was a forerunner of the type "Great Magnate," but was nearer to the elemental thrills and joys of wielding power and making money. The melting of the stubborn ore, the attendant panoply of fire and fume and noise that went with it, were not things whose effects he surveyed on a balance-sheet or understood by the advice of technicians. He himself was the ordainer, the master, the greatest master in the world. Since his boyhood in the bloomery of the Furness District, where they smelted with charcoal, just as they had done when the monks of the abbey owned the woods and the hearths, he had made iron, and iron had made him. While he was hard and quite unscrupulous, he was shrewd and inventive and very far-seeing and with it all, as Telford assures us, he was very good company, "a host in himself." Coming from the critical Telford in 1788, the formula probably meant that he was as much impressed with Wilkinson's sense of humour as with his good sense of the commoner sort.

Wilkinson's iron-mindedness and his long foresight, which no doubt logically reached to the Judgment Day and the probable condition of the usual grave furniture if that event should be long delayed, led him to insist that a man should be buried in an iron coffin, cast-iron from preference. Accordingly he had one made for himself at one of his own foundries and another (in the interests of publicity) as a free gift for any iron-minded proselyte who would accept it. With a just sense of fitness he kept these in the right repository for exotics, which was his greenhouse at the Lawns. The host's iron coffin was the show-piece after dinner for his guests, not for a moral reminder as the classic death's-head, but as a good tip (if you really wanted to turn out respectable before the Judge of all men and keep your bones neatly together for that resurrection of the body which the parsons, the quakers, and all the dissenters were commonly agreed about). And what a discouragement to the body-snatcher! Here was a spare ready-made; or you could have one made (in any style) to your own measure, exactly, just as his had been.

His monument had also been thought out. It was to be of solid iron weighing twenty tons. When at last the call came, Wilkinson was not at Broseley but at Castle Head, a mansion he had purchased in his native county, near Lindale. By the terms of the will it was laid down that he was to be buried in his iron coffin in his own grounds and be surmounted by the twenty-ton monument. But he who had made such long calculations had not reckoned on one thing. The coffin was now found to be too small and, being of cast-iron, it could not be altered. There was nothing for it but to give him a temporary grave and order a new sarcophagus from the works in Shropshire. This was 1808, not only before the time of telegrams but of railways. In due course, however, reinterment was correctly made and the huge monument set up. But very soon it was found that the earth would not support such a weight, so a new site in the garden was found where the rock cropped out. The rock was excavated and Wilkinson was again transferred. In 1828 Castle Head was sold, and the new owners, who had no sympathy with Wilkinson or his ideas, thought it unseemly and unpleasant to have a corpse in their garden. So the remains were lifted once more and taken to the burial ground of Lindale chapel. But owing to a fear of the second mishap repeating itself the monument was not permitted to accompany them. It was set up at the road-side. In a Lakeland guide-book published in 1934 occurs the following: "In its present position it is becoming a nuisance to swift-moving traffic, and probably in a few years the iron-work will be removed elsewhere." What a tail-piece for the Apostle of Progress!

As I said earlier, the forges and furnaces of Willey and Broseley have vanished so completely that you would never think that anything of the kind had ever stood there. But one industry has survived all the shifts of history and fashion for three and a half centuries and is still going stong, that is the manufacture of clay pipes. The discarded bowl of an old clay pipe is not an object of beauty, but it lends itself handsomely to the collector, because in the seventeenth and eighteenth centuries its flat, button-like base had the date stamped on it more often than not, together with the maker's initials. It was the very small early bowls which the Almark family used to find in the peat cuttings on Fenn's Moss and treasure in the belief that they had belonged to the fairies. Owing to this excellent old rule of dating and initialling and the imperishable nature of a clay pipe, the industry at Broseley can be traced right back to its beginning. It has always run in families, the three principal dynasties being the Legges, the Rodens, and the Southerns.

Mr Southern's manufactory (and it is a true manufactory, a place where things are made by hand) is very picturesque and homely. Here, at least, the old tradition of a craft is still maintained, for the master takes an active part with his own hands in the actual production of his wares. There is no machinery, only a few simple tools and moulds—such as the Bronze Age Celts used to cast their palstaves in. Broseley was one of the earliest centres for the manufacture of the tobacco pipe. It seems to have begun production about 1600 or shortly after, most probably within the life-time of Sir Walter Raleigh, which seems very odd, seeing how far away it is from the fashionable world in which early smokers must have moved. One thinks at once of the excellent local fire-clay. But the modern pipe is not made of fire-clay and Mr Southern, who has studied fragments of the old makes, doesn't think it ever was. The present material comes from the Bovey Valley in Devonshire and if that import was also used in old days the pipe-makers must have been much ahead of the potters. Even if the theory of imported clay is erroneous, the mystery of such a wide distribution of a cheap and very brittle article with the transport available to Broseley in the seventeenth and eighteenth centuries remains.

The next day I went to Coalbrookdale. This was the true fount of the New Iron Age in Shropshire and (I think it could be contended) in the world in general, and throughout its first intensive outburst it remained the solid immovable centre. It was probably never the size of any single plant of John Wilkinson's, but the best brains were there and the steadiest and most conscientious business-men. It was, moreover, the birthplace of that revolutionary principle in the reduction of iron ore which made both Wilkinson and the New Iron Age.

The foundry at Coalbrookdale is still active. I asked the works manager if he could show me the old furnace. It is in ruin now, so much piled up with debris as to appear almost ripe for excavation by the archaeologist. We peered into a cave on one side and he pointed out four solid iron bearers. The faces of two bore initials and a date which had been cast on them: "Abraham Darby 1777" and, on the lower, "Bl E W 1668." They reminded me exactly of similar iron beams at Gunn's Mill in the Forest of Dean, also cast, complete with dates and initials, in the seventeenth century.

I believe I felt almost as well rewarded by that peep under the brick arch as a collector does when, after long search, a rare specimen at last comes into his possession. Such thrills are the reward of the pertinacious sightseer. I had at different times visited the sites and ruins of the old bloomeries in Sussex, the Forest of Dean, and the Furness District, had, in fact, seen the relics near Greenodd of the one where John Wilkinson had worked as a boy with his father. I had read the local lore, and heard from word-of-mouth the local legends, and talked to charcoal-burners whose ancestors had been key-men in the industry of old-style smelting and who, themselves, were still using emplacements for their heaths which had been made when Cistercian monks owned the woodlands. And I had always hoped to see the *very place* where the actual discovery was made, which changed not only iron-founding but the whole of our economic history. And this was the very place! This was the mouth of the dragon beast from which issued that interlace which involved both men and gods.

The discovery I am speaking of was how to smelt iron with pit coal instead of charcoal made from wood. All attempts (except one in the seventeenth century, which perished with its inventor) failed, for the impurities imparted to the fluxed ore rendered the metal unusable. So the ironmaster was tied to the charcoal-burner and the charcoal-burner to the forest. Lucas, writing in 1740, reveals a state of things quite astonishing. He says: "The mighty destruction of wood occasioned by the great Quantity of iron made in this Kingdom has long been complained of in all Parts of the Nation; and not without very good Reason; for in the County of Sussex alone, there are, or lately were, no less than One Hundred and Thirty Furnaces and Hammers which, by an exact computation are found to consume yearly Ninety-four Thousand nine Hundred Loads of charcoal to the extravagent consumption of timber"—then in great demand for ship-building.

In 1709 Abraham Darby, a Quaker, came to Coalbrookdale—then spelt Caldbrook (a name allied to other streams called Calder and only linked with coal by an obvious association of later date). There was already a "smithy place" here, as appears in the manorial records of Madeley Court at the time of Henry VIII. It would be like those other vanished forges in Corvedale, a place in a wood where charcoal was available and by a stream which could work bellows for the bloomery furnace and a trip-hammer. Darby acquired the manor of Madeley with its ancient rights and lived at Madeley Court like a gentleman. Whether he came to the coal-field because he had inklings that he was on the verge of discovering the great secret is not known, but in 1712 he solved the first part of it and was able to substitute *coke* for charcoal. In 1717 he died at the grand old manor-house. His son, another Abraham, made the necessary second step. In 1737 he "first used coal instead of charcoal for converting pig iron into bar iron at the forge."* And this

---

*It is claimed that Dud Dudley of Worcester, Master of the Ordnance to Prince Rupert during the Civil War was the first to effect the smelting of iron by coal. But if his process was really successful its secret perished with him.

was no doubt the very thing which brought Wilkinson to Broseley, and in fact the credit for the discovery has wrongly been awarded to him.

It was in the time of the third Abraham that the Iron Bridge was cast at the Coalbrookdale works. In his time Richard Reynolds came to be manager at the works. He, too, was a Quaker and a man of outstanding character. True to the Quaker tenet of himself and the owner, he steadfastly refused to make armaments for the French war while Wilkinson did a tremendously thriving trade in them both for the British Government and the French, getting his castings smuggled abroad by all manner of means (until he was stopped, as narrated). All the same, Reynolds became immensely rich. He distributed largesse in a princely way to the deserving, but anonymously where possible, and with great discretion. He actually employed almoners in London and Bristol who sent in weekly accounts of free gifts dispensed.

It is not a little diverting to observe that the government (then led by William Pitt the Elder) when it became aware of a new source of national wealth immediately proposed to tax the very means that produced it, and endeavoured to levy two shillings per ton on coal. This was strenuously opposed by Richard Reynolds, the most effective spokesman for the ironmasters. One of his letters on the subject is given by Randall. It is of interest for what it reveals of its own time and in the light of things as they are today, so I will quote. The letter is dated 1784 and is addressed to Earl Gower, President of the Council.

"The advancement of the iron trade within these few years has been prodigious; it was thought, and justly, that the making of pig iron with pit coal was a great acquisition to the nation by saving the woods and supplying a material to manufactories, the make of which, by the consumption of all the wood the country produced, was unequal to the demand; and the nail trade, perhaps the most considerable of any article of manufactured iron, would have been lost to this country, had it not been found practicable to make nails of iron made with pit coal; and it is for that purpose we have made, or rather are making alterations at Donnington-Wood, Ketley, &ct, which we expect to complete in the present year, but not at a less expense than twenty thousand pounds, which will be lost to us and gained by nobody if this tax is laid upon our coals. The only chance of making iron as cheap as it can be imported from Russia, is the low price of our fuel, and unless we can do that there will not be the consumption equal to half the quantity that can be made, and when we consider how many people are employed on a ton of iron, and the several trades dependant thereupon, we shall be convinced the Revenue is much more benefited even by the consumption of excisable articles, &ct, than by the duty on a ton of foreign iron; nor will it, I believe, escape observation that the iron trade, so fatally affected by this absurd tax, is only of the second, if indeed, it is not of the first importance to the nation. The preference I know is given, and I believe justly, as to the number of hands employed, to the woolen manufactory; but when it is remembered that all that is produced by making of iron with pit coal is absolutely so much gained to the nation, and which, without its being so applied, would be perfectly useless, it will evince its superior importance, for the land grazed by sheep might be converted with whatever losses to other purposes of agriculture or pasturage; but coal and iron stone have no value in their natural state, produce nothing till they are consumed or manufactured, and a tax upon coal which, as I said, is the only article which in any degree compensates for our high price of labour, & ct, or can be substituted in the stead of water for our wheels, and bellows, would entirely ruin this very populous country, and throw its labouring poor upon the parishes, till the emigration of those of them who are able to work shall strengthen our opponents, and leave the desolated wastes, at present occupied by their cottages, to the lords of the soil."

The measure was successfully defeated, and shortly afterwards Reynolds, Watt, Wedgewood, and Wilkinson formed themselves into an association for the protection of trade called the United Chamber of Manufacturers of Great Britain.

William Reynolds, the son, who made the Ketley Canal with its inclined planes, was a very versatile and charming person. His natural high spirits modified the sterner Quaker stuff in him and he also has left a legend. He was a pupil of Dr Joseph Black, who first propounded the theory of latent heat, and, as a chemist, Reynolds made many great contributions to the coal-and-iron industry. His leisure hours were spent in collecting the fossils of the Coal Measures, so that we hear of him from many people who were not in any way connected with engineering or business, notably the geologists Murchison, Buckland, and Prestwich.

Reynolds lived for some time at the Haye but removed across the river to the Tuckies at Jackfield. The house is another which has an ancient and a modern history. Reynolds appears to have acquired it from that interesting admiral peer, the tenth Earl of Dundonald, whose secret weapon for blowing up the Russian Navy has never yet been disclosed. Among the things he patented was a lamp to burn "oil of tar," now better known as petroleum. There was a rich seepage of this in a tunnel which had been bored by Reynolds in the hill opposite the Tuckies. Dundonald appears to have had some connection with the getting and distribution of it. The yield at one time is reported to have been as much as a thousand gallons per week, but as there were then no internal combustion engines and Dundonald's lamps had not come into production it must be assumed that, like the nearly allied product from the well at Pitchford, it was made up somehow in the form of medicine.

A long chapter, this! I fear that there will be some who will complain that I have made it disproportionate, who would have preferred me to have said less about this part of Shropshire and more about others that are more frequented. But I felt that the paramount role which the county played in the Industrial Revolution was little known and perhaps not fully appreciated. Also I was, myself, so much surprised by what I found in my four days' stay in that little town made in 1777 that I was tempted to dilate. What impressed me to the last minute about Iron Bridge was its absolute non-bogusness. It was an "old-world" place without knowing it. No one had ever pointed out the Dickensian charm of the little bow-fronted shop on the Tontine Hill or the picturesque vista up the 108 steps which rise against the terraced hillside to take you to the church. And that very building is one in which the parishioners do not take much pride, for when I went to get the key the woman said, "You won't find it any more beautiful inside than out."

Perhaps not, but it was singularly fitting. The exterior in warm russet local brick was a very simple and direct interpretation of the Early English style as they understood it in 1836. Inside, it was a perfect period piece of that exact date, with galleries and pewing. The latter speak eloquently of the social grading of that time and may be compared with the first-, second-, and third-class of railway travel. The middle aisle (that *via optima*) gives access to box-pews *with* doors. Adjacent to these are box pews *without* doors, opening on the side aisles. Between the side aisles and the walls are bench-pews with narrow seats and rails at the back to make the inferiors sit bolt upright. But then, within living memory, Dr Webb was always known as the *gentlemen's* doctor. He wore a top-hat. The other doctor only aspired to a Homburg. It was Dr Webb's brother who was the first to swim the English Channel—his picture still appears on a match-box—and Dr Webb's son who married the inspired authoress.

Last of all, I would like to take you to a view-point on the terrace of the Haye, where John Rose lived. He must have seen it on every clear day, and it is very reminiscent of certain scenes I seem to remember on old Coalport plates. You look out over the Severn Gorge in its renewed greenery. The river tumbles through it and, at that distance, the Iron Bridge appears to hang in air like a willow-pattern make-believe in filigree. Above it, just through the cleft of the gorge, rises the sharp hill configuration of the Breidden on the Welsh Border, blue as blue (if the day is clear). You are looking right across Shropshire to the place of the old romance, while, below you, is the valley where the new romance was made, which is not yet far enough removed in time to have received its canonization. Accompaniments to both were the glow of fires and the clash of iron. The dead of the old wars cannot be counted, neither can those of the new strife. If death be indeed a necessary contrast in romantic perspectives, you may bear in mind how the dreaded cholera came again and again to the valley so that hundreds and hundreds were dumped in plague-pits without a mark on grave or in register.

It is a view which stimulates the imagination as well as the aesthetic sense, for it seems to show the crudeness of fact exalted by the mystery of fancy and is, indeed, something altogether Salopian.

APPENDIX

THE MORTIMERS OF WIGMORE
Their motto: "Not we of Kings, but Kings of us."

1 RALPH — Fought at Hastings. First saw Wales under the banner of William Fitz Osbern, 1st Earl of Hereford (the founder of Chepstow Castle). In the rising of the 2nd Earl, he remained loyal to the King and was given the forfeited manors of Wigmore, Cleobury, and Bridgnorth, all keypoints, which he fortified. Died c. 1104.

2 HUGH — During the Stephen-Matilda trouble he remained at home strengthening his castles and ventured to oppose the accession of Henry II. Henry attacked and defeated him but only deprived him of Bridgnorth Castle. He founded Wigmore Abbey and died in 1181.

3 ROGER — Chiefly occupied in fighting the Welsh. Died in 1215.

4 HUGH — A strong supporter of King John. He died in 1227.

5 RALPH — Hugh's brother. Very aggressive towards the Welsh but presently married Black Gladys, daughter of Llewelyn the Great, Prince of Wales.

6 ROGER — Married Maud de Braose, an heiress who added Radnor Castle and wide lands in that shire and Brecon to the growing Mortimer domain. He stood by Henry III in the Baron's War and planned Prince Edward's escape from Kenilworth Castle providing the horse which enabled him to make it. Commanding the rearguard at the Battle of Evesham, it was his men who slew Simon de Montfort. The severed head was sent as a trophy to the Lady Maud at Wigmore Castle. He died in

1282. His third son, Roger, built Chirk Castle and founded the second strong line of the *MORTI-MERS* of *CHIRK*.

7 EDMUND Married Margaret de Finnes, a kinswoman of Queen Eleanor of Castile and was as much in favour at the English court as his father. Edward I stood the expenses of the wedding. He died in 1304.

8 ROGER Married Joan de Geneville, an heiress who brought him Ludlow Castle, half the great Lacy fief, and lands in Ireland (Co Meath). He withstood Edward II's Dispenser favourites and took arms against the king but was captured and imprisoned in the Tower with his uncle, Roger Mortimer of Chirk. After two years he escaped with the connivance of his neighbour, the Bishop of Hereford. He made his way to France where he was given shelter at the court of Charles IV. Here he met Queen Isabella of England as told on page 49. Died the traitor's death at Tyburn in 1330.

9 EDMUND Lived in retirement.

10 ROGER Married Philippa, daughter of Montague 1st Earl of Salisbury. Fought at Crecy. Earldom of March and all the immense Mortimer inheritance restored after the reversal of his grandfather's attainder in 1355. He made Ludlow Castle the chief seat of the family instead of Wigmore. Died in 1360.

11 EDMUND 3rd Earl of March, married Philippa, daughter of Lionel Plantagenet, Duke of Clarence. She brought him the Earldom of Ulster and their union placed his heir in direct succession to the crown. Their eldest daughter, Elizabeth, married Harry Percy (Hotspur). Edmund died in 1381.

12 ROGER Married Eleanor Holland, daughter of the Earl of Kent and niece of Richard II. By right of his mother he was acknowledged as heir presumptive to the throne in 1385. He was killed at Kells on his

Irish estates in a local feudal war in 1398 and brought to Wigmore Abbey for burial.

13 EDMUND Was only ten years old when Bolingbroke seized power and deposed King Richard, having himself crowned as Henry IV. The new king took custody of the young rival claimant and made him and his younger brother, Roger, royal wards. They were brought up at court. Roger died. Later, Edmund fought in the wars of Henry V and made no trouble about his superior claim to rule the land. He died childless in 1424, the last heir male. Henry V founded a chantry to the two brothers in Chichester Cathedral. Their sister, ANNE, had married Richard Plantagenet, Earl of Cambridge and grandson of Edward III. His sudden end at Southampton was dramatized by Shakespeare in *Henry V* Act II Sc 2. Their son, Richard Duke of York, was killed at the Battle of Wakefield, fighting for the claim inherited from his Mortimer mother, already that *cause célèbre* known as the Wars of the Roses. But his son achieved success and was crowned as EDWARD IV.

The succession was from father to son except where mentioned (4–5). Like the Corbet family they came from the Pays de Caux in Normandy. The place-name remains on the map—Mortemer-en-Brai.

PRONUNCIATION OF SHREWSBURY

The traditional pronunciation of the *ew* in Shrewsbury survives in the word sew. In earlier days when spelling was phonetic the name appears as Shrosebury and Shrowesbury, e.g. Speed's map of 1610 (the *ow* being evidently sounded as in show). A very handsome word when thus enunciated, as it is entitled to be, and not given the shr*ew* sound.

INDEX

INDEX